Able Underachievers

Able Underachievers

Edited by

DIANE MONTGOMERY CERTED, MPHIL, CPSYCHOL, AFBPSYS
Middlesex University

W

WHURR PUBLISHERS

LONDON AND PHILADELPHIA

© 2000 Whurr Publishers
First published 2000 by
Whurr Publishers Ltd
19b Compton Terrace, London N1 2UN, England and
325 Chestnut Street, Philadelphia PA 19106, USA

Reprinted 2001, 2004 and 2005

British Library Cataloguing in Publication Data
A catalogue record for this book is available from the
British Library.

ISBN: 1 86156 193 8

Printed and bound in the UK by Athenaeum Press Ltd,
Gateshead, Tyne & Wear

Contents

Foreword

This book first suggested itself at the European Council for High Ability (ECHA) conference in Budapest in 1990, when a group came together under the leadership of Nava Butler-Por to give papers on the needs of the able but disadvantaged. This was not then a well-researched subject in gifted education circles, except for underachievement in women and girls. Since then this group met at ECHA, WCGTC (World Council for Gifted and Talented Children) and NACE (National Association for Able Children in Education) conferences and this book has evolved.

During this period attitudes and perspectives have changed, particularly in the UK. For example, girls are now outperforming boys at school in almost every subject at every level. However, as women they will still earn only three-quarters of the income of men and they will not break through the 'glass ceiling' in significant numbers, except where men have moved out of a sector. Culturally different people and cultural underclasses will suffer a worse fate and will have difficulty getting employment at any level.

The UK government has set up an Advisory Group on the Gifted and Talented to help it develop a national policy for schools, having been persuaded that the National Curriculum (NC) has not met the needs of the most able students. Cuts have been made in NC content with little effect, and yet we see more cuts in the offing.The problem may have been that there has been too much 'teaching' and teacher focus and not enough learning.

Because education is now centrally driven and little autonomy is given to professionals, advice given by experts tends to be ignored by government. Wholesale changes to the system have been made, over the last 20 years, although none appears to be evidence based, or evidence is selectively used. In the special strand for the able in the Excellence in Cities Project (Department for Education and Employment, 1999) we can already see the direction in which the policy for the more able is being driven, and that is for schools to select their top 10% for special and segregated provision. 'World class' tests are going to be developed to aid selection and are intended to make international comparisons possible and more accurate. This ignores the fact that there are already such tests available, which are frequently used by international schools (Meno Research Project, Thinking Skills Service, 1998), and that different systems have different methods and objectives in education.

Instead of analysing and improving what presently exists based on current theory, research and practice, surveys are carried out of what exists in schools and seems to work in particular settings. This is then disseminated, whether or not it is what *should* be going on and whether or not it has any kind of rational theoretical base.

At the UNESCO conference in Salamanca in 1994 an agreement was drawn up which most nations of the world, including the UK, signed. Each agreed to work for *inclusive education*. In the UK, since the Education Act (1981), a policy of integration has been developed and implemented in which the vast majority of children would be educated in primary and secondary mainstream schools. It was never total, as in Sweden, but some local education authorities were more successfully integrational than others. However, the provision varies across the country and within and between schools. Inclusion means that schools must adapt to meet the needs of children, whereas in integration children must be helped to adapt to meet the needs of schools.

Integration was enabled by differentiated provision or learning support in the classroom, and/or remedial withdrawal for short periods of intensive tuition for pupils with learning difficulties and recently for pupils with emotional and behavioural difficulties (EBD).

Special provision for the more able in the UK is rarely seen in primary schools, where teaching is generally in mixed-ability groups. In state secondary schools, which are mainly comprehensive, the vehicle for provision is setting by ability in key subjects such as maths, English and modern foreign languages. Some schools 'stream' pupils by ability, and there are still some grammar schools and a system of private education which about 7% of the school-age population attends and which runs a grammar school type of system in both primary and secondary sectors. Both setting and streaming involve moving selected pupils through the curriculum at a faster rate – accelerated content methods – and thus are against the principle of inclusion, as are pull-out programmes, enrichment groupings and so on. This is an issue that will be dealt with in this book. That is not to say that we cannot learn from what is included in special programmes for the gifted and talented, but we need to find ways for them to become accessible to the majority. All children are entitled, in my view, to an enriching and enriched inclusive education.

For a number of years the terms 'highly able' and 'high ability' have been promoted in the UK to try to move away from the notion of 'gifts' that people either have or do not have and which are immutable. In much of the rest of the world the term 'gifted and talented' is still used and has been adopted by the UK government for its programmes, while the recent House of Commons Select Committee of Inquiry (1999) used the term 'highly able'. Both terms are used in this text and reflect the international contributions.

Contributors

Professor Joan Freeman is the author of 11 books on the development of abilities, many of which have been translated into other languages. She has also written hundreds of scientific and popular publications. Her major overview, *The Education of the Very Able: Current International Research*, was published by the British government in 1998. She has given presentations on the development of abilities in most parts of the world, to universities, schools and conferences, based on more than 25 years' research in this area.

Joan Freeman received her doctorate in educational psychology from the University of Manchester, and is a fellow of the British Psychological Society and a Chartered Psychologist with a private practice. She was the Founding President of the European Council for High Ability (ECHA) and until recently Editor-in-Chief of the refereed journal *High Ability Studies*. She is Visiting Professor at Middlesex University and a member of the government's Advisory Group on the Gifted and Talented.

Dr Eva Gyarmathy graduated in psychology from Eotvos Lorand University (ELTE) in Budapest in 1985 and then from ELTE in postgraduate educational psychology. In 1996 she gained her PhD degree from Kossuth Lajos University in Debrecen.

She worked as a school psychologist for seven years until 1992 and led training courses in the Municipal Pedagogical Institute for teachers.

Since 1992 she has been a researcher at the Institute for Psychology of the Hungarian Academy of Sciences. Her main field of interest is learning-disabled gifted children. She has been a part-time tutor at Kossuth Lajos University in Debrecen since 1993.

She is a committee member of the Hungarian Association for the Gifted and a member of ECHA.

Barry Hymer is a graduate of the Universities of Cape Town, Port Elizabeth, Cambridge and Southampton, and is presently engaged in further research at Newcastle University. Since 1991 he has been employed as an educational psychologist in Cumbria, and he coordinates that county's Able Pupil Project.

Barry Hymer is a national trainer for the National Association for Able Children in Education (NACE), and was co-founder of a network of British educational psychologists with an interest in the needs of able pupils.

With his wife he runs occasional enrichment workshops for children. He is presently coordinating a working group of teachers and consultants which is preparing a resource pack of strategies for combating boys' underachievement in primary-aged English.

Dr Janice A. Leroux is a former school teacher and elementary school principal. She has taught at McGill University, Queen's University and is currently Professor at the University of Ottawa. Her teaching and research focus 15 on gifted children and adults, creativity and gender differences. She has been a consultant for school systems and teacher education in Canada and many other countries including Russia, Portugal, the United States and England.

Janice Leroux is author and editor of two books on high-ability learners, and has written numerous publications on gifted adolescents and the achievements of high-ability females. Her current research deals with gifted students and gender differences in self-regulation and motivation for learning.

Professor Diane Montgomery is a qualified teacher, chartered psychologist and Emeritus Professor of Education at Middlesex University where she was formerly Dean of Faculty and Head of the School of Education.

Professor Montgomery is Director of the Learning Difficulties Research Project in Maldon and Course Leader and author of two distance learning programmes for Middlesex, the MA SEN and MA SpLD. An MA EBD and MA High Ability Studies are in preparation.

She has books published on *Classroom Observation, Reversing Lower Attainment, Spelling and Handwriting: Spelling: Remedial Strategies*; *Educating the Able*; *Managing Behaviour Problems*; *Learning Difficulties*; *Classroom Management*; *Appraisal*; *Teaching Learning and Strategies – Study Skills*; and *Early Reading Skills*.

She is a member of the government Advisory Group on the Gifted and Talented and Editor-in-Chief of the NACE journal *Educating Able Children*.

Dr John Munro (BSc, DipEd, BEd, BA Hons, MA, PhD) is Senior Lecturer in Educational Psychology and Giftedness in the Faculty of Education, University of Melbourne. He lectures and researches in areas of effective learning and teaching, learning difficulties in numeracy and literacy, educational psychology and giftedness.

Originally he was a secondary maths and science teacher, and retrained as a psychologist because of an interest in maths and literacy learning problems. He works in schools with parents on strategies for enhancing opportunity for effective learning.

He has written books and articles for teachers in the area of effective learning and teaching, cognitive style, individual differences and giftedness.

Dr Jane Piirto is Trustees' Professor and Director of Talent Development in the College of Education at Ashland University, Ohio. She also teaches qualitative research methodology at the doctoral level. She is an award-winning poet and novelist, author of 12 books, among them *Understanding Those Who Create*, *Talented Children and Adults* and *My Teeming Brain: A Psychology of Creative Writers*. Her latest project is a collection of her own Christmas poems from the past three decades.

Dr Barbara Schlichte-Hiersemenzel studied in Kiel, Vienna and Hamburg where she did her Doctorate in Medicine. After having trained as a general practitioner and family doctor, she specialized in Psychoanalytic Orientated Psychotherapy and Psychotherapeutic Medicine. She qualified in different therapeutic methods and as Balint group leader and runs her own practice in Hannover, Germany.

Her work includes the treatment of highly able children with developmental problems. Both professional experience with highly able adults and a private confrontation with the needs of the gifted have led her to gain in-depth knowledge of the problems encountered by highly able children in a 'normal' environment. She has published articles on psychosocial conflicts of gifted children and for some years she did voluntary work for the German Association for Highly Able Children. After having set up workshops on different health topics as chair of the Arbeitsgemeinschaft Arzt-Lehrer in Niedersachsen (Working Group of Doctors and Teachers in Lower Saxony) she is now personally involved with the further training of teachers, paediatricians and family doctors, focusing on the psychosocial situation and developmental difficulties of highly able children and adolescents.

Professor Dorothy Sisk (EdD) specializes in the field of gifted education, focusing on creative behaviour and leadership development. She holds an endowed chair and is currently a professor in education at Lamar University, where she directs the C.W. and Dorothy Ann Conn Chair for Gifted Education and the Center for Creativity, Innovation and Leadership. She also coordinates teacher training in gifted education.

Dorothy Sisk is world renowned for her leadership in gifted education over the past 20 years. She is co-author with Doris Shallcross of *An Inner Way of Knowing: Leadership: Making Things Happen*; with E. Paul Torrance of *The Growing Person: How to Develop Healthy Emotional Development in Children*; with Hilda Rosselli of *Leadership: A Special Type of Giftedness*; and with Charles Whaley of *A Primer for Future Studies*. She was the author of *Teaching Gifted Children in the Regular Classroom* and *Creative Teaching of the Gifted*. She has also authored and co-authored numerous chapters, articles and papers.

She served as Director of the US Office of the Gifted and Talented, playing an instrumental role in increasing the cadre of professionally trained consultants for the gifted, thereby expanding opportunities for students.

She held the positions of the President, Vice-President and Executive Administrator of the World Council for Gifted and Talented Children and President of the Association for the Gifted (TAG). She was the first President of the American Creativity Association (ACA) and currently serves on the board of directors. She also served as Editor of *Gifted Education International* and *Gifted and Talented International* and is an associate editor of the *Journal for Creative Behaviour*.

Dr Lorraine Wilgosh is a Special Education Professor in the Department of Educational Psychology at the University of Alberta, Canada. She is also Special Education Program and Field Experience Coordinator for the Faculty of Education at the university.

Her research has focused on issues in parenting of children with special needs, as well as career development for students with special needs. In the latter area, in the past decade her research interests have been extended to the impact of media messages on the development of gifts and talents of women and girls, particularly as they have an effect on their underachievement and failure to develop their full potential.

Lee Wills (BEd, TPTC, ITC, MACE) has been a teacher and administrator in state primary, secondary, independent schools and tertiary institutions in Australia since 1960. From 1986 to 1993 she worked as an Education Consultant privately and in industry.

In July 1993 she was invited to Ruyton Girls' School to develop an enrichment programme for boys and girls aged five to 12 and so the Victoria Enrichment Centre at Ruyton was born.

In 1994 she attended the European Council for High Ability (ECHA) conference in Nijmegen in the Netherlands and has since then presented papers on her work at ECHA conferences in Vienna in 1996 and Oxford in 1998.

Currently she is Assistant Principal and Head of Junior School at Ruyton Girls' School, Kew, Victoria.

Introduction to Part 1

My interest in the subject of underfunctioning able people first developed two decades ago when I was researching some background for a course for Surrey Local Education Authority on the gifted and talented. I came across the research of Lewis Terman and his colleagues at Stanford University. They had undertaken a long-term follow-up study of about 1500 gifted children in primary and secondary schools over more than a 20-year period. The average IQ of the children was 154, but, when reflecting on his findings, Terman (1954) expected that no more than about six of them would achieve national eminence, and perhaps one might be remembered in a hundred years' time. It struck me then that with such vast potential how could it be possible for such a group to underfunction on this massive scale? They had been pre-selected for the study by their teachers and I wondered how many more children had been left out who were not likely to be teacher nominees but who were able and talented in many ways other than in school tasks.

In my own extended East Anglian family there were numerous examples of successful entrepreneurs who had had little or no schooling, a cadre of powerful women who should have been entrepreneurs, and a millionaire who insisted that if he had been able to read and write adequately he would still be serving in a shop.

As a teacher-educator supervising students on teaching practice it became easy to be the 'fly on the wall' and observe vast numbers of pupils in their various modes of inactivity and underfunctioning. This has been reinforced in appraisal research with experienced teachers in a variety of schools (Montgomery, 1999). Even in the fast-track streams of the top grammar schools that still exist, it was possible to see pupils spending acres of time off-task, unengaged, bored and underfunctioning.

Underfunctioning as we currently perceive it arises not from a single source but from the complex interaction of many sources, and from a variety of critical incidents and experiences. Therefore an ecological

1

analysis (Mittler, 1990) of this is required, as it is in the area of special needs in general. After this, an *ecosystemic* approach (Molnar and Lindquist, 1989) to intervention should follow.

> The ecosystemic approach derived from systemic family therapy, draws on humanistic and behavioural psychology as well as social systems theory to create ways of constituting and intervening in problem situations that take account of the full range of psychological, emotional and social influences that may be relevant. (Cooper, 1999: 42)

This approach is common in the emotional and behavioural field and needs to be adopted in studies of high-ability individuals, especially in the area of underachievement, for there are significant overlaps with emotional and behavioural difficulties. Simple solutions such as 'accelerate' or 'provide mentors' are not going to resolve the complex problems associated with the needs of the more able, even those individuals without problems.

The book opens with a philosophical analysis by Piirto of some key issues and concepts for the education of gifted pupils. This year is probably a pivotal point in the education of the more able in the UK and, because of likely changes to be made by the government, it is crucial that the issues involved are clearly set out so that we may think them through. Already it can be seen that having entered postmodernism in the 1980s, the education system in the UK has been thrust back to modernism. Having been through a period of denial that giftedness exists, we are now in a state of acceptance and promotion of the interests of gifted pupils at the expense of others with needs. Piirto's analysis of the grand narratives of gifted education is powerful and demands to be addressed. It raises issues for the book as a whole, both in the analysis of the problems in Part 1 and the interventions proposed in Part 2.

Patterns of underachievement

It was generally thought in earlier decades and even now that ability is a gift that would enable 'bright' children to succeed against all odds, whatever their circumstances. Kellmer-Pringle's (1970) research showed that able underachievers as a group showed a characteristic profile, and this has not significantly changed according to Butler-Por (1987) and Wills and Munro in Chapter 7. Underachievers generally show:

- a sense of inadequacy and limited ambition,
- a dislike of school work and book learning,
- poor work habits,

- unsatisfactory relationships with peers,
- a high incidence of emotional difficulties, and
- behavioural problems in school.

However, we can also identify, if we observe carefully, the RHINOS (Really Here In Name Only) – those pupils who move quietly through the system without touching the sides. They do the minimum to avoid being noticed and merge into the background whenever possible so that they do not need to participate. They may daydream their time away, or quietly socialize and spend most of their time off-task.

When we speak of the able, the talented and the gifted, clever or bright children, there are far more of them than most people think. In any classroom of mixed-ability children there will be at least five who are able; one may be gifted and many may be talented. Fifty per cent of them or more might show untapped gifts and talents or potential for high achievement if we can only provide them with an appropriate curriculum that enables them to find or reveal their abilities. High achievement does not seem to follow a normal distribution like IQ does. It is not over-optimistic to think that giftedness and talent are widely distributed in the population (Goldberg, 1965) rather than the narrow preserve of the few.

What makes children underachieve and what is the ecological perspective? The rest of the chapters in Part 1 seek to answer these questions.

Some pupils may arrive at school already sure that education is not for them, or they may come to perceive it as irrelevant to their needs given the way they are treated. For others, their social context may predetermine their first hostile reactions to education and these may be reinforced by some random early schooling experiences.

In Chapter 2 Freeman gives a developmental analysis of the origins of underachievement in the linguistic, social and cultural backgrounds of children. She draws on data from her worldwide studies of children who do and do not have access to education. This gives an important insight into the underlying problems of underachievement. This chapter provides the foundation and rationale for what the chapters on practice in Part 2 seek to address.

Although teachers may work exceptionally hard to interest their pupils, what they offer and the way it is presented may give insufficient challenge to motivate large groups of children for long. There may also be a tendency for teachers to underestimate pupils' cognitive capabilities, even when they know they are able, so that they may be 'spoon fed' and lack sufficient challenge. Able pupils are particularly vulnerable to underfunctioning where there is a lack of cognitive challenge. This has been a concern of both Her Majesty's Inspectorate (HMI) (DES, 1977; HMI, 1992) and the National Association of Able Children in Education (NACE).

Chapter 3, by Schlichte-Hiersemenzel, illustrates only too clearly in her experiences from a psychotherapeutic practice the distress and 'disorders' that can arise when highly able and talented children are understimulated at school and where their creative abilities have to be suppressed. The system of education to which her patients are exposed is essentially didactic and has a punitive assessment system.

In Chapter 4 Wilgosh examines the barriers to the aspirations and achievements of women and girls. It seems that the media and the social environment still provide the strongest sex-role stereotyping, which can militate against girls' and then women's achievement, and even endanger their lives. She examines a number of strategies and policies that can help girls. She concludes that they require positive classroom and school environments which value boys and girls equally, and says that simply providing maths and science scholarships for bright girls will not solve the problems.

For underachievers, the progressive lowering of attainment in comparison with peers can lead to a lowering of their sense of self-esteem and self-worth. This can result in their seeking esteem in other ways which are attention-seeking or disruptive and which will leave even less opportunity for learning and lower their attainment still further. Pupils showing challenging behaviour can come to be regarded as working against the school goals and school ethos. When they do try to make an effort these attempts are not valued and supported, and then further and deeper problems can arise.

If, for example, the mode of teaching is didactic, with long periods of teacher talk and explanations, followed by closed questions requiring one-word answers, followed by long periods of writing, then it may be wholly unsuited to many learners' needs. Such a system is not geared to valuing and educating the emotions; it favours neat writing and perfect spelling frequently over content. Hymer in Chapter 5 emphasizes the needs of underachieving boys to participate more in their learning and to do more oral work, and this is equally true of a wide range of lower attainers (Montgomery, 1998).

It may well be that the skills and abilities many pupils bring to the curriculum are insufficient if that curriculum is delivered in an inappropriate mode. It can be inappropriate in the sense that information is, for example, highly verbal and given in such a way that the sense of it cannot be grasped because it has not been planned properly and carefully structured. The sense of it also may not link with anything already known by culturally disadvantaged learners, as Freeman points out in Chapter 2, and so it can remain isolated and incapable of use. Pupils' literacy skills may also be insufficient, in that reading and writing abilities are insecure or poorly developed. In Chapter 6 Gyarmathy shows, in her work with learning-disabled groups, that traditional IQ tests are not suitable or sufficient in the identification of the highly able or the underfunctioning able. She uses, among other instruments, Raven's Matrices and emphasizes the holistic aspects of learning. She identifies a trend in current thinking that suggests that many learning-disabled students have compensations in their other hemisphere's development and have different talents. This also suggests that we need to be educating them differently. How can this be compatible with inclusion?

Pupils in both primary and secondary classes do in fact complain that they have far too much writing to do. The education system for many years has been one in which hordes of pupils each day compile personal textbooks and so become copy scholars. It is still common to find that 70% of pupils' time in school is spent on writing. Woe betide any pupil who has not mastered the skill of handwriting legibly.

Downloading information from the internet to complete homework exercises is no different in its low cognitive demand on the learners. In the rest of their lives they may enjoy a far more exciting and interesting time, gaining information in many different ways from dozens of different sources, but seldom, except at university, sitting down to listen to a lecture and take notes. School must seem a strange place and learning too passive a process.

Relevance in the curriculum is frequently recommended, but it was noted in the Scottish Education Department survey report (SED, 1978) and Lower Attaining Pupils Project (HMI, 1986) that pupils' failure to see the relevance of the curriculum on offer was a significant contributing factor in the development of their underfunctioning and learning difficulties. It is indeed a problem to demonstrate the relevance of a great deal of what is contained in the current National Curriculum – or in its revision, which will 'free up' 20% of pupils' time. Nevertheless, it is important for teachers to consider relevance and share it with pupils.

Other underachievers may seek cognitive stimulation in that favourite pastime of all pupils – tormenting the teacher. Able pupils, however, are so much cleverer at this and think of many different ways to disturb others. They may clown and fool about, enjoying the excitement and thrill of making their peers laugh and driving teachers to the brink of distraction without necessarily pushing them over the edge. They may also be provoking by asking endlessly creative questions or knowing answers not in the teacher's repertoire. These activities are interpreted by teachers as 'challenging' and misbehaviour, and all too easily a pupil may become set on a career in disruption as people fail to recognize the signs and overreact in their disciplining techniques.

Problem pupils such as this are said not to fit into the school régime and are excluded as soon as feasible. Nevertheless it must be said that there are many schools that go to great lengths to try to counsel and keep such pupils on track. It is, however, difficult to break these habits once they are well established, especially when they are driven by some inner emotional need or tension arising from personal or family conflicts and fears or a daily diet of intense boredom – as Schlichte-Hiersemenzel discusses in Chapter 3.

We can also suggest that the more imaginative and creative the pupils, the more likely they are to be switched off a didactic form of curriculum and pedagogy. Even the most able and least creative pupils, after mopping up all the knowledge and skills of the primary and early secondary years, may perceive increasing redundancy in the knowledge input or feel that the brakes are permanently on. The disparity in ability and knowledge can become so wide that didactics can no longer reach them. The better memories often observed in the highly able can mean that the threefold repetitions of all material in classrooms can prove stultifying, requiring them to switch off.

Although there is a wide range of learning disabilities as well as impairments in vision and hearing, the most common and the most detrimental to educational progress, resulting in underfunctioning, is dyslexia, together with other literacy difficulties. Pupils with these difficulties, however able, cannot reveal their abilities when asked to write down their ideas, unless they are shown how to overcome these problems. We need to ask: When is withdrawal remedial education consistent with inclusivity?

There is also a group of able and underfunctioning pupils that we may call the 'career gifted', first identified by Freeman (1991). In her longitudinal study she found that the 'career gifted' had been nominated by parents or identification procedures as gifted at an early age. These children had enjoyed the aura that the title could bring, but feared failure and also suspected that they might not really be worthy of it and would be found wanting. Consequently, they would say that they could not be bothered to try with schoolwork, that the work was too uninteresting and boring or that it was beneath them. By failing to involve themselves in schoolwork they fell further behind so that eventually the only sign of high ability was on tests that required very little prior knowledge.

As can be imagined, any one of these underfunctioning individuals in the classroom could be a sore trial to the teacher. Because they are avoiding work there is much time that can be spent on other, sometimes disruptive, activities. It is upsetting for the teacher to be told that everything provided is 'boring' and it can also be catching, so that other children may decide to tell the teacher this and so obtain some more attention or freedom to choose something different.

Sometimes the promise seen in the early years of education is not fulfilled and once again a range of reasons is given – misassessment, favouritism, burn-out, laziness, or challenge of the more advanced curriculum when often the reverse is the case. There may be insufficient challenge and a mundane curriculum, with days of boredom stretching into infinity. Trapped in this 'psychic prison' (De Mink, 1995) the pupil switches off and daydreams the time away.

Where there is a stereotype that the highly able must 'look bright' (Karnes and Johnson, 1991) then those who look different in some way may be considered to be less able than they really are. The UK stereotype is in fact of a white male, weedy, bespectacled, given to solitary reading, referred to as the 'little professor' or 'boff' by peers and often by teachers, and sounding and looking old-fashioned (Freeman, 1991: 22). This can thus disqualify girls and children from other cultures and ethnic origins from being considered as potentially able and being referred for 'special' treatment such as enrichment, depending on who decides and who prevents whom from trying (Holland, 1998).

This ecological perspective shows a wide-ranging group of under-achievers who have learning needs. For a variety of interacting reasons their needs result in or from disaffection with the learning environment and, as such, learning must be the focus of any intervention. Underachievement may be progressive and lead to more extreme forms of alienation, to opting out, to personal harm, or to challenging behaviour and exclusion – unless it is identified and dealt with. In 'dealing with' it, we need to adopt an ecosystemic approach and this is introduced in Part 2.

CHAPTER 1

Some questions for the education of the gifted and talented

JANE PIIRTO

Introduction

In two books critical of the field of gifted education, Margolin and Sapon-Shevin in 1994 wondered about the reality of a giftedness construct. Margolin, a social worker, and Sapon-Shevin, a special educator, both critics from outside the field, believe that gifted and talented education benefits the privileged classes. Benn (1982) in the UK also raised such issues. Along with many others within the field, they also believe that giftedness is not absolute – the results of a test score – but is a socially constructed phenomenon.

In 1996, Borland asked the field to criticize itself in the following areas:

- Is there such a thing as a gifted child?
- Is gifted education racist, sexist and classist?
- Is there a need for ability grouping?
- Does gifted education interfere with community?
- Is the field irrelevant?

Let me attempt to put these criticisms into perspective. In recent years, a group of educational foundation thinkers known as the curriculum reconceptualization movement (Pinar et al., 1995) called for a rejection of the modernist conception of curriculum as a list of objectives, books and concepts to be mastered according to the plan set down by Ralph Tyler in 1949 (and essentially unmodified since he set it down). Tyler's four goals were:

- What educational goals and purposes should the school seek to attain (objectives)?

- What educational experiences can be provided that are likely to attain these purposes (design)?
- How can these educational experiences be effectively organized (scope and sequences)?
- How can we determine that these purposes are being attained (evaluation)?

The 1960s civil rights movement, the opposition to the Vietnam War and the development of the counterculture in the USA all contributed to a rejection of curriculum as behaviourism – with its 'observable' goals and objectives. The rejection of positivism and structuralism led to a crisis of meaning. Experiments in the 'open classroom', and neoprogressivist calls to treasure childhood for its own sake, resulted in an emphasis on humanistic education, with the stress on the affective and the personal rather than the corporate and the patriotic.

During the 1970s, the thinking about curriculum focused on the dangers of curriculum engineering, emphasizing freedom and aesthetics, with a call to tie the curriculum not to technique but to the human spirit. Educators were urged not to conceive values as goals or objectives but to design an educational environment that values educational activity and to pursue a wider view of what educational activity is, as well as to foster creativity. They urged us to value the arts and humanities as well as the sciences and mathematics.

Parallel to the writing of curriculum reconceptualists in the 1980s, a move back to the political right focused curriculum on psychological stage theories of development, with an emphasis on what learning was appropriate during various stages. In the 1990s, curriculum theorists, including the reconceptualists, showed a fascination for the socialist theory of Vygotsky (1984) and with the assessment emphasis of Gardner (1991, 1993). Higher-order thinking became the emphasis at the same time as a call for going back to the basics. Studies such as the Third International Maths and Science Survey (TIMSS) (1995, 1997), comparing the US science and mathematics curriculum with, among others, the Japanese and German curricula, have noted that the US curriculum is 'a mile wide and an inch deep' (Avery, 1998). The recent proficiency testing movement in many states has also influenced what is taught. Again, these trends would seem to herald a more conservative trend in curriculum development.

The reconceptualists are calling for a move from a consideration of curriculum as a set of behavioural goals and objectives – that is, a consideration of curriculum development as a field of 'design' – to a consideration of curriculum development from the point of view of understanding on a deep level what our in-school and out-of-school conscious and unconscious curriculum choices and predispositions mean (Slattery 1995a, b). As well-meaning educators of talented students, we need to continue to engage head on the critiques of our field, our attitudes towards the curriculum and our ingrown biases, defensiveness and prejudices. Postmodern curriculum and theorists provide a framework for doing so without resorting to personal attacks and finger pointing.

Gifted education and curriculum theory

Perhaps the questions this movement raises have been inadequately addressed by workers in the field of the education of the talented. Perhaps we have been so engaged in an effort to establish a foothold for the special curriculum based on the deficit model of special education that we have focused on the trees and not on the forest. A historical look at the curriculum for talented students in the USA must take into account the work of many scholars who have had an influence on the development of thought about curriculum for the talented. All say that the main reason for the education of talented students is to provide a differentiated curriculum because academically talented students learn differently, especially in rate and in ability to think abstractly. All emphasize that the curriculum for the academically talented should be different in kind and in emphasis but not specifically in type. They call for a 'defensible' curriculum that is differentiated. To my knowledge, they deal little, if at all, with the reconceptualist view of the curriculum theory described by Pinar et al. (1995), although mentions of progressive educators, such as Bruner (Maker and Neilson, 1996a), and of teaching for creativity (Piirto, 1998a) are common.

Eisner (1994) delineated five different orientations to curriculum. Most descriptions of curriculum orientations in gifted education speak of content, process/product and concept orientations (Maker, 1982a; Maker and Neilson, 1996b; Van Tassel-Baska, 1988, 1994a, b). Eisner's orientations provide a convenient and comprehensive approach to thinking about the curriculum for the talented. What follows are his proposed five orientations:

1. *Personal relevance* (Renzulli's Enrichment Triad). 'Building educational experiences around student interests is probably one of the most recognizable ways in which schoolwide enrichment programs differ from the regular curriculum' (Renzulli and Reis, 1989: 230).
2. *Technology* (Maker's Problem Type matrix; Van Tassel-Baska's various matrices; Tannenbaum's Enrichment matrix). 'Use boxes 1–5 to indicate results; check appropriate box if mastered (use other codes as

needed, i.e. "N" – not appropriate, "A" – absent, "1/2" – achieved at least half mastery' (Kemnitz et al., 1982: 15).

3. *Academic rationalization* (William and Mary Language Arts and Science Models; Van Tassel-Baska's 'Integrated Curriculum Model'; Talent Search curricula). 'Most of the outcomes that have been officially defined are lacking in specific academic content. This vagueness about content is a continued evasion of our collective responsibility to provide academic guidance. To be genuinely useful, outcomes-based guidelines should spell out ... by clearly defined grade-by-grade content guidelines for at least fifty per cent of the curriculum' (Hirsch, 1993: 1).

4. *Social adaptation and social reconstruction* (Javits grant authorization; postmodern curriculum thinking). Javits 'targets grants to school-wide efforts to provide challenging curricula and enriching instruction (often offered in gifted and talented programs) to all students; at least half of the grants will go to high poverty schools' (Elementary and Secondary Education Act, Title IV, Part B, 1988). In relation to postmodernism there is the issue of power – who will decide? Who decides what the learners will learn and what the teachers will teach? Does the Advanced Placement Company decide? Does the International Baccalaureate Company decide? (Piirto, 1999: 407)

5. *The development of cognitive processes* (Project Zero's 'Teaching to Understand'; Sternberg's 'Componential Model'; Taylor's 'Multi-talent Totem Pole'; Maker's 'DISCOVER Problem-solving'; Meeker's SOI; Betts' Autonomous Learner Model; Van Tassel-Baska's 'Integrated Curriculum Model'). 'The characteristics are that the student will develop Divergent Thinking Processes such as Fluency, Flexibility, Originality, Elaboration' (Ohio Gifted Students Course of Study, 1989: 11).

The essence of the DISCOVER assessment process is that the children engage in problem solving activities in their regular classroom setting: 'they use materials that are novel, fun and versatile, and they interact with their peers while a trained observer records their problem solving behaviours and describes their products' (Maker et al., 1994: 9).

Your belief system informs what you think should be taught. Elsewhere I added two other orientations to curriculum that should be considered by curriculum theorists in the field of gifted education/talent development:

6. *Teaching for insight* (Project Zero's Teaching for Understanding – Gardner, 1991). 'Performances can only be apprehended and appreciated if they are performed by a student ... students need to begin to

"practice" these performances from the first day of class' (Gardner, 1993: 191)

7. *Postmodernist* (Piirto, 1994, 1997a/b, 1999). 'State organised education is an attempt to create what we have repressed in ourselves. But this act is an act of violence' (Block, 1997: 162). Many of the common recommendations for the curricula for the academically and artistically talented were indeed postmodern: for example, pre-assessment for individualization; development of student interests; autobiography used to reconceptualize; time as a variable; talent development based on specific talents (Piirto, 1998b: 132).

One could argue that teaching for insight is subsumed under Eisner's 'curriculum as the development of cognitive processes', but, given the recent push in schools for a multiple intelligences approach brought on by the Project Zero research (Gardner, 1993), I have made it a separate category.

What are modernism and postmodernism?

Before discussing the issues that are the subject of this chapter it is important to frame the argument historically to contextualize it. What modernism is depends about which domain you are talking and the shift you are discussing. In religion, some say that modernism began with the Protestant reformation in the 16th century, which signalled a repudiation of the traditional authority of the Roman Catholic Church and the cultivation of incredulity by such thinkers as Montaigne or Erasmus. Some say that modernism began in the 17th century with the scientific reformation signalled by the works of Galileo, Descartes and Newton. Some say that it began in the 18th century with the republican rebellions in France and the United States. Some say it began with the industrial revolution in Europe in the 19th century. Whatever the preference for its beginning, the age of modernity denoted a sea change in the way humans lived their lives.

Postmodern was a term first used in 1917 by Rudolf Pannwitz, a German philosopher, who used it when speaking of the nihilism of 20th-century culture (Cahoone, 1996). It was used again in 1934 by a Spanish literary critic, Federico de Onis; in 1939 by theologian Bernard Iddings Bell, who used it to signal a return to traditional religion; and by historian Arnold Toynbee to describe the rise of mass society after the First World War. The term postmodern was widely used in the 1950s and 1960s in literary criticism to describe the backlash to artistic modernism. Architectural critics began to use the term in the 1970s but it did not appear in the *Oxford English Dictionary* of 1971 or in the *American Heritage Dictionary* of 1982.

In the 1980s, the term was widely used to refer to poststructural philosophy, especially in the work of young French thinkers who rejected the existentialism of Sartre, the focus on the self of Freud and the phenomenology of Merleau-Ponty. These thinkers embraced new versions of Marxism after the Stalinist horrors were revealed by writers such as Solzhenitsyn. Poststructuralist thought was considered radical, as it questioned whether there could be such a thing as rational inquiry, detached truth, a single self and objective meaning. The term postmodern has been more widely used than poststructural, and that is the term I choose to use here.

Postmodern curriculum theory

Postmodern curriculum theorists seem to fall into the category of what Eisner (1994) called the 'social reconstruction' orientation to curriculum. Postmodernism in education typically criticizes grand narratives as explanations for the way things are. Grand narratives are explanations that have been accepted unconsciously by most people. In the field of gifted education, grand narratives would be educators' commonly held beliefs: giftedness exists and can be identified by a test score; that giftedness is good; that education of the gifted and talented should be the training of intellectuals; that gifted students should have the chance to go to colleges that will help them change their social class; that certain curricular practices, such as grouping or cooperative learning, are or are not effective with gifted students; and that the school system is resistant, unfriendly or discriminatory against gifted students. These and other grand narrative-related beliefs are seldom questioned by practitioners in the field.

Postmodernism has been shown to have five overarching themes: presence (issues of discourse); origin (issues of the body); unity (issues of canon and gender); denial of transcendence (issues of power and class); and the theme of constitutive otherness (all issues) (Cahoone, 1996). These take the form of types of critiques offered. After reading and thinking about what the postmodern critique offers to the field of gifted education there seem to be 12 issues (Piirto, 1997a, b, 1998a, b, 1999). These are issues of time, power and class, the body, the spirit, the canon, justice, diversity, language, discourse, desire and passion, gender and imagination. These are not inclusive and are perhaps idiosyncratic. Only five of these will be discussed in this chapter: issues of discourse, of the body, of the canon, of gender, and of power and class.

Five themes and five issues

So as not to indict the field, no names of educators in gifted education are used, but the issues themselves are described in the spirit of engaging in scholarly discourse.

Presence: Issues of discourse

This theme criticizes *presence*, that is, the idea that anything is really there, or can be directly apprehended if it does exist.

One common argument in the field of the education of the gifted and talented is that the nation is at risk and that properly educating our bright students will save the nation. This argument has been used since the publication of the Marland (1971) report, which evoked national interests to argue for the special education of the gifted. Bright students have even been called 'national resources'. One wonders what people whose children are not so bright think about such talk. Are their children not national resources also? Educational discourse is much more than the latest model or strategy with lines and diagrams within a bound curriculum guide.

That we think we pose or solve a problem when we discuss it is naive, as is thinking that problems have solutions. Luke (1995–96), in a discussion of the new research in educational discourse in and out of the classroom, noted that every time we make a judgement about a textbook, about the truth of an argument, and about the validity of information in a text, we are making a context-bound analysis of discourse.

Several curriculum models in the field of the education of the gifted and talented emphasize problem finding. In thinking about problems to solve or to find, perhaps we as teachers could pose questions in this vein: What about this problem or curriculum model have we unconsciously accepted? What have we unconsciously rejected? What are the hidden features in the models we adopt? What are the ways we are compliant, complicit or blind? All discourse has its hidden, implicit assumptions. 'Problems solved' are few. The analysis of the process might reveal where unconscious processes take over, if only for a moment, and where they direct the assumptions that the problem is 'solved'.

Many of the conversations held between students and the text are seen in their faces, bodies and questions at home and outside schools, and not in their test scores and products judged according to a rubric. Does the knowledge demonstrated in informal settings matter, even though we cannot measure it? Yes. Selection of curriculum materials, modes of encountering the material, and valuing of the material necessarily involve decisions that entail a knowledge of consequences, both implied and spoken.

Perhaps too many of the curriculum developers and practitioners seek quick fixes – a lesson to do on Monday morning – without engagement in the two critical issues of curriculum: What shall we teach the gifted and talented?; and For what purpose? Much of the discourse literature concerns children who have trouble in school because of their cultural difference from what the school expects. Researchers in the high-ability field could also conduct discourse analysis research of the 'good' kids, as Margolin (1994) called them. This research could shed light on cultural likeness and resiliency.

Other matters in this field have to do with talent development and gifted education (terminology), the development of expertise (process), historical definitions of giftedness (Marland, 1971), definitions, (definitions of IQ, domain definitions), assessment (authentic, test-driven identification) and so on.

Origin: Issues of the body

'Inquiry into origin is an attempt to see behind or beyond phenomena to their ultimate foundation' (Cahoone, 1996: 14). Postmodernists often deny that there is an inherent truth behind phenomena, and this theme will be discussed focusing on the issue of the *body*.

In our field, we call for the life of the mind. Yet cultural critics, multiple intelligencists and special educators have begun to emphasize that there are many more ways of learning than intellectual ways – that learning gets into the 'intellect' through bodily means. 'Identity is lived before it is taught' (Grumet and Macedo, 1996: 17). Lewis (Lewis and Macedo, 1996: 33) noted: 'The body of knowledge that is the curriculum and the body experience of being schooled – learning to be still and be quiet – are not separated from each other in the process of education'. Gifted students are known as 'good', according to Margolin (1994), because they obey, they are curious and witty and have good memories; they are crowned with haloes by adults; they sit politely in classes, helping the slower students without making a fuss; and, as such, they may not receive the attention they deserve as frazzled teachers wrestle with the troublemakers or the physically active students. Some bright young students are branded with labels of Attention Deficit Hyperactivity Disorder and subsequently drugged for their bodily, physical activity while learning.

On still another level, current pedagogical wisdom advocates that teachers subsume their essential teaching selves from 'teacher as interpreter' to 'teacher as manager'. In my state (Ohio) and in others such as Georgia, the model of intervention/facilitation/inclusion specialist that is beginning to dominate how the gifted and talented are taught may mitigate against a close, human relationship between teacher and student. Teaching as 'performance' is a bodily act, and an act of love and spontaneity. Teachers as 'facilitators' may not be able to create the relationships with each individual student that make teaching a theatrical reaching out and coming back. The facilitation model may dehumanize the teacher such that the teacher becomes a function and not a person. Teaching is an act of passion and engagement with certain, specific children – 'my kids', 'my class'. On the other hand, the model may encourage such relationships as well.

The picture of the teacher who gains emotional validation in our popular films is of the teacher leaping on the desk in *Dead Poets Society* (Weil, 1989), or the socially engaged and innovative inner-city teacher in *Dangerous Minds* (Smith, 1995). This is the teacher who grabs our minds and emotions. That is the teacher we seek to be, not Ditto in the film *Teachers* (Hiller, 1984) who had the students fill out dittoed work sheets while he sat in the back of the classroom and read the newspaper.

When we teach as performers, we bewitch our students, and they bewitch us. I, as a teacher, am an artist, a dancer; I can change the focus from moment to moment; I can read the temperature and mood of my class; I can speak up and say something to make that sleeping student in the back sit up and participate; I can 'cover' the material or not, as the moment suits me; every moment of every day in my classroom I am tripping the light fantastic. I am not a 'facilitator', a 'guide on the side' – I am a partner in my students' learning.

hooks (1994) noted that the more intellectual the teacher, the more he or she is permitted to deny the body, to be just a mind up there, immobile, behind the desk or podium in front of the class or lecture hall, proclaiming and personifying the 'body' of the knowledge he or she holds in the 'mind'. hooks thinks that part of the separation of social classes has to do with how little or how much one uses the body. 'When the teacher walks out from behind the desk or the podium the body becomes engaged with the student body' (hooks, 1994: 139). hooks made the provocative statement that: 'The person who is most powerful has the privilege of denying their body' (hooks, 1994: 137). The intellectual is seen as holding knowledge in the mind, and no one questions what the body is doing while it is standing behind the podium or lectern, professing the contents of that mind from lecture notes. That intellectual is most frequently male and no one cares that his tweed jacket smells of cigars or pipe tobacco, whether he is animate, or that he spends most of the time with his back to the students writing on the blackboard. The intellectuals who are the most respected and perhaps viewed as being most powerful are those who profess at élite colleges. Those with the least respect, the least pay and perhaps the least power, are the early childhood (mostly female) teachers who must bend, twist and be bodily and actively involved with their students – even though they have studied for several years, have college degrees (even doctoral degrees) and have trained themselves to be experts on young children.

However, such denial of the body may also be part of the lives of female teachers as well. On a recent evening, in a course called 'Counselling and

Creativity for the Talented', one-third of the 24 female beginning teachers revealed, after reading Mary Pipher's *Reviving Ophelia* (1994), that they or their daughters had or are wrestling with eating disorders. If the experience of these professional, well-dressed, caring and perfectionistic female teachers of the talented is any indication, these female teachers specifically, and women in general, have still not resolved the bodily issues raised by the visions of women in mass media and by the consequences of being silenced and made to conform in their school days.

Unity: Issues of the canon and gender

This third theme is the critique of unity. Postmodern thought attempts to argue that what has been thought of as one, a unity, will ultimately be shown to be many. 'For example, a text can be read in an indefinitely large number of ways, none of which provides the complete or true meaning' (Cahoone, 1996: 15). *Canon* is a religious term that has come to mean the inviolable course of study that students should read and discuss in order to become 'educated'. Of course, there has also been argument that some books have more value than others as materials to be studied in our classes. Postmodernists argue that popular culture should also be an academic concern. 'Who reads must choose', said Bloom (1985: 15).

While these observations have been made by feminist and minority theorists, feminist critic Moi (1985) noted that even feminist critics, who do not believe that the curriculum should include only DWMs (Dead White Males), have a canon – and that this is usually novels and poems by women writers of the 19th century. The underlying belief is that if students read 'great works' by 'great authors' they will become better and finer humans. The definition of 'greatness' is that the version of life that has been conveyed in the work is authentic, real and true. The reader views the work with respect and awe. The danger of using more recent works is that they may present experience that is less respectable for school purposes. Moi called them 'those deviant, unrepresentative experiences discoverable in much female, ethnic and working class writing' (1985: 78). What is human is necessarily censored by the choice of material that is included in the canon. The history that is conveyed through these works is most often a 'whitewashed' history. This is convincingly demonstrated in books such as *Lies My Teacher Told Me* (Loewen, 1995), a book that deconstructs current history textbooks and the stories they tell.

Questions of what the canon is must particularly engage educators of the talented as their gifted students must take the tests that give them the credentials to move out of their towns, communities and cultures to join the technocratic information producers. The question arises: What are the basics? Grumet (Grumet and Macedo, 1996) said, 'In the name of the basics, relation, feeling, fantasy, anxiety, aggression, memory, irony are all banished' (1996: 17). Texture and wonder are missing from many of these books, and then, when students enter high school and college, they are relegated to 'ancestry worship, oblivious to the world students actually live in and care about' (1996: 17). Grumet said we have focused on ends rather than means.

The engagement of bright students in social criticism is not encouraged. Yet the very basis of the democratic ideal is that all people must participate in criticism and thought in order to make the decisions of the people. In history classes, students learn from textbooks and get into their minds the timelines and dates so that they can pass proficiency tests. Seldom are they taught critical history, that is, a historical view that critiques what the power structure has done, and what decisions it has made. The 1991 Gulf War is never portrayed as: 'evil phallic posturing of insane men who have learned the lessons of their unexamined privilege well: the ritualised game of exclusion, violation, and obliteration of the many for the narcissistic pleasure of their own power to destroy' (Lewis and Macedo, 1996: 39).

Joanne Pagano, a highly educated social and educational foundationist, agreed: 'The literary canon so jealously defended as source and sustenance of our highest and most noble aspirations is featured prominently in my educational history' (Pagano and Miller, 1996: 142). She appreciates and interacts with music, art, science and mathematics, and she had high scores on both her SAT and GRE. 'And yet these seem not to have made me a better person' (1996: 142). She wonders whether the current education debates will focus on 'the sort of person education should produce. They are moral issues and not simply matters of skill and content. Our education ought to help us to be better persons' (1996: 142). In many states, the outcomes that stated such sentiments were vehemently opposed by parents, who thought that the schools should not teach morals, but that the children's parents and churches should. Of course, a postmodern position would be that one cannot teach without unconsciously infusing one's character into what is being taught.

These are old arguments, and, by now, many of us in the field of the education of the gifted and talented have made our own internal answers to these arguments. We may go along with Hirsch (1996), who argued that we must be able to talk with our grandparents, that educational theory has failed, that 'skills' divorced from engaging content are useless skills, that the romantic principles on which these theories are based have been just that – well taken, but too romantic – and that a democracy fails if there is not a shared body of knowledge that is conveyed to our students. Yet there remains a nagging doubt in the mind of this working-class girl.

Many critics of the canon are themselves privileged and conversant. Then they stipulate that the poor, the disenfranchised and the despairing do not have to be conversant in the canon. On the other hand, to deny a student's worth by ignoring that student's heritage in the name of the canon is also arrogant. As a child of the working class with all four of my degrees obtained at low-tuition state universities, I have, true to my calling as a teacher of literature, advocated a 'core knowledge' curriculum. My reading in critical theory made me wonder how much I have devalued my own experiences as a child of a miner from a Finnish American culture in doing so. Why is my culture, its literature, and its regionality marginalized? Why did I aspire to be Holden Caulfield from the 1951 novel *Catcher in the Rye* by J.D. Salinger, seeing the 'phoniness' of the bourgeoisie, and not Daisy Miller, the naive and feckless American social climbing character in the eponymous novel by Henry James (1915)?

The studies of the American Association of University Women (1995) and of Sadker and Sadker (1995) led to the conclusion that the academically talented female is at risk. Such statements as the following by Lewis (Lewis and Macedo, 1996) are common: 'In the seventeen years of formal education that preceded my graduate studies I had not studied the history, culture, and political realities of women, of labouring classes, of racial and ethnic minorities, of gays and lesbians' (1996: 43). Pagano (Pagano and Miller, 1996) said: 'As a student, I was exposed to all sorts of studies and "ologies" that taught me, objectively and disinterestedly, against my own experience, that women are, in more ways than I can count, inferior' (1996: 145).

Yet the issue of gender among the gifted and talented is more than this. The personality characteristics of androgyny are known to be present in talented creative individuals. Androgyny is characterized by a flexibility whereby the sexes take on similar personality characteristics. Women can be aggressive and men can be sensitive. The presence of androgyny as a personality attribute common to creative people is sometimes acknowledged (Barron, 1968; Heilbrun, 1988; Csikszentmihalyi et al., 1993; Piirto and Fraas, 1995; Piirto, 1998a, 1999).

Another gender issue has to do with same-sex attraction. Yet the presence of gay academically talented and creative students has received no attention in the literature or the field of education of the talented, and these students' needs for role models, approval and humanness may not be addressed by educators in our field. We are only now beginning to acknowledge our shame in how we have ignored our talented gays, lesbians and bisexuals. The 1997 World Conference of the World Council for Gifted and Talented Children and the 1997 conference of the National Association for Gifted Children posed a beginning as there were several sessions given by parents of gays and lesbians as well as by gay and lesbian teachers of the gifted and talented.

Issues of gender are seen in two other arenas. The push to engage girls in science and maths has not been followed by a complementary push to engage boys in the arts and literature. This has led to a gender bias that favours scientific and mathematical discourse over aesthetic discourse. One could even say that there is a revulsion towards encouraging male participation in the arts, especially dance.

Furthermore, the makeup of our field itself indicates gender issues. The vast majority of teachers of the gifted and talented are white women. The vast majority of coordinators of programmes for the gifted and talented are white women. The lack of presence of men and of minorities must have an unforeseen and unconscious influence on the development and direction of this field. Are there solutions to this situation? Probably not, as recruitment of men and minorities seems to fail whenever we try. When we do attract men and minorities, they often shoot to the top of the field as we white women clamour to elect them to offices to indicate how equitable we are.

Denial of transcendence: Issues of power and class

> Where most philosophers might use the idea of justice to judge a social order, postmodernism regards that idea as itself the product of the social relations that it serves to judge, that is, the idea was created at a certain time and place, to serve certain interests, and is dependent on a certain intellectual and social context. (Cahoone, 1996: 15)

Norms do not exist. For example, exactly what *is* truth, goodness, beauty, love, intelligence, talent? This theme brings forth from the critics of postmodernism accusations of relativism and of nihilism. Issues of power and class are collected under this theme.

The critiques of our field, that we are educating students in the positivist paradigm to duly and without protest assume their roles in society, must be considered. How is power viewed in certain school settings by men, women and children? Are our teachers aware of their complicity with the power structure, their docility in training students towards outcomes that may preclude self-examination?

The illusion of the rationality of the technocratic society pervades our field. Although our goal as teachers and professors is to teach students that all beliefs are relative (that is, to bring students to an appreciation of one another's beliefs and views of the world), postmodern theorists insist that truth is not relative but relational. That is, what is considered true depends on who is in power, on what is the student's and teacher's relation to that power, and on the *Zeitgeist* (the 'spirit of the age' or prevailing paradigm). This implies that there is no such thing as neutrality. Much of the rhetoric justifying the existence of an effort for special education for intellectually talented students is so that they can 'save the world' as 'natural resources'. Essentially, we are educating the students to assume power and privilege. If someone has power, someone else does not, and when the subordinates accept their status as natural, inherent, destined, or random, oppression and power are securely entrenched.

National Excellence (1993) argued that international comparisons of test scores should drive the education of the outstandingly talented (that is, these individuals' 'quiet crisis' is that they do not score as high on tests as bright students in other countries). The federal government wrote this report and drives the policy towards achievement of domination by capitalist interests through manipulation of the education of the brightest students in the USA towards achievement on international tests (for example, TIMSS, Avery, 1998). The justification for these practices is that the USA is 'good', that our capitalist free enterprise system is good for the world, and that bright students should be educated to carry out its intrusions into other cultures. A one-sided hegemonic view of power may influence bright students who may not be taught to see US policy in differing lights. For example, bright US students may not be encouraged to read editorials in the foreign press. The power issue in the 1998 bombing of Iraq was looked at quite differently by Indian editorial writers.

On the power issue of social class, hooks (1994) noted that when she, as a child of the working class, entered Stanford, she never encountered a professor who was from the working class. Her professors espoused classless values but were themselves members of the privileged classes. Most or many teachers in public schools are from the working classes – many fathers, like mine, were staunch members of trade unions who sent us to college to fulfil a dream they had. Educators of the gifted and talented still behave along lines where class counts. As teachers of the talented who see their mission as one of training intellectuals, they may have been taught to admire the intellectuals of the 'East Coast establishment' more than the intellectuals in their own home towns. So it is no surprise that educators of the gifted and talented have complied with one of the implicit goals of the field – to move bright students into a higher social class.

When asked what is the purpose of a special education for the academically talented many would say that it is to get them into a good college and help them to move social classes. They will rise above their parents, their culture and their teachers from the working classes. This goal is seldom even questioned. What is left behind when you leave your geographical place, your social class, your roots, to join the technocratic élite? Perhaps it is a sense of family, continuity, closeness, belongingness; a relationship to grandparents, aunts, uncles, community ties and family traditions. Leaving these behind is perhaps endemic to US culture because of its immigrant heritage (except for African Americans who were brought unwillingly and Native Americans who were here already). Immigrant ancestors left all behind in the old countries to seek a better life in the new world; why should this risk-taking not continue?

But what is the price of leaving home, family and tradition behind? Are these worth leaving in order to make more money and gain more intellectual respect? Perhaps yes and perhaps no. In a current study of creative writers, writers often asserted that they had to leave their home place in order to be able to gain the distance required to write about it.

Another issue of power may be how certain educators of the gifted and talented may have been silenced by a majority who propound current paradigmatic models in this field. For example, those educators who are practising artist-educators may have difficulty with the limitations of the linear positivistic psychology-driven models of others. They may find themselves stifling their own intuitive ways of knowing, their own instinctual questioning of positivistic models, fearing censure and ridicule if they seem disingenuous.

Another issue of power is, who decides? Who decides what learners will learn and what teachers will teach? Teachers of advanced and honours classes often feel that they have so much material to cover that they cannot breathe, teach or be free. They feel relegated to positions of curriculum delivery woman, much as the milkman of yore. What is the power of the committees who choose what texts to teach and read?

Still another issue of power is that of the small test-driven field of the education of the gifted and talented within the huge education establishment. The field has served as bellwether and has pioneered many teaching strategies and philosophies over the years. The proponents in this field have not received validation nor recognition for this and have pulled back into their shells, licked their wounds and whimpered as they were accused of racism, classism, élitism and test scorism by critics (Margolin, 1994; Sapon-Shevin, 1994). Some professors in the field feel powerless against the onslaught of criticism levelled against them. They know they represent a field that has no money, no prestigious following, no government cachet, although it strives towards educating and serving the needs of students whose learning needs are different from those of other children. What is their recourse? Perhaps to just continue as they have been, to be the pioneers of an innovative educational practice that may begin as education for the talented but will soon be adopted as education for all. Or maybe the pedagogy of the powerless is not so powerless at all, given the clientele that can take a gem, a germ, a smidgen and expand, magnify and extend.

Constitutive otherness

Constitutive otherness engages many of the issues mentioned above, especially those of power, of discourse, of gender, of the body and of the canon. Accusations and comments about the cognitive meritocracy that has been created by the sorting mechanisms in the school system have been propounded by Lasch (1995), among others. Kaplan and Kaplan (1997) wondered whether:

> we, in a world increasingly structured by technology and increasingly directed by the interests of the new elite, can create an order that respectfully includes people, whatever race they turn out to be, who are average or below average in intelligence. (1997: 427)

Educators of the top 5–10% of students (the cognitive élite) seldom portray the world as a place where those who are capable of being symbolic analysts (Hernstein and Murray, 1994) are separated from their communities (the others) by frequent job relocation and by the walls of the gated communities in which they live, communicating with each other by email, fax and private carrier, and travelling on aeroplanes. Perhaps such separation of the brightest from the 'others' will create a population unable to criticize government and commerce. Perhaps, as Kaplan and Kaplan (1997) say: 'America is no longer a country that provides a lively democratic alternative to rule by an aristocracy. It is merely a country in which entry into the aristocracy is based upon merit, rather than heredity' (1997: 430).

Of course, many educators and parents of highly intelligent students would assert that these students are themselves treated like the 'other' in their elementary and secondary schools, that they are discriminated against in both the classroom and the curriculum. The postmodern conception of the constitutive otherness can be a two-way street, as can the other issues discussed above. However, here at least, perhaps the discussion has been framed and the taboos against talking about these issues can be mentioned and found, maybe, to be straw.

Conclusion

The field of the education of the gifted and talented has embraced curriculum models such as creative problem solving, future problem solving and problem-based learning. We were teaching critical thinking, higher-order thinking and creative-thinking processes before they became part of the regular curricula. Educators in the field advocated for advanced placement courses, the international baccalaureate, junior great books, brain-based thinking, thematic curriculum, interdisciplinary curriculum and the like before regular education did. The innovations pioneered are seldom recognized. Now the postmodern curriculum theorists also go beyond the development and elaboration of curriculum models. They ask educators to engage in understanding what they are doing, why they are doing it and whether they should continue to do it. They ask us to question the grand narratives. The Indian philosopher Krishnamurti (1974), in his discourses on education, urged teachers and students not to rely on their predispositions but to consider everything with fresh eyes. He differentiated between knowledge and intelligence, knowledge being what one acquires in order to get a degree and a job, and intelligence being the ability to see without prejudice. He asked: 'now that you are aware that you are conditioned, what next?' (1974: 34). What next, indeed?

Note

This is a condensed version of a case example that first appeared in Piirto, J (1999). *Talented Children and Adults: Their Development and Education*. Columbus, OH: Prentice-Hall. Another version of this appeared in the Journal for the Education of the Gifted in Fall, 1999.

CHAPTER 2

Literacy, flexible thinking and underachievement

JOAN FREEMAN

Introduction

The concern of this chapter is to explore relationships between literacy and quality of thinking – that is, the flexible and creative aspects of thinking that enable children who have the potential to demonstrate excellence in a variety of situations. Using developmental evidence, the argument is presented that, without literacy, children with the highest level of potential will underachieve. The processes of literacy and flexibility of thinking begin from birth and so are first dependent on the family, and then on outside educational provision, which are influenced by social context.

The conditions in which children of all abilities grow up vary widely throughout the world. Some provide only very limited possibilities of literacy. In the favella slums of Brazil, for example, where children have to earn money to live, teachers are obliged to use their ingenuity, such as enticing children into school with food. In South Africa, children in the shanty towns are struggling with the break-up of the apartheid system of education; classes are large and teachers are often not fully trained. In some strict religious cultures, children may not only be illiterate but may be prohibited from questioning and thinking for themselves (Freeman, 1992).

Literacy

Basic literacy is usually considered to be the ability to read and write to some extent, and numeracy is sometimes included in this. Most definitions place literacy firmly in the context of a particular society. In some areas of deprivation, it may mean simply being able to read the letters of the alphabet or sign one's name. But in more technically advanced societies, which demand a higher level of literacy competence in daily life, even someone who has had a primary school education may be seen as functionally illiterate. The usefulness of literacy depends on how much material people are obliged to read: in general, the more complex a society's economic and social structures, the more an individual must read and write to a higher and even technical level (Street, 1990).

The Commission of European Communities (1988) stated that the term illiteracy does not apply to people incapable of reading or writing on account of physical or mental handicap, but to people who:

> experience difficulties in, or are totally incapable of, for example, filling in official forms, reading public transport time-tables, understanding bills; all of which obviously restricts their access to information, excludes them from rewarding social function and confines them to the role of socially assisted persons (1988: 5).

Illiterate people, however, can now be reached in ways other than the written word, owing to the immensely increased opportunities for communication through radio, television, the telephone and so on. But the extent to which such media are available in developing countries differs widely. In some, the daily circulation of newspapers is less than one per thousand inhabitants, whereas others have no national broadcasting network and not even a reliable telephone system.

Being literate not only implies the mechanics of reading, it means being able to present ideas by using the written word, as well as understanding, storing and analysing words to react appropriately. The International Bureau of Education defined literacy as 'the application of a set of skills to a set of general knowledge areas, which result from the cultural requirements that are imposed on the members of a culture' (UNESCO, 1988). Without literacy, people are limited in the information they can acquire and which they need, such as directives about farming, health or population planning.

The chances of becoming literate differ with different levels of a society (Dubbeldam, 1991). At the family level, for example, a literate family both improves a child's chances of going to school, and encourages familiarity with the written word. However, compulsory schooling is not in itself sufficient to eliminate the problems of illiteracy. Disadvantaged or differently cultured children, for example, may come under the care of teachers who are not adequately prepared to cater for their needs and who may mistakenly accept some reading failure as inevitable.

Literacy is probably the most important foundation stone of lifelong learning. Yet millions of people all over the world leave school never having acquired the ability to read or write – a social and intellectual disablement that is not likely to be due to any deficiency in themselves. Given enough time and suitable help, most normal children should be able to read. But before any individual can reach the stage of reading and numeracy, he or she must first be acquainted with adequate language and numbers.

The development of language

Babies have to learn to make sense of what adults say, not only to understand the direct meanings of their speech, but also the unspoken implications of their gestures and body movements (Messer, 1994). Learning to speak correctly requires yet further effort. This includes pronouncing the individual sounds, ordering words correctly into sentences, and placing sentences into groups that communicate comprehensible thoughts. Conversation involves getting one's own meanings across, as well as interpreting what other people are saying, which means sharing some assumptions about the way in which language is used in the society. Sentences that do not express intended meanings will not be socially adaptive, even if their grammar and pronunciation are perfect. Part of the reason why children acquire languages so quickly and with such apparent ease seems to be their keen desire to communicate.

First, infants cry, then they coo, then they babble, then they produce words. All languages reflect those first sounds by making them the names of caretakers – mama, papa, abba, ima and so on – so that the first words and word meanings of children throughout the world are similar. The first words refer to people, animals, toys and other relatively concrete objects that both interest and attract children. Learning names for objects makes it easier to group them into categories, and categorizing objects helps children to learn more new names. By the end of the first year, language and thought become bound up together, each affecting the other's development (Mehler and Pupoux, 1994). Language continues to influence thought by firming up the growing sets of categories of words. Thought influences language by making it easier to learn words that fit into the existing categories.

The early lives of children who grew up to be of world status have been found to be highly verbal and interactive (Radford, 1990). Generally, future high attainers at school peak earlier and on more fronts, giving them a head start in thinking skills. Additionally, the highly intelligent child aged under five years often demands and so receives more stimulation from the family, and so, in this sense, alters his or her own learning environment. Girls usually develop language skills earlier than boys.

Competent language development is helped considerably by verbal interaction – not just what is exchanged in passing, but systematically with adults (Fowler, 1990). This is an aspect of wider intellectual development, which includes acquiring knowledge and thinking skills. Children who emerge from infancy with exceptional verbal ability, reading to some extent before they are five years old, are well prepared for exploring broader educational fields on their own.

Language is developed with feedback – being heard, corrected, using words to demand – and the rate and breadth of the feedback is clearly related to the language of the adults who look after the children. Underprivileged children can miss this necessary feedback from parents, and the gap in communication ability between them and better-off children widens in just a few years. Developing spontaneous complex speech in children who are not used to conversing in this way is not easy, because children with poor verbal ability are often also impoverished in their perceptual and other intellectual abilities.

In most homes, conversation between adults and children is more evenly balanced than at school. Even in nursery schools teachers tend to dominate children's thinking by constantly asking questions with an answer already in mind, which can actually inhibit the child from thinking up questions (Tizard and Hughes, 1984). The teacher's well-educated style of speech can also be confusing to young children from less favoured backgrounds. It is important for teachers to encourage children's questioning and to listen to them, allowing them to think out loud and use all their powers of imagination.

Learning to read

According to interactive models of children's reading, reading is a deliberate cognitive process of actively constructing meaning both from previous background knowledge and from ideas suggested by the text. This model emphasizes the reader's ability to control and regulate comprehension, a process of metacognition. Reading, though, is a high-level thinking skill which demands flexibility. In trying to understand what an author had in mind, the reader has to check the new ideas, and then organize them and compare them with what she or he already knows. The newest of readers selects from the text, leaving out details that do not seem central to the message, while adding extra information from memory (and the wider culture) that is needed to make it intelligible.

Even in a generally literate culture, individuals vary considerably in their exposure to print. Any group of people with the same level of assessed reading comprehension can be found to have remarkable differences in their contact with the printed word (Stanovich, 1993). A difference in just the amount of reading can show measurable variation in important cognitive skills. These include vocabulary size, verbal fluency, general knowledge and a variety of other verbal skills. Exposure to print seems to be a powerful and unique predictor of content knowledge. It follows that as content knowledge is closely related to cognitive change, so is print exposure. In brief, the more you read, the livelier your mind.

However, children may have an advanced ability to pronounce the words, yet lag behind in understanding the meaning of the text. Guided word play (a form of cognitive practice) is effective in closing this gap (Yuill and Easton, 1993). Young children who are able to remember and repeat word-play jokes, such as 'How do you make an apple puff?' (Chase it around the garden!), have better reading comprehension skills than children who can only remember jokes with little linguistic ambiguity, such as 'How do you get six elephants in a car?' (Three in the front and three in the back!). By the time children can make up their own jokes they are already fluent concept manipulators.

Looking at 5600 Australian children, Rowe (1991) and his team found that their age, sex and socioeconomic levels had neither direct nor indirect effects on their reading levels: the significant differences were due to reading at home, which also had a positive effect on their general attentiveness and achievement. Indeed, parental involvement is consistently found to increase reading skills, as shown in the study of London primary schoolchildren (Tizard and Hughes, 1984). Those whose parents listened to them learning to read were more advanced than others who only learned at school. Not only do little ones need to be taught specific reading skills, they also have to be given the chance and encouragement to practise them. This is considerably helped by the involvement of parents in their play and conversation, and the same seems to be true for learning to write (Blatchford, 1991).

Highly intelligent children are sometimes said to be able to teach themselves to read, but this depends on the materials they have to learn with and their language experience. Early apparently insatiable reading is one indication of an intellectually gifted child. Clearly, though, however high a child's natural potential, without access to literature and permission to learn the child will not read.

Learning numbers

What is true for words is also true for numbers. Babies start to learn numbers by listening to parents counting things, such as fingers or steps, over and over again. Many children's rhymes have counting in them, and the language of mathematics can emerge quite naturally in a lively home.

Seymour Papert (1980), the US mathematician, says that a home should be mathematically literate, which means that in the same way that children are expected to learn their letters, so they should learn to use numbers. Papert views the child as a builder who needs materials to build with. Children who fail at mathematics usually come from environments which are poor in 'maths-speaking' adults, so that they arrive at school lacking the basic learning that is necessary if school mathematics is to follow on easily.

Papert also refers to 'cultural toxins'. These are negative ideas which contaminate people's images of themselves as learners and lead children to define themselves as incompetent in any subject area. In this way, their deficiency becomes their identity – 'I can't do maths'. Learning then deteriorates from the child's early free exploration of the world to a chore, limited by insecurities and self-imposed restrictions. Many children who grow up with a love and aptitude for mathematics owe this positive feeling at least in part to picking up what Papert calls the 'germs' of their 'math culture' from adults who, you might say, know how to 'speak' mathematics. It's not that they know how to solve equations, but rather that they are marked by a turn of mind that shows up in the logic of their arguments. Such fortunate children's preferred play is often puzzles, puns and paradoxes, and they may be seen as mathematically advanced.

Maths phobia is a block that is endemic in Western culture, and especially affects girls. It prevents people from learning anything that they perceive as mathematics, although if they do not recognize it as such they may not have any trouble with it. Such phobic children are forced into school learning situations where they are doomed to generate powerful negative feelings about numbers, and perhaps even about learning in general. This sets up a downwards, self-perpetuating cycle. When these individuals become parents themselves, they will not only fail to pass on mathematical 'germs', but will also infect their children with the intellectually destructive germs of 'maths phobia'. This self-perpetuating cycle has to be broken. It should be done as early as possible in a child's life, although it could also be done by a good teacher in the child's first school.

The context in which school mathematical questions are presented has a big influence on children's ability to answer them. For example, the tangled wording of many arithmetic problems is a burden on a child's memory, simply increasing the difficulty of the problems, in a way that has nothing to do with the arithmetic. Even when the wording is not over-complex, unfamiliar contexts often strain children's competence, and prevent them from applying the procedures that they use successfully in other contexts.

This is illustrated in a study of 9–15-year-old Brazilian street children, who were the sons and daughters of poor migrant workers who had moved to a large city (Nunes et al., 1993). The children contributed to the family financially by working as street vendors, selling coconuts, popcorn, corn-on-the-cob and other foods. Their work required them to add, subtract, multiply and occasionally to divide in their heads. (One coconut costs one cruzeiros, five coconuts will cost...?) Despite little formal education, the children could tell customers how much purchases cost and how much change they should get. They were quick-witted and articulate in their own environment, with excellent fluency in 'street' language.

In an experiment, the children were asked to solve three types of problem. The first type of problem was typical of buying and selling trans-actions, and the second involved similar problem-solving situations, but without the goods the child was used to. The third type was problems that were arithmetically identical, but which were presented without a problem-solving context, such as how much is 85 + 63? The children were able to solve 98% of questions that could arise at their food stall, and 74% of the items that involved selling unfamiliar goods, but they could solve only 37% of those outside a problem-solving context. These children clearly knew how to add, but were not flexible enough in their thinking to transfer it to other situations.

The children were not, in fact, understanding the fundamental laws of mathematics, but only a limited selection of techniques. There was almost no insight or reflection involved in what they were doing, so that it was difficult, if not impossible, for them to transfer their techniques to other mathematical situations or subjects. What they were using were basic coping skills that made use of numbers, rather than any genuine compe-tence in numeracy. Obviously, it was possible to get by with enough super-ficial information to live, but without tuition and practice in cognitive skills, no child can reach the level and flexibility of thinking of which they are capable.

Flexible thinking

Flexible thinking can be seen in the ability to deal competently both with information and with other people. But it does not develop spontaneously to a high level, no matter how high the potential: children need emotional support and good teaching if they are to improve beyond the minimum needed for short-term everyday problem-solving. Yet the human potential for learning and flexible thinking has been seriously underestimated. The decoding and learning of the spoken language is, of itself, a brilliant feat that is accomplished by just about everyone to some extent, including slow learners.

However, it cannot be assumed that because bright children are well educated, they are also capable of thinking and acting flexibly and creatively. This was seen in the results of the British 14-year-old comparative study of 210 gifted and non-gifted children (Freeman, 1991, 1994). Some of the academic high-flyers, the ones who were keen to learn, and whose parents and teachers were keen for them to learn, left school flushed with examination successes but with their curiosity dimmed and their outlooks narrowed. But others did not. The differences in their lifestyles and personalities seemed to be responsible. Successful academic achievement, which is involved with considerable learning and its reproduction, seemed to be more closely related to control of the emotions and fear of experimenting with new ideas. Those who were able to show flexible creative thinking had greater emotional security and had been brought up to think for themselves. This provided them with the courage to explore intellectually and artistically, and was a highly significant feature of their creative production.

Thinking is social. From birth, individuals adjust their behaviour according to the people they live among. Assessing the capacities of other people and predicting their behaviour is an important part of intellectual growth. The ways in which we behave can be seen as ongoing 'experiments', their results providing feedback from the environment which helps to determine future behaviour. One can see the effects of the social context in the ways an individual deals with a problem, which may change radically in different situations. For example, a child may think more creatively at home but conform at school, or may fail with problems set at school but be highly successful in the demands of the street gang.

Indeed, good performance in one place may be inappropriate in another. Flexible thinkers should be able to operate in a great variety of situations, especially when these are complex, to exploit their opportunities and adjust their own behaviour to others. As research findings from psychology, the social sciences, neurobiology and medicine show that the way people think and behave is directly related both to their experiences and to the way they receive them, it would be a good idea to look at where this begins.

The roots of thinking skills

Once a baby is in the world, every sense is active, though usually with a bias towards vision and hearing. From the first days of life, infants are curious and look around for what interests them, staring at some objects

and events more than at others. The refinement of their earliest perceptions is very rapid, and what they are learning then provides an important
foundation for their future mental life.

Even in babies, intellectual development can be thought of in terms
of problem-solving skills (Mayer, 1992). By a few weeks old, they begin
to use their own experiences for simple problem-solving, and so must
have begun to store them in memory – however fragile and unreliable
that memory is. But the human brain is never passive; we always try to
make sense of our experiences by transforming them into simplified,
coded versions, which become models to work from. Adults have
thousands, probably millions, of these short-cut codes and models in
memory.

An example of a short cut is judging distance by using perspective cues
learned from experience. The earliest coding starts with coordination of
sensory impressions, such as feeling the way a ball is round and then
watching it roll. But good perceptual skills do not just happen, they must
be learned through experience. Improved performance requires practice,
and so the best children's toys are those that provide physical characteristics to be explored, problems to be solved, and the possibility of classifying
things.

Obedience is an emotional model, which may be useful in some childhood situations. But if it becomes fixed because children are not allowed
to practise making decisions for themselves, children are more likely to
continue to accept others deciding for them. Independent questioning,
thinking and stepping out of line can then be difficult.

The most valuable and sophisticated ordering of experiences is
'metacognition' – the awareness of your intellectual activities, such as
thought processes, concentration and memory, so that they can be used
most effectively. Individuals who make use of effective planning and self-
monitoring perform better than those who do not regulate their actions
(English, 1992; Span, 1995). They can become self-organized and are free
to learn from experience. They can use themselves as a reference 'test' for
validating new experiences, both to negotiate what they need and to carry
it over into future learning. To be at their most effective, it is important for
children to be familiar with ways of thinking that are appropriate to the
area in which they are working.

In all analyses of complex task performances, the prime characteristic is
smoothly working metacognition. Normally, this improves as children
grow up and gain experience. The experienced car mechanic, for
example, when reasoning about breakdowns and repairs, does not work
unthinkingly through a routine checklist but makes good use of the
mental models acquired of the behaviour of engines.

Culturally disadvantaged children find it more difficult to practise and increase the complexity of their early perceptual learning and modelling so that they can reach the stage of metacognition. This can be seen in little children who are below average in recognizing objects and situations, and who are also less able to describe them (Siegler, 1991). British children who come from homes where they are unstimulated, and where play is scarce, have been measured as falling considerably behind other children by the time they are five years old (Mascie-Taylor, 1989).

The strongest early indicator of a future lively mind is the ability to communicate, which is traceable from the age of three months (Bryant, 1992). Vygotsky (1978), in his 'socio-historical' approach, described how, while children are learning their language, they are also taking in 'ready-made' parcels of culture to use in communicating and thinking. The system works, he wrote, because adults have learned it and share these cultural assumptions. In addition, almost all words carry emotional meanings from the situation in which they were learned, although this can change.

Language thus mediates our perceptions, resulting in extremely complex operations – the analysis and synthesis of incoming information, the perceptual ordering of the world and the encoding of impressions into systems and models. In this way it serves as a basis for highly complex creative processes. The linguist Noam Chomsky argued that babies are born with an innate knowledge of a universal grammar – a system of principles, conditions and rules that are elements or properties of all human languages (Chomsky, 1968). That is why, he said, toddlers can grasp any particular grammar quickly, despite its complexity.

Effects of complexity

Language and culture

The development of speech is the clearest single indicator of intellectual growth, although it is not an infallible guide. But words are symbols representing ideas which are emotional as well as informative. They carry emotional meanings from the situation in which they were learned, although this can change as the experiences associated with them change. So, learning to speak, read and write is affected by a number of factors, such as the baby's emotional security and the need to communicate with words.

Mothers usually provide a baby's introduction to the prevailing culture by mediating or filtering experiences of the world. The mother's own emotions play a role in this, which can significantly affect the intellectual life of the baby. Even at the age of 10 weeks infants can recognize the difference between happiness, sadness or anger in their mothers (Collins and Gunnar, 1990). The mother's happiness encourages the infant to explore; her unhappiness produces sadness or anger; and her distress causes the infant to withdraw.

Any condition that causes stress to infants increases their need for their mothers, and decreases their urge to explore. What is more, the ill-effects of anxiety-arousing experiences (such as poverty) are cumulative. As a result, children raised in a stable, happy home are more likely to be curious and to persist with their own explorations, especially when tasks become more complex. In a comparison study, three-and-a-half-year-olds who had been classified as securely attached when they were babies thought of new ideas and participated more in nursery activities and also attracted more friends than the less secure children. Their teachers rated them as more curious, eager to learn, self-directed and effective (Waters et al., 1979).

Human beings are social by nature. They come together in groups which have their own particular cultural identity, made up of what their members have learned and how they behave. Cultural influences, such as historical origins, mythology and religion, legitimize this behaviour, as in the division of labour or status. Culture filters downwards through generations, but it also spreads horizontally. In this way it affects other cultures, the most notable example of this being the world wide influence of US culture. Culture can also move upwards, as when new expressions in language, coined by the young, are absorbed into general speech. Changes also come from creative endeavour, for example the psychological ideas of Sigmund Freud or Pablo Picasso's new concepts of art, which become absorbed by the cultural network. With any change in culture, the language changes accordingly: new words are introduced, and others become obsolete or disappear altogether. With all these currents and cross-currents, the culture that is inherited by a particular generation can never be the same as the one it later passes on.

To understand each other, people have to learn the specific codes, signs and language of their culture. In almost all countries, people are marked as belonging to different subcultures by using different words and dialects within the common language. Their ideas about social values are equally varied. Non-verbal, physical expressions, such as the way people greet or insult each other, are just as culture-based. Indeed, sometimes dress or a hairstyle can be more informative than any words in identifying groups.

Deprived children

For millions of the world's children, schooling is almost an irrelevance in the daily battle for survival. Working children lack choice, career goals, and hence any incentive to persevere with formal learning. Indeed, absenteeism from school, whether voluntary or not, has a poor prognosis in many respects. For example, longitudinal British research has found that truants are significantly more prone to breakdowns in marriage, health and achievement (Hibbett and Fogelman, 1990). This individual human loss is enormously significant in world terms.

When children are obliged to earn money, it interferes with the time they can spend at school and also with their inclination to acquire school-type knowledge. Non-school work is not necessarily bad. It can be a source of personal fulfilment at any age, and can provide a positive stimulus that enhances the quality of life. But it can also be mind-numbing for small reward – no more than destructive drudgery.

Even now, in the third millennium, a conservative estimate of the number of children under the age of 15 in full-time work is 52 million. For most, there is no alternative because they are contributing to essential life support, and may even be the family breadwinner. Child soldiers are recruited in countries such as Sri Lanka, Nicaragua and Peru; in Bangkok, girls and boys as young as 6 years old swell the ranks of prostitutes, of whom about 30 000 are under the age of 16. At the start of the 21st century, half of the world's population is less than 25 years old. Their chances of their receiving the education they need in order to achieve their potential are minuscule.

Children who work from an early age can bypass some stages of vital psychological development, producing stunted maturation. Their intellectual development may also suffer, as a minimum amount of mental stimulation is needed at any age for intelligence to develop. If that minimum input is missing, intelligence may not develop to its full potential. Although the children may learn to cope with everyday obligations, they may have difficulty in thinking and planning beyond the present – and the younger they are when they work, the worse the problem is likely to be. Child workers are often given the most menial and boring tasks, during which they survive by 'switching off' mentally, so damaging their developing ability to think and to acquire a feeling of control over their lives.

A child's development of his or her potential also depends on the less tangible nourishment of the social environment. For example, in most parts of the world, the least attractive work is done by immigrants – and their children. In addition, they usually have the major handicap of not speaking the host country's language as their native tongue. Consequently, when they do go to school, the children's lack of verbal fluency may appear to be stupidity. Underachievement by immigrant children, such as gypsies in Hungary or Turks in Germany, has been found in many schools. The majority language of a country implies much of the outlook on which the culture is based. But when the children are brought up without that language basis they are somewhat barred from those ways of thought. Effectively, they remain 'foreigners' in the country of their birth.

This is not to say that all immigrant children succumb to such problems, as evidenced by the current brilliant performance of Vietnamese and Korean children in California, or of Jews in Western Europe and the USA in the earlier part of the last century. The essential difference seems to be in parental attitudes to education. In families where children do have to work and miss school, they may still get some education if there can be some form of alternative at home.

Literacy and women

In poor countries, education, especially basic literacy, is identified with status, self-esteem and empowerment. But this can be unfortunate, because not all members of the family may be seen as having the same rights to this status. For example, where women's lives are restricted to the home, they may be denied literacy, and all communications with the wider society may be selected for them by their male relatives. In some countries, such as Pakistan, Nepal, Afghanistan and Yemen, more than three-quarters of young women have no education at all.

Girls may also get a raw educational deal because of their parents' ignorance and cultural attitudes. In India, for example, education is far less frequently given to daughters, just as the best food is often given to the boy and not 'wasted' on the girl. As a result, there is widespread illiteracy among girls and women, just as there is often a poor nutritional base with which to face a life of hard physical work. Relatively few Indian women have access to the printed word or know their rights.

But literacy for women has proven value. Female literacy is associated with better family health and nutrition, lower maternal and child death rates and lower birth rates. Important research in the areas of high illiteracy, where one group of mothers was taught to read and a control group was not, found that women with even a little education produced healthier and intellectually brighter children (Hundeide, 1991). Such information suggests that where education is in short supply, that of females should take precedence over that of males, rather than the other way round, as at present.

This may be compared with Britain today, where girls and boys follow a National Curriculum with a common course from 5 to 14 years of age, with the exception of physical education, and there is a formal commitment to equal opportunities at all levels of education, which inspectors check for in classroom teaching. In every school subject, at all ages girls are scoring higher than boys. An increasing proportion of girls are staying on at school and going into further and higher education; indeed, from 1992 more women than men entered university – a trend which is continuing. Girls-only schools produce consistently higher overall grades than boys-only schools. Consequently, boys' examination performances have become the subject of national concern.

This fear of allowing people to learn – especially to learn to read – seems as though it is a fear of loss of control over others. If people are able to read, they may learn other ways of doing things, and who knows what they could then do with this knowledge? The first printing of the bible by Gutenberg, for example, was condemned by the Church because it presented the threat of non-church, non-approved literature being widely available: the authorities could then lose control over what the people might believe – and achieve.

Conclusions

A child's will to strive for high-level achievement comes not only from personal experiences, but is usually intergenerational. Children will accept ideas from those who are close to them, although these ideas will be modified by individual personality and ability. Feelings about your place in society, which are based on the cultural environment, largely determine feelings about yourself, and have a strong effect on whether or not there is to be any change in the next generation's attitudes.

Feelings of being worthwhile affect children's belief in what they are capable of doing. Those who feel good about themselves and who are confident about aiming high are psychologically much better placed to develop their education. This is helped by the increasing degree of control that they are allowed to assume over their working and living environments.

The major goals of good education are generally recognized as having spread beyond the mere accumulation of knowledge. They include helping children to develop curiosity, problem-solving attitudes and a love of learning that will last for the rest of their lives. However, these beneficial teaching aims have to be encouraged by specifically directed teaching, with provision of materials to learn with. They can be obstructed by children's lack of self-confidence, as well as by cultural prohibitions. People can act positively when they have enough self-confidence and courage to use experience in new ways.

The promotion of versatile thinking comes from acquiring knowledge in a manner which is meaningful to the learner, and which can be used in many situations. Individuals also have to learn to work with others, leading to greater interpersonal understanding. Flexibility in teaching,

concern for the individual child, the provision of free, high-quality education leading to literacy, as well as non-school educational provision for
those who want it – these are the facilities that enable potential to develop
in people from all walks of life.

CHAPTER 3

The psychodynamics of psychological and behavioural difficulties of highly able children: experiences from a psychotherapeutic practice

BARBARA SCHLICHTE-HIERSEMENZEL

Introduction

If people are not sufficiently valued and nurtured, especially in their developmental years, this may lead to a great deal of suffering and misfortune. Children who are extraordinarily gifted in a general sense often feel alienated, because they are different and in a minority in a world that wants to standardize them. They too often receive insufficient recognition and esteem from children and adults in their immediate environment. Thus they often develop an insecure self-concept and have to struggle to hold their ground. This can result in psychological and behavioural disturbances, which in turn may cause a chain of other problems that might continue throughout their lives.

By the time highly able children and their parents come to seek help in my practice, many of them are already exhausted from a hopeless struggle to develop themselves. Some are at the very end of a chain of negative experiences and I am then sometimes in the position where it is initially not possible to do more than simply keep a suicidal child alive.

From July 1995 to June 1998 I was contacted by people looking for help in 93 cases where problems were thought to be connected to high ability. In 89 cases this could be confirmed, mostly by standardized intelligence tests with results corresponding to an IQ of 130 or higher. In some of these cases people were concerned about themselves, and in others parents sought help where problems were thought to be due to the high ability of their child. While most of the children had done an intelligence test before coming, some parents approached me with the expressed purpose of having their child tested.

Up to the age of 17 years boys represented three-quarters of the total number. This proportion changed for adults, when three-quarters of the group were women and one-quarter were men. However, the size of this sample was much smaller.

In a remarkable number of cases as compared with previous years, teachers were the first people to suspect that the child might be highly able and encouraged the parents to look for further investigation and counselling. Paediatricians and family doctors have also begun to pay more attention to highly gifted children as a result of further training courses and have since referred more able children when they suspected special competence was called for. However, it was still usually parents who first sensed that there was something different about their child and they themselves then decided to seek help. Occasionally parents had only a vague feeling that something needed to be done, but sometimes they were convinced that the child required a different kind of emotional and intellectual nourishment than was usually offered. Often they had already sought help from various other sources and had encountered discrimination in the process, yet these parents continued their search for means to prevent their children from withdrawing, diminishing their joy of life and even stifling their abilities.

The characteristics of the group

The parents

There were two main groups of parents. One group just wished to get more information about highly gifted children. These parents wanted to know how they could provide appropriate support and challenges for their own child. In many cases there was telephone contact only, and occasionally one sometimes a few hours, of investigation and counselling, but only seldom specific therapy.

The parents in the other main group were troubled by the situation of their child. They felt a great deal of frustration and annoyance with an education system where teachers at kindergarten or at school were not responsive to their child's needs. Often parents themselves experienced being dismissed and devalued when they tried to get help, and they then felt as despondent and isolated as their child. I think that most parents were courageous not to give up. At first they had expected competence from teachers and the education system, but after a period of remaining patient, hoping and searching, they learned that they could only rely on themselves. Then they began reading the literature or asking questions in order to find other ways out of their predicament. Many no longer dared to discuss the problem with the school. Nearly all of them did not wish to involve the school psychologist, because of their impression that they would be seen as parents who wanted to make something special out of their child. They feared that confiding further in a member of the school system might do more harm than good. In some cases parents invested heavily in time and money to seek help. This shows the severity of their despair and indicates that experts could not be found in their region for the psychosocial problems that were imposed on their child. Many parents were also concerned about confidentiality, and therefore preferred to see a physician rather than a school psychologist or a teacher.

In addition there was a third, small group of parents who tried to deny that there was something special about their child. They were afraid that if they were to admit that their child had started life with an extraordinary potential, they had to accept the responsibilities thereby imposed on them and feared that they would not be able to cope. Their aim in seeking advice was to be reassured. They wished for everything to be 'normal' and, in their inner image of themselves, the child and the family, tried to deny the child's ability. Fathers seemed to fear the personal challenge of having a gifted child more than mothers did. When this fear could not be admitted, but instead remained hidden behind principles, high emotional pressure arose in the family, especially for the gifted child. In these cases the pressure was reduced when I expressed understanding for the difficulty involved in taking an unusual path, without an obvious social network to support parents of highly able children. Some of these parents started to become receptive to new ideas after having received further information and counselling. But others did not wish to be confronted with the need to change their own attitude, and instead withdrew.

The children's problems and difficulties

Although the very early years of childhood are fundamentally important for the child's development and self-confidence, the problems described in this chapter focus mainly on the school-going years. School is the only situation in Germany that is by law compulsory for all people for many years, and it thus has an incomparably powerful effect on children during their formative years.

The circumstances that affected the children I saw were the same ones that forced parents to look for help further afield. At school a child can encounter a wide variety of negative signals from teachers. These range from cynicism and disparaging the child in front of peers, to subtly pointing out what is different about him or her, and insinuating that they will be integrated only when they adapt 'properly'. The child also receives such signals from classmates, people in the neighbourhood or even family members. The message the gifted child gets from the surroundings is: if you wish to be accepted, do not be different. The inner self of the child – of any person – has the deeply rooted need to be loved and to belong. This need then comes into conflict with another deep-seated need, namely the need to develop one's self. Both needs can hardly be completely suppressed, but are instead expressed in a disguised form as psychological and behavioural disorders.

During the formative years of childhood and adolescence, a child's personality is still coming into being. In these years the sense of self in children depends to a much higher degree than it does in adults on the way they are mirrored in the reaction of the environment. The same is true of highly able children. Although they might be able to comprehend intellectually that the outside world's judgement about them could be wrong, emotionally they nevertheless require an affirmative reflection.

When the described needs come into conflict with one another because of the reactions from the outside world, the child is often forced to give priority to one only. If the need for self-development dominates, the highly able child will be in danger of being isolated and of being seen as strange and bad. Eventually they can then come to feel that they are strange and bad, although another part of the personality feels that they are right. If the need to belong receives priority, the child's urge to develop the self will be put under enormous pressure.

When the soul finds itself entangled in a basic conflict, this causes angst. One of the most common emergency solutions it could resort to in order to diminish this angst is to keep one need isolated from the other. During the vulnerable years of childhood, the people responsible for the child's development should guard against such conflicts arising to an extreme degree, as such conflicts may even tear the child's self apart. In order to prevent this from happening, the child's self finds solutions that, while allowing him or her to cope with the problems to some extent, nevertheless produce severe reductions of a positive self-concept by means of withdrawal and inhibition. On the other extreme the child could develop aggressive behaviour in order more easily to draw the attention that could not be obtained before. Such aggressive behaviour could include disrupting lessons, behaving demandingly in an uncontrolled way, being the class clown, biting and otherwise physically attacking their playmates (this happens mostly during the years of kindergarten), and especially arguing and quarrelling endlessly at home.

The main reasons parents had for seeking help in a psychotherapeutic practice were that they had noticed a change in their child's behaviour. Parents also received complaints from teachers about the child not paying attention, not doing homework, and about so-called provocative behaviour that did not conform to the teachers' expectations. Teachers were disturbed by the child being too quick or showing more knowledge and thinking capacity than was required or expected. At home parents noticed that the child had a general lack of interest, was depressive, had sleeping disorders, had difficulties getting up for school in the morning and even had psychosomatic symptoms which led to consultations with their physicians.

When the child became depressed or even no longer wished to be alive – which happens to many children – parents understandably were alarmed and frightened, but often did not dare to talk about their problems with people in their immediate environment. This made them feel very isolated.

Fortunately, in a considerable number of cases the families did not suffer from any special problem, but were simply confronted with the fact that an intelligence test had shown their child's high potential. They therefore wanted further counselling to find out how they could support their child appropriately and to decide which school to send their child to. Many parents expected there to be schools that provide special support for highly able children, and then had to cope with the frustration that in Germany, schools with a specific curriculum for the highly gifted are few and far between. Nearly all of these special programmes start only in secondary school and even then provide places for only a small number of highly gifted children.

The children seen in my practice were, of course, quite different from one another. However, certain categories of behaviour and symptoms could be observed, resulting in the different therapeutic approaches. For example, there were 57 consultations in all (6 girls and 51 boys). Of these, four received an intelligence test and focused counselling only (1 girl, 3 boys). Twenty-seven received one to five sessions of counselling or psychotherapy (4 girls, 23 boys). Seventeen children received six to fifteen sessions of psychotherapy (all boys), and nine received longer-lasting psychotherapy because of serious disturbance (1 girl and 8 boys).

A rather large group did not show any striking behaviour during the consultation and there was no reason to consider a pathological diagnosis. Nevertheless it seemed to be necessary to make it clear to the parents that there was nothing wrong with their child, and that the child's behaviour was typical of his or her age and quite understandable when considering the special situation of a highly gifted child in a standardizing world. I also advised the parents that critical attention should not be drawn to the child too much in daily life. This information and encouragement mostly acted as a trigger for the family system to deal with their problems in another way. The parents were relieved and instead of criticizing their child, the child rose in their esteem. The feedback often received was that the family had found a new balance and no longer needed expert help at that time.

It was frequently the case that a child was thought to be hyperactive, had been diagnosed as such, but did not entirely fit into this category. Sometimes such a child could not sit still during the consultation. On the basis of my esteem and empathy for the whole person I then addressed the child in a way that challenged his or her intellect. This could provide release from high restriction/pressure. As the child enjoyed this, he or she could then sit still and concentrate on what we were doing. This is a change that could also be observed at schools when a so-called hyperactive child – but actually an underchallenged one – skipped a grade, or when his or her capacity was challenged by a high-level task in any other way. This would seem to indicate that when the 'grey cells' are not stimulated sufficiently, the unused energy is redirected and released through the muscles: as a typical transfer into body language, the muscle cells express the child's urge to be active.

There was another rather large group of children that suffered serious crises in their relationship to their normal surroundings. Mostly the source for this was the situation at school, and often the crisis also covered their behaviour in their personal environment. These children began to withdraw and showed psychosomatic symptoms as well as anxieties and depression. They felt quite confused about themselves and started to lose hope of finding a response to their needs in the outside world. Serious tendencies towards resignation had to be counteracted through further sessions of specific psychotherapy and additional consultation with the parents.

Strategies for intervention

In cases where it was obvious that the interaction that took place at school day by day and lesson by lesson showed a lack of understanding on the part of teachers and peers, I suggested giving general information about gifted children to the teachers. Mostly the parents needed encouragement and ideas on how to address the teachers. They had to hold their ground as individuals struggling against an institution. They feared that when they dared to offer information, teachers would think that they were trespassing on their field of expertise and react negatively. This sort of behaviour characterizes the kind of relationship where one side seems to be too easily offended when confronted with the fact: 'There is a field I do not know enough about, perhaps I made mistakes or even caused harm to a pupil.' Often I wished I could have had both parties in my practice in order to encourage the teachers too, thereby stimulating both sides to enter into better communication.

In some cases the parents agreed that I could telephone or write to the school. Even if general consent had been given to reveal details about the child concerned, this remained a particularly delicate situation. Although I had been released from my medical secrecy, I did not wish to give away details about a patient if I could not be sure how reliable my opposite number would be about confidentiality. It was understandable that parents feared that details about their child's psychological situation would be exploited to disparage the child even more, or to place the responsibility for the difficulties at school only on the side of the child or the family. When authorized by the parents to write to a school to suggest a telephone conversation or a meeting, the child was involved in this decision whenever it was justifiable. It was a rather negative experience that no answer was obtained from most schools – not even an acknowledgement that the letter and the enclosed literature had been received.

There was one encouraging example, though, where a teacher was even prepared to travel nearly 200 km to my practice to discuss the topic and learn more about gifted children. The situation for the child concerned, a seven-year-old boy in the second grade, was singular in that his class was an 'Integrationsklasse', which means it was a class that integrated so-called normal children with slow learners and mentally handicapped children who would usually have attended a special school. The teacher told me on the telephone, 'If I meet the special needs of children who are not normally integrated because of their handicap, why should I not also learn to support a child that has special needs because of extraordinary abilities?'. I had some longer telephone calls with this teacher and sent her information and some literature. The cooperation between parents, teachers, psychotherapist and the child worked well.

At an early age this child had assumed his parents' attitude of great social commitment in different fields, which also included accepting every child into the community of a normal school. He took care of his classmates and was considerate towards them while he himself managed with great ease to be nearly top of his class. But gradually, and unnoticed by others, he began to fall short. Nobody noticed that acceptance and support were given mainly to handicapped children, but that this gifted child had needs that required the same basic right of response. The boy could read between the lines only too well and found an appropriate answer to a message that is far too often also given to gifted children who are in normal mixed-ability classes: 'Do not be further developed and ahead of others as you indeed are, but retrace some steps in your development in order to be equal to the others.' The child did so and regressed – his 'symptoms' showed, how he experienced what was going on in his classroom to be far removed from his needs: he started to crawl around on the floor like a toddler, used baby language and was no longer willing to fulfil the tasks during lessons. The final solution was that he skipped a grade, although parents, teachers and the boy himself were sad that the next class was not an 'Integrationsklasse'. But had he not been put into a higher grade, he would not have obtained what he needed to develop all parts of his personality, including his high intellectual-creative potential. After some time, feedback from the school and the parents showed that the child's regressive behaviour had immediately disappeared, and after two weeks of mourning the loss of his familiar environment in his previous class, he was happy and keen to step forward.

There were a few children who were suffering from severe depression and were periodically suicidal, or walled in by a mode of aggressive defence. When I explored their biographies in more detail, I noticed that they had experienced an especially negative chain of events during their school lives. Such events could, for instance, be a situation where classmates bullied too hard and teachers did not accept responsibility for the deteriorating dynamics in the class community. The group had needed a scapegoat, the gifted child, who was then ostracized. It could also just be that teachers refused to accept that a gifted child had special needs; or it could be that teachers were too insecure themselves and could not bear a child who was perhaps ahead of them, both in potential and in many specific skills.

Usually I try to keep counselling and therapy sessions to a minimum. With these children, though, it was necessary to start a specific psychotherapy with the aim of accompanying child and parents over a longer period. I did not limit myself to the therapeutic sessions, as I usually do with adults, but also tried, in cooperation with the parents and the school, to influence circumstances at school.

School is not the only influence on how a child copes with difficult problems. This ability also depends on the child's natural disposition, on the early relationships in the family, on the family's typical strategies for problem solving and on other influences. But the school occupies a central position in the child's developmental years. As school is compulsory in Germany, there is no chance of escape when parents and child realize that the school system does not meet the child's needs. Even if school becomes a hindrance to the child's development, and even if the school structure and the people there cause lasting damage to a child, he or she is still required by law to go to school.

This reality means that it is necessary to find ways to make the education system more flexible, and for teachers to become more aware of their responsibility to use unusual – but nevertheless legal – possibilities to support and challenge an unusually gifted child. Teachers should not set inappropriate hurdles, thereby neglecting their obligation to support each and every child. Although the structure of our school system is effective for the majority, it does not allow sufficient latitude for the highly gifted minority. But, for the highly gifted too, school still remains compulsory.

Summary and conclusions

The largest group of children seen in my practice were just beginning to develop serious disturbances. The disproportionately high number of boys as opposed to girls (61:20) that were counselled could be attributed to the seemingly gender-specific reactions of boys to crises: they express their suffering more strongly through their behaviour than girls tend to do. Parents and teachers may also take greater note of discomfort signs in boys than in girls.

It was a wise decision of the parents to look for help further afield when satisfactory solutions could not be found in the education system. In most cases the feedback was that at least in this phase of the child's life further serious psychological problems and imbalance of the whole family could be avoided through only a few therapy sessions.

The seriously affected children made better progress during psychotherapy when circumstances at school also changed, thus allowing these lonely children's needs to receive more respect and support. When the school structure remains intransigent, the highly able child is forced to continue the great inner struggle to survive with basic needs both to belong and to develop. This struggle is often not noticeable to the outside world and not perceived at all by the school. In such cases the psychotherapeutic work can be likened to a sisyphean task, due to the rigidity of the school system. The success of psychotherapy then often lay only in preventing a child from committing suicide, in keeping alive the hope and trust that a way out of the strenuous struggle would be found.

The importance of circumstances at school was evident also in the less threatening crises of the other children. Even when there was only a small but reliable change at school, this gave the child a little push which resulted in the feeling of new hope. The child could thus develop a new balance and restore an appropriate concept of reality more easily. That means that the child's developing self-concept was given a chance to free itself again from being linked to unreflected reactions and inappropriate negative signals of others. Supported by the psychotherapeutic relationship, the child then emotionally recognized his or her place in the world better, his or her relationship to others in a more realistic manner, and emotionally started to distinguish: 'That strange and bad reaction of others has more to do with them than me; I can nevertheless feel that I am right.' Thus the child's devalued self began to recover, and self-confidence began to grow again.

The significance of what was going on at school was immense in all cases. Probably the most serious disturbances of the children I saw could have been avoided, had the education system and the people working in it shown more respect towards the highly gifted minority.

An aspect I became aware of while working with gifted children and their parents was that many parents were socially committed to a high degree. They felt a conflict between their principle of social equality and modesty, and their wish to take care of their own child in the right way. This conflict significantly contributed to their contacting a teacher. The parents seemed to be more defensive than offensive, and perhaps could not demand confidently enough what they thought the school ought to have given their child. The conflict present in our society between the ethical aim of equality and equal opportunities on the one hand, and the need to allow the existence of an elite of high achievers on the other hand, was thus individually enacted in these parents and also burdened the single gifted child.

In many of the families I saw, the children had adopted their parents' attitude and covert message: 'Is it a shame to be ahead?' They had tried to solve their problems at school in a self-reducing way, inhibiting their strength to comply with this message. Finally, they were willing to be satisfied even by mediocrity, and already felt privileged when, on rare occasions, they received even the tiniest true challenge. Nevertheless, many boys, had been able to demand enough attention to their distress and their parents reacted fittingly.

However, we should be concerned about the fate of highly able girls. They are under-represented among the children I saw, but are over-represented (13 girls to 8 boys) among twenty one children whose parents had had only telephone contact with me, who hesitated to make an appointment, or even cancelled it later. Are highly able girls not affected by the described problems to the same extent as boys? Are they even more willing to adapt and to put their social skills at the service of others, instead of using them adequately for their own progress, but suffer from conflicts as young women rather than young gifted men? Then was a striking distribution among highly able youg adults (age 21–32) with only two men but nine women. Are both girls and their parents more willing to be patient and adapt to the common expectations towards girls in our society?

Often results in counselling are better when you do not concentrate on the children's behaviour and psychosocial-somatic disturbances only, but recognize that these are also an indicator that something is wrong in the system in which they have to live. A constructive problem-solving strategy demands that attention be given to the personality and style of interaction of those who have to take care of children – that is, parents and teachers.

When a gifted child comes into the practice, time and time again I have the impression that it is not the child who should be the patient. High ability is not a disease and I try not to categorize the child as a patient. Sometimes the parents obviously suffer from problems themselves and should be the patients, but often they do not wish to reflect about their problems more deeply.

At times, perhaps, the teachers concerned should instead be the patients. For even though I know that the child's experience is only one side of the coin, I have learned that the teachers are often psychosocially unbalanced. They often seem to be controlled by difficult, unreflected feelings that they are unaware of, or cannot deal with, or suffer from long-term problems. Intrapersonal conflicts seem to be acted out in the relationship with a child who, simply by being extraordinarily gifted, produces anxiety and envy.

Probably the whole system with all its constituent parts should be the patient: the gifted child as the individual concerned, the parents as representatives of the primary socializing group, and teachers as representatives of the school as a powerful state institution and secondary socializing system for children and adolescents.

As a model, the teacher of the integration class should be encouraged. This teacher took the important step of adding new skills to her existing ones and of cooperating with others from outside the school, in order to respond to a gifted child's needs in the school. It worked.

Acknowledgement

I would like to express my heartfelt thanks to Nico Benadie, whose generous and sensitive assistance was invaluable in enabling me to present the results of my work experience in this chapter. My gratitude also goes to the boy of the integration class and his parents for allowing me to publish their story, and to all my patients who confided in me about their experiences and feelings.

CHAPTER 4

Understanding and overcoming underachievement in women and girls

LORRAINE WILGOSH

Introduction

The first part of this chapter summarizes general issues and concerns related to historical and societal influences on women and girls, and the often negative effects on their achievement levels and career choices (Wilgosh, 1993, 1996). This is followed by an examination of educational issues and innovative approaches to enhancing gifts and talents and facilitating achievement of young women and girls, particularly in the adolescent years.

General issues and concerns

Ognibene (1983) discussed how myths about 'True Woman' have perpetuated, over centuries, prejudice against women's work. Although more than half of American women work, marriage and family are still viewed as ideal for women: 'Myths about "True Woman" undergird and define the political, economic, social, and personal structures that determine women's working lives. Because they exert control both internally and externally, we need to recognise their power and try to counteract their effects' (Ognibene, 1983: 8).

In her history of women in management Alpern (1993) reviewed the 19th- and 20th-century view of middle- to upper-class women as (potential) wives and mothers – that is, placing women at home rather than in the business world – and stated: 'This chapter has shown how structural barriers, institutional practices of discrimination, exclusionary laws, and attitudes regarding proper sex roles for upper- and middle-class white women have had a negative impact on women's advance into managerial positions' (Alpern, 1993: 47).

It is Alpern's hope that legislative change and the presence of larger numbers of women in the workforce and in management (with their contribution of a more interactive leadership style) may break down barriers against women in management. Ciccocioppo (1998) described the continuing existence of attitudinal barriers (the 'glass ceiling'), preventing all but a few women from reaching corporate and university executive levels, although there is some evidence that recently more women are making inroads.

Alpern (1993) has noted that some defensiveness of women in management has come from uncomplimentary media portrayals – for example, of these women as efficient 'go-getters' without feminine sensitivities. She recalled Friedan's (1963, as cited in Alpern, 1993) book *The Feminine Mystique*, wherein the case was made that the identity of women in the 20th century was equated with their femininity. Furthermore, as an aftermath of women's increased prominence in the workforce during the Second World War, the media and educational institutions strongly reaffirmed women's primary roles as wife and mother.

Pyke (1997) reflected back to the 19th-century view that women's smaller brains confirmed their intellectual inferiority. Thus, their education, consisting of such teachings as needlework, drawing and dancing, was directed towards the primary role of pleasing and being useful to men. If one steps back to the writings of the time, the origins of contemporary views and attitudes can be traced. For example, the 'feminine ideal' of that century depicted women's existence as focused on meeting the needs of others, particularly their husbands and families. The prevailing ideology of womanhood was powerful, which still retains some potency:

> In the Victorian period the feminine ideal became sentimentalised and, especially in the minds of men, trivialised ... the prevalence of the leisured lady in popular fiction suggests strongly that many, possibly most, middle class women aspired to the idle, refined life of the 'perfect lady'. (Pyke, 1997: 155)

If we examine the writings of female novelists of the 19th century, for example Jane Austen, we can gain a first-hand impression of the female roles that potentially influenced women and girls of the time. In a contemporary preface to *Northanger Abbey* (Austen, 1818; as republished in 1993), Rowe (1993) noted parallels to current concerns about corruption from television and film. In Austen's depiction of the effects of novels on the attitudes and behaviours of individuals such as her heroine, Catherine, she described Catherine thus: '... from fifteen to seventeen she was trained for a heroine: she read all such works as heroines must read ...' (p. 4), '... her mind about as ignorant and uninformed as the female mind at seventeen usually is' (p. 6). Catherine expressed some views on gender equality: 'In every power, of which taste is the foundation, excellence is pretty much divided between the sexes' (p. 13). Later in the novel, more cynically, Austen stated:

> To come with a well-informed mind, is to come with an inability of adminis-
> tering to the vanity of others, which a sensible person would always wish to
> avoid. A woman especially, if she have the misfortune of knowing anything,
> should conceal it as well as she can. (p. 71)

Clearly, this single example demonstrates that contemporary attitudes towards women and girls can be traced to influences well before the 20th century.

Lack of contemporary gender equity in the workplace is well documented (Dick and Rallis, 1991). Tomini and Page (1992) cited research showing disadvantages to women and girls in career choice, with women over-represented in lower-level jobs relative to men and choosing career paths other than science, mathematics and engineering. They identified factors that contributed to this state, including gender-role conditioning, family and peer influences, fear of success and media content. Their own research illustrated that counsellors' recommendations to students tended to be towards traditionally gender-appropriate careers. Not surprisingly, Masson and Hornby (1986) had cautioned that girls receive 'wrong information' about the importance of education and employment in their lives from poorly informed educators and counsellors. Their recommendations included educating counsellors about non-traditional occupational choices and labour market needs, and developing mentorship programmes for girls to inform them of career options.

Although many writers (for example, Hyde et al., 1990) promote gender-equity strategies to allow equality of opportunity for girls in traditionally male-dominated fields, others (Fuchs and Fuchs, 1995) propose separate educational approaches for girls to allow their development in more gender-specific career directions.

Consistent with this dichotomy, Kimball (1994) has identified two different feminist perspectives on gender differences and similarities, which lead to vastly different social outcomes. Those feminist psychologists who focus on similarities between men and women (similarities tradition) are motivated to promote full participation (that is, political and social equality) of women in a 'male dominated public world' (p. 388). They emphasize the lack of differences in skills and competencies between the sexes and the impact of situational variables on gender inequity. By contrast, feminist psychologists who focus on gender differences (differences tradition) have the goal of creating a different world order where women's qualities of caring, connection and reciprocity are valued over power, separation and hierarchy (Kimball, 1994). The differences tradition advocates separate spheres of influence for women, on the basis that positive human qualities have been undervalued because they are associated with women.

Operating within a differences tradition, Reis (1991) suggested that we need to study problems and challenges facing women: 'We may find it useful to redefine achievement in a way that adequately reflects the conscious choices and decisions made by high ability females' (1991: 197). Kimball (1994) argues for the necessity of both perspectives (that is, justice and care) in understanding women's and men's lives. She warns that the similarities perspective, which demonstrates that women perform as well as men in a male-dominated society, 'reinforces and justifies a symbolic male system' (1994: 400). There is a need to challenge the existing order and to question the values we want to promote as human values.

In recent decades, many adolescent girls have come into therapy with such serious problems as anorexia, desire to hurt themselves or as victims of sexual violence, whereas others have less serious problems such as school refusal or underachievement (Pipher, 1994). The causes lie in the culture, which Pipher called 'girl-poisoning' (1994: 12). Pipher identified the mixed messages that girls receive: 'Be beautiful, but beauty is only skin deep.... Be independent, but be nice. Be smart, but not so smart that you threaten boys' (1994: 36).

Wilgosh (1993, 1996) examined media images of women and girls, sampling newspapers and news magazines, to raise the awareness of counsellors and educators to the impact of the media on young people, particularly girls and young women. Articles clustered into eight themes, which are summarized below from the 1996 study, in which they were further classified as those depicting the feminist similarities and differences perspectives (Kimball, 1994), and those presenting more traditional societal views of women. For all eight themes, almost one-third of articles were classified as portraying or challenging the similarities perspective, and almost half the traditional perspective. Thus, the differences perspective – that is, valuing women's unique contributions to society – was given little attention in the press.

The messages conveyed bear consideration. Stereotypes of women (Theme 1, 'Women's Image and Stereotypes') emphasize physical beauty, but the dominant (and confusing) Theme 1 message was that girls and women should be beautiful, and tough but also dependent. There is some current emphasis on gender differences, with girls winning the gender competition, at least on some dimensions (Theme 2 'Gender

Differences'). There continues to be much violence against women (Theme 3, 'Violence Against/by Women'), with an undercurrent of gaining equality by violent acts: the primary message of Theme 3 for women and girls was that they should fight back, but the world is a dangerous place for them. There is recognition of women's achievements in both traditional and non-traditional occupations (Theme 4, 'Women's Outstanding Accomplishments'), but there is still much evidence that women are 'underdogs' in employment (Theme 5, 'Women and Jobs'). Although Theme 4 messages were positive in terms of women's career success, the clear message from Theme 5 was that women are still second class in the working world and there is resentment when affirmative actions attempt to improve the professional options for women in male-dominated professions. In education of girls (Theme 6, 'Education/Achievement of Girls'), there is evidence of confusion on which models of education (for example, separate schools or classes) to pursue for girls. Finally, there continues to be concern about decreasing women's disadvantages and increasing women's advantages (Theme 7, 'Feminism/Affirmation'), but fundamental disadvantages prevail, for example in health care (Theme 8, 'Woman/Gender and Health'), where the 'male' model of health is prevalent. It should be made clear that the press coverage often presented negative or confusing messages to women and girls.

By documenting and confirming the confusing media messages to women and girls, Wilgosh (1993, 1996) provided a context in which to examine the issues and concerns for educators working with girls. There is a body of writings that reinforces and confirms the general findings addressed above, and provides innovative models and practices for educational change.

Issues and approaches in educating girls

Initiatives within schools

Mirkin (1994) affirms that, with the onset of adolescence, girls learn to deny their knowledge to protect their relationships; counsellors and teachers must respect their relationship needs while helping them to 'voice their knowledge' (1994: 81). Mirkin expressed the hope that girls will begin to recognize the outstanding women in society, counteracting the forces, for example the media, which work to undermine their identity development. Pipher (1994) encourages girls to trust their sense of self, to observe the culture critically in terms of the messages being delivered, to separate thinking from feeling, to make conscious choices and take responsibility for their lives, and to define their own boundaries and limits. However, she warns that we must also change society: 'Our daughters deserve a society in which all their gifts can be developed and appreciated' (Pipher, 1994: 13). Schlosser (1999) has recommended that self-reliance and leadership skills must be promoted in girls, and that their achievements must be valued and supported, so that they develop responsible career orientations and experience career success.

A number of writers have dealt directly with the role of teachers and schools in countering and overcoming the impact of the media on gender stereotyping. For example, Turnbull (1993) proposed media education using stereotyped portrayals to teach students to question the stereotypes, rather than moving to provide students only with politically correct portrayals. Steinke and Long (1995) proposed that educational science programmes must be changed to provide positive role models for girls, to encourage them to choose science as a career, and Reinen and Plomp (1993) have encouraged the involvement of women and girls in school computer courses and usage, as teacher role models encouraging girls to be involved, and as students.

Horgan (1995) has provided a workbook of strategies for teachers, with case studies, checklists, worksheets and other resources, to guide teachers in helping both boys and girls to build self-confidence and competencies for success. Similarly, Kleinfeld and Yerian (1995) have produced a casebook of situations in classrooms to assist teachers in developing ways to handle gender-equity situations. Teaching tools, such as the programme *Sexual Stereotypes in Media: Superman and the Bride* (Films for the Humanities and Sciences, 1998), have been designed to encourage examination and discussion of the role of the media in nurturing and reinforcing sexual stereotypes.

Also, Grossman and Grossman (1994) have published a text to help raise teachers' awareness of gender inequities, and of how to develop and employ appropriate educational approaches to eliminate gender bias. They have raised the critical question of whether teachers should prepare boys and girls for similar or different roles, and outlined four distinct viewpoints which cause controversy among educators:

1. that natural, physiological sex differences warrant preparation for different roles;
2. that androgynous role preparation will bring about societal change;
3. that individual teachers should determine which of the first two positions to take in their teaching;
4. that teachers should assist students in making their own determination on which of the first two directions to take.

Acknowledging that schools are not solely responsible for under-achievement of girls, Measor and Sikes (1992) nevertheless placed some of the responsibility with schools, and offered suggestions for changes in schools to facilitate gender equity. These involve placing more women in administration to bring more 'feminine' qualities to school management – that is, more collaborative and personal styles of management. Teachers, student teachers and students must all be helped to question their gender-related assumptions and expectations and moved to action for gender equity. These issues must be addressed at the level of school organization, curriculum and instruction, assessment and career counselling; and there must be monitoring to ensure implementation of gender-sensitive practices.

Measor and Sikes (1992) drew attention to two different feminist approaches to education: namely, equal opportunity approaches (equal access to the same curriculum for girls) and anti-sexist approaches (developing new school curricula and structures which are 'girl friendly'). Both approaches acknowledge the need for change to bring about gender equity, with little clear agreement on strategies for change. Measor and Sikes noted that single-sex and mixed-sex groupings and classes are still being evaluated for relative effectiveness. They reviewed national and local equal-opportunity initiatives, concluding, 'There is little systematic evaluation of what has been done, and it is difficult to assess how much progress has been made' (1992: 145).

I (Wilgosh, 1999) am in the process of developing a three-category rating scale for classifying depictions of women and girls and their roles (for example, in print and audiovisual materials), based on the Wilgosh (1996) categories of similarities and differences, and traditional perspectives of women, for classifying media messages impacting on women and girls. The rating scale will assist educators and counsellors in undoing influences that reinforce underachievement. At a basic, practical level, the act of classifying media messages raises awareness to the existence of different media messages. This can be effectively used in in-service settings to raise teacher and counsellor awareness, or as a student activity in classrooms, promoting discussion and awareness of media messages and their effects on attitudes and behaviour. This is one more way of potentially bringing about change in societal attitudes and perceptions through educational intervention at an individual and group level.

Administrative and government initiatives

Supportive school and district administration, as well as government policies and initiatives, provide a context in which teachers can work towards educational changes to increase support and encouragement for young women and girls. Measor and Sikes (1992) cautioned that government and administrative policies do not guarantee equal opportunities and access for girls.

School boards have been urged (Scollay, 1994) to be aware of the status of women and girls in the district, by tracking participation rates of girls, representation of women on staff and so on. Boards must also be informed of government prohibitions against gender discriminatory practices; must analyse their policies, programmes and practices; must advocate for gender equity; and must show strong leadership in eradicating biases (Scollay, 1994).

Government departments of education have a role in providing support to classrooms and schools through educational policies and legislation, as well as in preparation of gender-neutral or expository curriculum materials and practices. Development of such resources as 'Raise Young Voices High: A Resource for Gender Socialisation', a discussion kit issued by Alberta Community Development (1995), is intended to assist educators and counsellors in promoting discussion on gender socialization and equity. This particular kit poses the question: 'If you woke up tomorrow and discovered you were of the opposite sex, how would your life be different?'

Burbridge (1992) proposed that governments must commit to more inclusion of girls and women in vocational education, because the current vocational programmes have not succeeded in drawing women into non-traditional fields. Where legislation has been enacted with these goals, it is still necessary to evaluate vocational teachers' gender-role attitudes and beliefs, and to provide instructions to teachers so that they understand the harm of such attitudes and can design appropriate learning activities for all students (Lasonen and Burge, 1991).

Post-secondary initiatives

It is necessary to consider post-secondary initiatives briefly because a welcoming post-secondary environment is essential to preparing girls to go on to higher education. Astin (1990) encouraged higher education to provide 'creative responses' to women's increasing aspirations, transforming course content and the ways in which science is taught, to facilitate women's continuing in science studies. Opening science to women will not only allow 'new people' in, 'It will gradually change how the system works, and science will almost certainly be better for it' (Prentice, 1996: 9).

Caplan (1993) has provided a survival guide for women in higher education, for both academic staff and graduate students. She has outlined personal and institutional ways to overcome inequality, for example advising women in academia to choose appropriate mentors. 'Determine for yourself that your goals include retaining your humanity, helping others to retain theirs, and acquiring and maintaining self-esteem and self-confidence' (Caplan, 1993: 81). She places the power with women to choose their studying and working environments (that is, to be selective). Her checklist for selecting a 'woman-positive' institution gives guidelines such as examining the hiring and promotion records for women in the institution, and verifying the existence of policies prohibiting discrimination. Welch (1990) also emphasized the importance of networking and mentoring to provide supports for women in higher education, so that woman can bring about change in campus environments. She concluded that appropriate classroom activities can be used to empower young women and develop self-confidence.

Conclusions

The themes identified by Wilgosh (1996) are confirmed by counsellors' and therapists' experiences with troubled girls (Mirkin, 1994; Pipher, 1994) as well as being reflected in educators' concerns (Meagor and Sikes, 1992). The range of difficulties that girls experience, particularly in adolescence, extends from underachievement to life-threatening difficulties (Pipher, 1994). Many of these concerns require more than simply providing maths and science scholarships for bright girls. They require positive classroom and school environments which value girls and boys equally, with guidance and counselling available to help all girls, particularly bright girls who may be at even greater risk (Pipher, 1994), deal with the underlying concerns and pressures that lead to underachievement.

The negative impact of societal influences on girls and women has been well documented (Pipher, 1994), and the roles and responsibilities of the education system have been defined (Measor and Sikes, 1992). Many of the above writers have addressed educational changes that will strengthen girls' coping with their learning environments (Mirkin, 1994; Pipher, 1994), and influence all students in order to create more gender-equitable educational environments.

These writers have also reinforced the need for changing schools and society towards greater support and valuing of girls and women (Steinke and Long, 1995). Unfortunately, at the educational level and in the broader society, the directions for change remain ambiguous and uncertain. Grossman and Grossman's (1994) 'critical' question was, should teachers prepare boys and girls for similar or different roles? There is no clear 'ideal' to direct change. At least two models exist: creating equal opportunities and access for young women and girls in the current common curriculum and educational environment; and creating a new 'girl-friendly' curriculum and environment. This dichotomy is reminiscent of Kimball's (1994) similarities and differences distinction. It seems likely that compromises must be found, valuing both perspectives to the extent that they create equality of opportunities for girls and boys. There must be women in teaching and administrative positions to provide a more caring environment and appropriate role models for girls; curriculum and classrooms must be supportive of all students and provide reasonable preparation for all students for post-secondary opportunities in society.

In conclusion, we must examine cautiously approaches that make the assumption that girls must be changed rather than recognizing the need for educational and societal changes (Briskin and Coulter, 1992). Encouraging girls to succeed in mathematics is valuable, but not if it devalues other options. We must expand the options for individuals, supporting all individuals' learning preferences and styles. We must focus on changing and improving society, moving away from male-dominated structures towards greater valuing of caring and connection over power and hierarchy (Kimball, 1994).

CHAPTER 5

Understanding and overcoming underachievement in boys

BARRY HYMER

Introduction

> The intellectually gifted underachiever is a ubiquitous phenomenon, identifiable in all schools at all academic levels, but he appears a most significant challenge at secondary school level. He may appear in many guises – lazy, disinterested in school, bored, rebellious, unable to relate to teachers, or having difficulty with one or more subjects. Nonetheless, no matter what the appearance, he is generally a youngster who is not using his intellectual potential in meeting the academic demands of school. As generally defined, the high ability underachiever not only fails to reach the academic excellence which his outstanding ability suggests he is able to attain, but also is found lagging behind the achievement level of students of average ability, or, at best, only managing to hold his own with them. (Ralph et al., 1966: 1)

Why 'he'? Passow, in Supplee (1990), noted that in describing their early study into high-ability underachievers, he and his colleagues followed the writing convention of the time in using the masculine pronoun. At the same time, however, it was acknowledged that underachievement is not the domain of one sex alone, and Passow himself '... found *equal* numbers of boys and girls (able underachievers) – a first in the field, but a phenomenon that has persisted over 5 years' (Supplee, 1990: xi; emphasis in original).

In the United Kingdom, what has generated the massive transfer of focus in academic writing, the media and in the applied fields (notably schools) from female underachievement in the 1970s and 1980s to the 'discovery' of male underachievement in the 1990s, has been the publication of data accumulated since 1988 – when the General Certificate in Secondary Education (GCSE), the National Curriculum and new assessment procedures came into being in state schools. There had been early warning signs before then, but, until the 1980s, the 'conventional wisdom was that girls had only an initial cognitive advantage, related to their reaching physical maturity at an earlier age, but that boys overtook girls in the teenage years' (Northern Ireland Council for the Curriculum Examinations and Assessment, 1999: 37). The emerging data, however, were compelling and seemingly unidirectional in their conclusions, revealing, for instance, that girls develop a lead in reading at Key Stage 1 which is maintained at Key Stages 2 and 3 (this finding is from the 1995 data). By 1998, the gender gap in reading had widened between Key Stages 1 and 2. In 1995, boys were already lagging behind girls at GCSE in terms of the proportions obtaining five or more higher-grade passes (grades C to A*), and this trend has continued, with the gap between girls' and boys' GCSE performances widening to 10% by 1998: 51% of girls achieved five or more higher-grade passes, compared with 41% of boys. Although national pass-rates were improving generally, girls' improvements were outstripping those of boys. Looking at the upper end of the performance spectrum, at the highest level of GCSE achievement (A and A* grades) in English, 14% of girls secured these grades in 1995 as opposed to 8% of boys. At A level, having trailed behind boys since 1951, girls gained better average results than boys in 1998 (Department for Education and Employment statistics).

Closer reading of all the available data, however, suggested a far murkier picture, with boys' and girls' performances in mathematics and science being more similar – from KS1 through to GCSE – at all levels of attainment. At A level, even in 1998, boys still had the edge over girls in traditionally 'masculine' subjects – physics, maths, computer studies and economics. As noted by Arnot et al. (1998): 'Blanket statements about girls performing better than boys or vice versa are difficult to justify, reference should always be made to a *specific aspect* of the curriculum' (1998: 8; emphasis in original). In an article by Sarah Cassidy in the *Times Educational Supplement*, Jannette Elwood of the Qualifications and Curriculum Authority observed that,

> These huge benchmark figures make it seem that girls are surging ahead on every level. However they mask areas where girls do not do as well at A-level despite outperforming boys at GCSE. A-level choices are still very gendered. (Cassidy, 1999: 7)

There have been other cautionary voices too: some have urged a more considered look at the possible impact of test construction, administration and marking on gender differences in attainment and on assessment data in general (Black and Willam, 1998; Davies and Brember, 1998). There have been careful critiques from the feminist perspective, noting, for instance, the historical antecedents of boys' underachievement and the attributions placed on boys' scholastic successes and failures (Cohen, in Epstein et al., 1998), or more generally the risks of ignoring the knowledge and insights obtained through feminist research (Skelton, 1998). There have also been attempts to encourage schools and teachers to eschew stereotypical assumptions about boys' underachievement in favour of action-based research based on their own unique circumstances, and to intervene accordingly (Pickering, 1997). Moreover, addressing the subgroup of able underachievers, Joan Freeman had also advised caution in the wholesale transfer of attention from female to male underachievement (Freeman, 1996), noting that school achievement, however welcome, is imperfectly correlated with achievement in post-school life, especially for girls. The notorious 'glass ceiling', it seems, has not been shattered yet.

In the public domain cautionary voices have had little effect: the overwhelming government and media interest since the mid-1990s has been in 'failing boys' and the search for solutions. A few examples of headlines from the UK national and educational press illustrate this: 'Girls doing well while boys feel neglected', 'Girls outclassing boys', 'Failing boys – public burden number one', 'Gender gap widens to a gulf', 'Boys will still lag in literacy stakes', 'Anti-school bias blights boys for life', 'Hard and macho – and their own worst enemies' and so on. Having been so vigorously fanned, the flames of public anxiety have risen high. A variety of possible explanations for boys' underachievement as revealed in national school-achievement statistics have been explored, each with its own implications for intervention. Those explanations that fall most readily within the reach of the school will be of greatest interest to educationalists, but it may also be worth looking at others.

Explaining boys' underachievement

There has been interest in *biological* differences in the sexes' performances in educational tasks for some time. In 1977, drawing on a range of extant genetic and neuro-biological research, a vigorous argument for sex-differentiated teaching and learning was put forward by Stewart (1977), who spoke of the interplay of biological and cultural factors contributing to sex differences and of 'conclusive research findings ... that girls and boys experience more success and satisfaction with learning tasks which are selected with appropriate reference to sex differences' (1977: 1). He omitted to note that social and cultural experiences of the period could also define both the learners' needs and expectations and the researchers' methodologies and interpretations. More recently, the evidence has been regarded as less conclusive, at least in the area of cognitive styles and learning strategies, with Riding and Rayner (1998) for instance finding no significant differences between boys' and girls' performances on their Cognitive Styles Analysis – a heavily researched tool for exploring individuals' differing and habitual ways of organizing and responding to information. Cognitive style, it is argued, is independent of ability, personality and gender. Bray et al. (1997) discussed genetic differences between the sexes from the pre-natal stage and found that the research suggests, for example, that female babies in the womb respond better to sound and intonation patterns than do males. Such maturational effects have often been cited to account for girls' superiority over boys in literacy skills.

Biddulph (1998), for instance, one of the leading exponents of the 'Men's Movement', makes much of research that suggests that boys develop neurologically at a slower pace than girls, attributing to this delay boys' scholastic underachievement (relative to girls) in the UK, Australia and the USA. Pickering (1997) explores the notion, founded in brain studies, of girls as analysts and reflectors and boys as speculators and experimenters, and notes that: 'Given the current assessment system in the UK which is based on a sequential and analytical approach to learning, girls are advantaged considerably' (1997: 48). Interestingly, the same arguments have been advanced for some time in the area of learning disabled children, with many high-functioning dyslexic children for instance known to struggle in an educational system which exposes their weaknesses and cramps their strengths.

Where there has been reference in research specifically to gender differences and attainments at the extremes, it has often been in observation of boys scoring more at the extremes of the range in maths and English (OFSTED/Equal Opportunities Commission, 1996; Davies and Brember, 1998) – a phenomenon much noted in the literature. Referring to a range of studies conducted since Terman, McLeod and Cropley (1989) noted:

> Three facts have been established about able girls in comparison with boys: fewer girls than boys obtain extremely high IQ scores, there have been fewer girls than boys among prodigious achievers, girls as a group tend to achieve in different subjects from boys. (1989: 124)

Benbow and Stanley (1983) provided evidence that non-environmental factors make at least some contribution to the skewed representation of males and females performing at the highest levels in maths. More recently, Van Tassel-Baska (1998) summarized the results of further studies in the area of sex differences in mathematics, finding evidence of a range of differentials in test performance and strategy use (Becker, 1990), in tasks requiring high-level problem solving and untutored conceptual understanding (Mills et al., 1993), and in parents' expectations for student success (Dickens and Cornell, 1993) – all favouring boys.

None of the above can, of course, lead to one simplistic conclusion that in maths or in overall cognitive ability boys are abler than girls – or, more precisely, that exceptionally able boys are more able than exceptionally able girls. The incomplete fit between ability and attainment, alongside concerns around ability test construction and other cautions exercised previously when describing boy/girl attainment differences, is likely to apply at the highest levels of attainment too. This might co-exist with the observation that '... the incidence of some manifestations of giftedness might differ – at least actuarially – in males and females' (McLeod and Cropley, 1989: 126), and the overall conclusion that the weight of evidence is that there is no sex difference in intelligence (Sutherland, 1990; Golombok and Fivush, 1994). The preponderance of boys performing at the extremes of attainment may well give substance to the impression of boys' underachievement (notably in literacy) as much as it might to the impression of boys' exceptional achievements (notably in maths), but the empirical data may be serving to mask the nuances.

Given the likelihood of some degree of gender differences in relation to specific subject areas, the most extreme formulation of the biological determinist's argument would suggest that there is little point in seeking actively to raise boys' (or for that matter girls') achievements, because boys (and girls) would simply be playing out their genetic life scripts during their school years – boys' underachievement as an educational construct would by definition not exist at all. The fact remains, however, that even if the evidence for inequalities in innate linguistic (or mathematical or scientific) ability existed solidly at the level of *populations* (and OFSTED in a 1993 report failed to find firm evidence that the differences in boys' and girls' performances in English reflected differences in innate linguistic ability), at the level of the *individual* there are known to be far greater differences in ability and attainment within each gender group than there are between them. In broad terms, at least, underachievement remains a viable and gender-neutral educational construct.

In education, underachievement is more comfortably regarded as a behaviour than as a crystallized state. Behaviours are capable of change, as (at least in theory) are *social behaviours* – which, it has been argued, may also play a role in boys' underachievement in specific or more general areas of the school curriculum.

Demographic factors, including the changes in employment patterns in society leading in turn to altered perspectives on parenting roles, and particularly the role of fathers in boys' attainments, have been much discussed and researched. The Tomorrow's Men project carried out by a group of unspecified researchers at Oxford University was widely reported in the press. They surveyed more than 1400 boys aged 13 to 19 and found that over 90% of them who felt that their fathers spent time with them and took an active interest in their progress emerged as confident, hopeful, 'can-do' individuals. Seventy-two per cent of those boys whose fathers were perceived as having low levels of engagement fell into the group with the lowest levels of self-esteem and confidence, and with the greatest susceptibility to depression, poor attitude to school and delinquent behaviour. Whether this was a result rather than a cause was not explored. Exhortations to fathers to engage more actively with their sons and to listen more to them are a natural by-product of findings such as these. Biddulph (1998) even put figures to these exhortations, saying that fathers who spend more than 55 hours a week at work are failing their children.

School-based interventions using the male-as-positive-role-model theme have included attempts to redress imbalance in the gender ratio of primary school teachers, encouraging fathers into the classroom and playgrounds, and the drafting in of high-status sports stars to combine football or rugby coaching with literacy-related activities – with considerable reported success in terms of enthusiasm and pupil attitudes in individual cases. There has, however, been little by way of larger-scale and longer-term evaluation. Feminist critiques of this last mentioned approach include the concern that in seeking to boost areas of low male achievement by linking these to stereotypical 'male' achievement, we may be narrowing the range of acceptable male behaviours and entrenching the macho attitudes that may be contributing to underachievement in the first place.

Very little of the current flurry of activity in exploring boys' underachievement has focused specifically or even primarily on the area of the underachieving *able* boy, and it could be argued that much of the impetus for the 'failing boys' movement, in the UK at least, lies in the assumed link between underachievement and the social ramifications of disaffection. This is the traditional and stereotypical domain of the working-class, low-attaining boy: 'Underperformance among working-class boys has become a particular concern for the government, because it is associated with high rates of vagrancy and crime' (*Economist*, 1999: 36). But the possible manifestations of the underachieving able boy, as described by Ralph et al. (1966), still resonate at the turn of the century, and the boundaries between ability, attainment and behaviour are blurred – if they exist at all.

Related to social factors, another much-fingered factor in attempts to explain boys' scholastic underachievement is the area of *attitudes* – including boys' and teachers' attitudes. Pickering (1997), for instance, noted that: 'There is a considerable amount of research evidence to support anecdotal suggestions that the attitudes of boys towards education in general and school in particular explain partly their recent poor examination achievement in comparison with girls' (1997: 31).

Pickering is referring to the Keele University survey of about 30 000 pupils, which suggested that boys' measured attitudes to school differ significantly from those of girls – by 4% (roughly the same difference as exists in GCSE and A-level results!). The image of the disaffected schoolboy is widespread in the literature across many cultures. For example, Schneider and Coutts (1985) found that boys are particularly susceptible to anti-intellectual influences from peers, and a study by Warrington and Younger (1996) concluded that, for many boys, it was not acceptable to appear to conform to the school's expectations and values. A front of disengagement, or at least reluctant involvement, seemed necessary.

Going beyond external behaviours, a number of writers have commented on the attributions made by boys as opposed to girls about their academic successes and failures. Boys, it is thought, are more likely than girls to attribute their successes to ability and their failures to lack of effort (Licht and Dweck, 1987). The same research suggested that boys were more likely to overestimate their future performances given their past and future achievements. Arnold (1997) details later research which seems to support the findings of Licht and Dweck, and which at first sight sits rather uneasily with the image of the reluctant schoolboy racked with insecurities arising from reduced employment prospects, evolving perspectives on masculinity and peer group expectations about classroom performance. The 'average' schoolboy, it seems, is rather more confident about his school performance and future prospects than he should be. He may be responding to a male-orientated classroom and society – to the reality of continuing hurdles to girls' achievements in society, which is well summarized in Montgomery (1996) and Freeman (1996). Interestingly, Downes (1994) partially exempted higher-ability boys from this with the observation that:

> The prevailing 'macho' image to which middle and lower ability boys seem to be particularly vulnerable, is that it is simply not expected that heroes do well in the classroom. The powerful role models from the world of sport, television, popular music etc are rarely projected as having academic gifts. If anything they have got on in life in spite of 'being dim at school'. (Downes, 1994: 8)

The extent to which more able boys are less susceptible to anti-school activities is worth considering. It could be argued, for instance, that more able boys are less likely to take on their peers' definition of 'success', valuing more highly success in formal academic terms. Csikszentmihalyi et al. (1997), for instance, comment on 'the strong core of attributes that distinguishes the talented males and females from their average counter-parts' (1997: 75), attributes that included achievement motivation and endurance. Certain attributes were more prominent among the boys – notably a degree of conservatism and reluctance to seek rapid change. The boys also possessed '... an unusual need for social recognition, a desire that ... could also reflect concerns about social competence' (1997: 78). In a small-scale study into the attributions of nine underachieving but able boys aged 6 to 12 years, Sadler (2000) found that whereas the major attributions for underachievement offered by the boys were curriculum factors, her boys '... were far more concerned about their relationships with the peer group than with either their teachers or their parents and saw this as influencing their performance' (2000: 7). Leyden (1985) picked up on the dilemmas faced by highly able boys whose talents run counter to the peer group norms – talents in creative expression (in poetry or dance for instance):

> His talents can be crushed and driven out through mockery and insinuation. The desire to create an acceptable masculine image for himself can force a choice on a boy as unfortunate and as unnecessary as the one that can face the girls. (1985: 78–9)

The tension between seeking social acceptance by his peer group and remaining true to his talents, interests and inclinations, can be a source of great distress to an able boy – especially when the prevailing culture and attitudes in school encourage conformity. John, an exceptionally able and creatively gifted nine-year-old Cumbrian boy known to the writer, resisted huge pressures to conform in his primary school, but at appalling personal cost which was relieved only by a change of school. At the height of his distress he was asked to draw how he would be if things were better. He drew four lines of primitive stick figures and said, 'I don't care which of these I am as long as I know that there's someone else on my level'. For all his rejection of the attitudes of his peers and his fierce determination to maintain a sense of personal integrity, John, like all children, still needed a friend, a soulmate. Professor C.E.M. Joad expressed the tension well in 1948: 'My life is spent in a perpetual alternation between two rhythms, the rhythm of attracting people for fear I may be lonely and the rhythm of getting rid of them because I know that I am bored' (Gross, 1993: 233).

It is the uniqueness of John and of all children that confounds any routine prescription for the remediation of underachievement. Even in programmes focused specifically on the needs of underachieving able children, the uniqueness of the individuals needs acknowledging: 'The children identified for the special program to help them reverse their underachievement all displayed high potential and low achievement. But that is where their similarity to one another ended' (Supplee, 1990: 5). It is the reality of the *achieving* boy that gives the lie to stereotypical assumptions of underachievement, for perhaps every school, irrespective of its ethos, culture, organisational structures and curriculum, will have some boys who achieve even against the odds. But this is not a call for complacency or for minimising the role of the school, its structures and its curriculum (overt and hidden) in raising achievement for all its pupils.

There has been a good deal of investigation into the merits of single-sex teaching as an antidote to underachievement. The evidence in support of this seems to be equivocal, with a recent review of research on single-sex education over the past 20 years suggesting the strong performance of girls' schools in examination league tables owes more to social class, ability and school traditions than it does to gender (Elwood and Gipps, 1999). Individual schools, however, including mixed-sex schools operating single-sex classes in certain subjects, have reported evidence of improvements in behaviour and academic results for boys and girls. An OFSTED/Equal Opportunities Commission report in 1996 noted that even though the research in the area of single-sex schooling and teaching was inconclusive, boys' schools were well placed to address the issues of underachievement, being able to tailor strategies directly to the needs of boys.

The role of emotional literacy and of creating emotionally literate schools and classrooms has assumed prominence in the 1990s. Pickering in 1997 anticipated a possible connection with boys' underachievement in noting that, 'Recent research suggests that pupils are more influenced by the human relationships aspects of teaching, and, for boys, this seems to be particularly marked' (1997: 15). He recommends that teachers take carefully into account the views of their own pupils in responding to the question, 'What makes an effective teacher?', comparing these results with the competencies-based approach of OFSTED (1995). It is possible that the 'woollier' virtues of fairness, being a good listener, friendliness, treating each pupil as an individual and so on may be more significant virtues in the eyes of many pupils, despite their lack of prominence in the OFSTED list.

The salience of *language* and literacy skills in combating underachievement, and especially boys' underachievement, has been recognized at the level of government (witness initiatives in literacy summer school and pronouncements by ministers), at local education authority level (see also the summary of initiatives reported in a briefing paper from the National Literacy Trust, 1999) and by individual schools. As noted by Arnold (1997),

'Probably the most important ability that schooling demands is the ability to use language to acquire learning throughout the curriculum, and to express what one has learned' (1997: 23). In the UK, National Curriculum Orders across all subjects are now prefaced with the requirement that pupils be taught to express themselves both in speech and in writing, and to develop their reading skills. Arnold suggests that many boys can be regarded as underachieving readers, adequately decoding print but failing flexibly to interrogate text, to infer and deduce, to attend to detail, to cross-reference and to sustain their reading. Boys who do develop and implement these skills can reasonably be expected to achieve well not only in English but across the curriculum. Given the maturational sex differences referred to earlier and the evidence of boys' delays in the development of early literacy skills, attention is being given to the ages at which children, especially boys, are expected to acquire formal literacy skills. There is the suspicion in the UK that boys in particular need more time to develop their powers of expressive and receptive language – opportunities received more plentifully on the Continent. The primacy of oracy over literacy is being asserted, despite evidence of policy initiatives over the past decade being in quite the opposite direction – with many parents and teachers being concerned that boys as young as four years of age are being asked to grapple with fine motor and formal literacy skills beyond their levels of readiness.

Given the evidence of boys' underachievement in English detailed earlier, a recent report suggesting that boys are more sophisticated writers and better spellers is worth exploring (Qualifications and Curriculum Authority, 1999). The study was based on an analysis of 300 A, C and F grade 1998 GCSE examination scripts and the suggestion that boys' tendency to write short, action-based stories with less detail or explanation than is provided by girls (see Millard, 1997; and Hall and Coles, 1999 for detailed considerations of gender differences in literacy) is penalized in English examinations. Boys are thought to have a wider vocabulary than girls, also pointed out in Freeman (1996), and greater technical and punctuation skills. The mean sentence length was also greater. Again, as other researchers have pointed out, this study would seem to suggest that bald examination statistics may fail to reflect the gender implications of the forms of assessment used.

Considerations in trying to combat boys' underachievement

Many schools and Local Education Authorities in the UK have introduced initiatives to combat boys' underachievement, especially in literacy

(Arnold, 1997). One example is at the junior school level in which the writer is involved. Although there is no clear evidence for gender differences in innate linguistic ability, Cumbrian boys are being heavily outperformed by girls at all levels of English attainment, including the highest levels at Key Stage 2 (National Curriculum Level 5+) and at GCSE (A or A* grades). Cumbria Education Service has prepared a resource pack of materials for use in primary schools (Cumbria Education Service 2000), aimed at encouraging teachers to experiment with a range of strategies and techniques for boosting the achievements of junior-aged children in English. The strategies have been based around the knowledge and expertise of literacy consultants Paula Iley and Joan Stark, together with a group of class and headteachers, and the pack's effectiveness will be evaluated over time by the schools that use it.

The strategies in the Cumbria resource pack seek to make use of many boys' interest and expertise in communicating through the spoken word (for example, through role play and drama activities), in the harnessing of a rich variety of reading material (not confined to narrative fiction), in structuring their writing through judicious use of writing frames, through creative use of film and video clips, in applications of Information and Communication Technology (ICT), and so on. Central to the strategies explored in the pack are the recommendations as set out in the Qualifications and Curriculum Authority (1998) report *Can Do Better – Raising Boys' Achievement in English*, which explores boys' strengths and weaknesses in English.

The following are recommendations for consideration in putting together a programme for combating underachievement in boys. They are derived from the issues raised in this chapter and from the following main sources: Frater (1997), Freeman (1998), Grubb (1999) and the Northern Ireland CCEA report (1999).

At school level

- Recognize the significance of strong local effects underlying achievement and underachievement, for there are wide attitudinal and achievement differences between schools, and statistical trends at the level of national populations may not be reflected in these smaller samples.
- Engage with parents, pupils, governors and teachers in opening discussion of the issues.
- Obtain a clearer insight into the issues affecting your own school by gathering a range of primary and secondary evidence, with as much detail as possible. For instance, sample and survey the attainment statistics, teacher and pupil attitudes, classroom practices, samples of work and policies.

- Use resultant local data to challenge stereotyped thinking about boys, girls and underachievement, being aware that positions which are hard to shift may reflect deeply held beliefs and/or anxieties.
- Look out for stereotypical or prejudicial beliefs and language in school policies and practices.
- Consider in whole school policies the value of baseline testing of all new pupils, provision for the targeting, monitoring and mentoring of individual pupils, and explicit attention to staff development needs, for example for staff awareness of boys' needs.
- Develop a consistent approach to language across the curriculum.
- Accept and encourage differences in approaches to learning, and consider staff training in cognitive styles and learning strategies.
- Develop a partnership with parents.
- Agree targets and a timetable for action, observable criteria against which to measure success, processes for monitoring and evaluation and key personnel to take the action forward.

At classroom level

- Make the lesson targets clear and explicit.
- Sequence tasks carefully and provide information in bite-size chunks.
- Provide for curriculum compacting – allowing pupils to undertake extension or enrichment work when mastery of a core area has been demonstrated.
- Value the role of challenge over completion, especially for the more able. Accept alternative product outcome for some tasks – not confined to narrative writing alone.
- Vary the classroom groupings to suit the task; provide opportunities for groupwork, practical work, collaboration and active participation.
- Consider the merits of experimenting with single-sex or ability-setted teaching, but bear in mind the lack of definitive research evidence in these areas.
- Seat underachievers with high achievers for some tasks.
- Use homework for extension and enrichment of classwork.
- Take in and mark extended coursework in stages. Provide guiding comments and advice rather than grades alone.
- Listen one-to-one and provide time for self-evaluation.

In the area of language and literacy

- Survey boys' and girls' reading habits.
- Encourage discussion, role-play, oral contributions and structured story writing.

- Attend to the structure of English lessons and to the structuring of pupils' thinking, including 'thinking about thinking' (metacognition).
- Mark for content, use of vocabulary and technical accuracy, not just for quality of descriptions or dialogue.
- Provide writing frames as scaffolding for different kinds of writing.
- Provide a range of texts for reading which appeal to boys' and girls' interests – and not just narrative fiction.
- Value the range of boys' voluntary reading which may be non-literary.
- Encourage reading for pleasure, schemes for paired, silent and voluntary reading and for boys sharing their ideas about 'favourite reads'.
- Use ICT to develop reading and writing skills.
- Teach the techniques and skills of writing and reading. In writing, use examples from a range of authors, and in reading teach the techniques of scanning, reading for meaning and so on.
- Consider the merits of using high-status male role models to promote reading and writing, for example sports stars.

Affective and motivational factors

- Use verbal encouragement to increase motivation and reduce the risk of public failure. Attribute success to the pupil's abilities or interests, and failure to lack of effort or external factors, for example level of task difficulty.
- Encourage attempts, not just successes.
- Offer praise and other reinforcement, but do this privately, not in front of peers.
- Keep homework tasks brief and focused, mark and return quickly.
- Encourage extra-curricular interests and achievements.
- Accept that some pupils value learning over the achievement of grades – there can be a difference.
- Be fair.
- Involve the pupil in setting his own learning goals.
- Seek where possible a close match between task and personal pupil interests.
- Encourage a pupil to tutor younger/less able pupils in his area/s of strength.
- Consider the use of mentors.
- Communicate a genuine unconditional concern for and interest in the individual pupil.

Summary

Whether it is biological, social, attitudinal, pedagogic or linguistic factors which are most implicated in the underachievement of many boys in school, or whether the gender card has been overplayed, it is the range of possible factors associated with boys' underachievement that makes the task of addressing the need so difficult for parents, teachers, education authorities and governments. What is known is that more boys than girls are recognized by schools and local education authorities to have special educational needs, to be disaffected with school and to have poor attendance records (Grubb, 1999). What can be said with a good degree of certainty is that there is no one factor involved, certainly not at the level of populations and possibly not even at the level of the individual. But the difficulties of teasing out the relative weightings of different factors in addressing boys' underachievement, where it is found, should not deter practitioners from setting out to make a difference using the available evidence as a starting point, adapting this to their unique circumstances and monitoring the effects of any intervention. Be prepared to be led beyond the current theory. You may be developing it.

CHAPTER 6

Holistic learners: identifying gifted children with learning disabilities – an experimental perspective

Eva Gyarmathy

Introduction

With the realization during the 1980s of the need to differentiate between subgroups in the gifted population (see Figure 6.1), interest in research increased. However, clear identification of gifted persons belonging to these groups remains difficult owing to the problems of definition and preconceptions about giftedness. Most research deals with the learning disabled gifted child, due principally to the fact that this population shows the most contradictory and difficult to understand profile of abilities. Their profiles consist of peaks and troughs, yet their intelligence remains almost unaffected, and their development, at least until entering school, is less disturbed than we note in many other groups.

Numerous great creators failed or had serious difficulties in their school achievement. Many of them had some form of learning disability. Albert Einstein could not speak until the age of three, and was a weak learner at school. His headmaster affirmed that he would never achieve anything in life, yet he gained a Nobel Prize when he was 26. Leonardo da Vinci also started to speak late and Friedrich Nietzsche had similar difficulties (Briggs, 1990). Anatole France could read early but could hardly get his baccalaureate because of his bad spelling (Ambrus, 1935). Pablo Picasso the brilliant painter, William Yeats the poet, Gustave Flaubert and Agatha Christie, famous writers, had difficulties in reading. Benoit Mandelbrot, the creator of fractal geometry, could not count well (Briggs, 1990).

Learning disabled gifted children

There is considerable evidence to suggest that when high abilities and learning disabilities appear together, they may cause a special talent. In

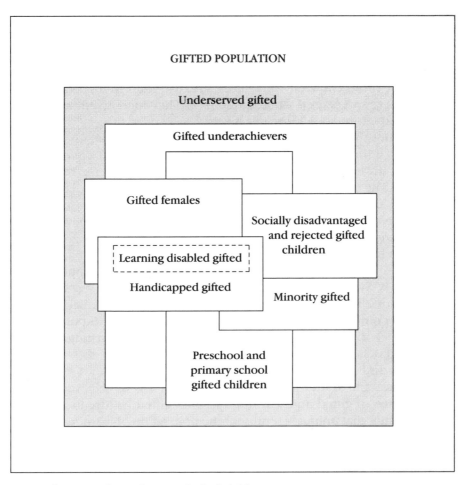

Figure 6.1: Special populations of gifted children

their studies of fetuses, Geschwind and his co-workers (1984) showed that there was a connection between the development of the brain hemispheres and dyslexia. They concluded that dyslexia is caused by a defect in the development of the left hemisphere. However, the same process may also cause a more developed right hemisphere. Although functions of the left side of the brain are poor, the functions connected to the right side can work on a higher level than average. They called the phenomenon a 'pathology of superiority'.

There is another interesting study to confirm this notion. Shaw and Brown (1991) assessed 97 sixth and seventh graders who presented with behaviour characteristic of attention deficit disorder, but who had high IQs. These children had more mixed laterality, used more diverse, nonverbal and poorly focused information, and showed higher figural creativity than did high-IQ peers without attention problems. The results supported Geschwind's prediction that high talent would be found in some types of learning disordered individuals. Shaw and Brown (1991) found that these children were more creative than their peers, when stimuli were presented simultaneously. They perceived and used background information more effectively.

Following the redevelopment of the WISC-R (Wechsler Intelligence Scale for Children) subtests, Johnson and Evans (1992) compared 14 children with high spatial and low information scores with 14 average children. The results indicated that the finding of less lateralized processing alone is inadequate to account for either the reading deficits or spatial strengths of the learning disabled children. There may be over-representation of spatial abilities in individuals gifted in some areas at the expense of language functions.

In a close analysis of learning disabled gifted children Yewchuk (1986a) examined WISC-R responses and profiles. She found that a seven-point difference on the verbal scale, a nine-point difference on the performance scale, a 10-point difference between any two subtests, or a 15-point verbal-performance discrepancy might be an indicator of a learning disabled gifted child.

Barton and Starnes (1989) compared patterns of WISC-R subtest performance and scatter indices, as well as patterns of achievement test performance of gifted and learning disabled gifted children to identify characteristics that uniquely represent the population of learning disabled gifted children. Eighty gifted and 41 learning disabled gifted children were tested on instruments that included WISC-R and subtests of the California Achievement Tests. Means and standard deviations showed a distinctive cognitive pattern of WISC-R subtest scores that reflected commonalities with the general gifted population, and discriminant analysis showed patterns in achievement scores that may serve as markers to target those identified for later in-depth evaluation for early identification. However, case cluster analysis showed the population of learning disabled gifted children to be heterogeneous, suggesting that a single distinctive pattern is unlikely.

Learning disability with high intellectual abilities causes more interfer-ence and makes identification difficult. According to Yewchuk (1986b), WISC-R subtest scatter may be an appropriate indicator of learning disabled gifted children for school psychologists, although other authors warn against too much reliance on them, because large scatters and Verbal Quotient (VQ)–Performance Quotient (PQ) differences are not unusual in gifted or learning disabled children. In fact, in a study of 300 dyslexics of average and above ability Montgomery (1997a) found that in nearly 70% of cases there was only a few points difference between verbal and performance quotients.

Patchett and Stansfield (1991) examined subtest scatter and verbal-performance discrepancies on the WISC-R of 290 normal children aged 9–10 years whose IQs ranged from 100 to 140. The higher-IQ groups exhibited substantially more scatter. The results suggest the need for caution in attempting to use WISC-R subtest scatter as an indicator of learning disability for gifted students. Differences between average and superior IQ groups on the verbal-performance discrepancy measure were not found. However, Herskovits and Gyarmathy (1995) did find significant differences between VQ and PQ in those with high intellectual ability.

After reviewing such studies Gyarmathy (1995) has concluded that the identification of learning disabled gifted children by the Wechsler scale's subtest scatter is dubious, mainly because of over-inclusion. For example, if Yewchuk's (1986b) criteria were applied, only 76 of the 123 gifted children did not present one or more 'signs' clearly referring to learning disability. This means that almost half of the gifted children would be identified as learning disabled/gifted.

Other research results suggest that the analysis of some subtests of the WISC-R may help identify learning disabled gifted children. Suter and Wolf (1987) discussed characteristics of various identification procedures and strategies for providing services that would meet the needs of both the intellectual talents and academic deficits found in these children. They also provided an overview of studies using the WISC-R in the identification of learning disabled gifted children. Large verbal-performance discrepancies were frequently seen. Subscales that assessed verbal reasoning abilities tended to yield high scores (Comprehension and Similarities) whereas scores on Digit Span, Arithmetic and Coding, reflecting attention and concentration, tended to be low. Suter and Wolf concluded that the WISC-R was helpful in identifying strengths and weaknesses as well as overall performance, but only as part of a wider multidimensional assessment procedure consisting of academic testing and different evaluations as well. Further analysis of these scales' results may help to find characteristics that can be used to identify and create tasks to reveal learning disabled gifted children's abilities more precisely. Silverman (1989) suggested that characteristics of this group which may aid in their identification include spatial strengths and sequential weaknesses on standardized intelligence scales.

Mishra and colleagues (1989) dealt with differences in information processes. They investigated an empirical basis for the interpretation of performance on the WISC-R of Navajo children. The children scored significantly differently in the subtests requiring sequential or simultaneous approaches. They found that the gifted learning disabled individuals typically encoded information in a different way, according to the Luria-Das model of simultaneous and successive cognitive processes.

The most promising approach would seem to be a recategorized use of the WISC-R subtests. Researchers such as Kaufman (1979) have suggested using shortened forms of the test for diagnosis comparing Verbal Comprehension (Information, Comprehension, Similarities and Vocabulary) with Perceptual Organization (Picture Completion, Picture Arrangement, Block Design and Object Assembly). Freedom from Distractibility (Digit Span, Arithmetic and Coding) has been described by Bannatyne (1974) as a sequencing factor and now a phonological coding deficit (Vellutino, 1979).

More recently, Birely et al. (1992) suggested omitting the sequential subtests from the results (Digit Span, Arithmetic and Coding) in order to gain a better indication of the intellectual abilities of the child with learning difficulties. This can then be compared with their attainments on reading and spelling tests and attainments in other school subjects.

The 'ACID' profile of dyslexics on the WISC-R has been frequently noted (Thomson, 1990). They generally perform poorly on the subtests Arithmetic, Coding, Information and Digit Span. It has been suggested that this is because each of these subtests depends on the subject's ability to establish and use phonological codes. This is a fundamental weakness in most dyslexics (Vellutino, 1979, 1987). The link between phonological ability and Information is perhaps more indirect than in the case of the other three subtests.

A possible way to identify gifted learning disabled students

The fact that both learning disability and giftedness are themselves heterogeneous, and that in origin and appearance many kinds of populations contribute to the definitions, makes identification more difficult. We have to use identification methods that aim to find the typical, irregular information processes of the learning disabled gifted individuals. Experience and research (Geschwind, 1984; Shaw and Brown, 1991) show that these children achieve in school well below what might be expected of them from their high ability, and they have a learning style that seems to be little suited for school success (Mishra et al., 1989). Their difficulties with verbal labelling and coding tasks such as mental arithmetic, Digit Span and Coding result in their having difficulties with verbal sequential ordering. This is seen in reciting tables, and in recalling the days of the week, months of the year and the sequence of the alphabet. This may cause them to adopt different strategies in learning or they may be more able in different forms of processing. They can thus seem bright when a holistic approach is taken.

In an earlier study Gyarmathy (1995) selected a group of learning disabled gifted children based on their irregular information processing. These children used somewhat parallel, holistic processes and had difficulties in tasks requiring successive, step-by-step approaches which are more useful in the school environment. This group will be referred to as the 'holistic' learners. This group scored at least three points lower on the Digit Span or Arithmetic subtests than on the Similarities subtest on the WISC-R. Most of the children identified by this method were, despite their high intelligence, either diagnosed as learning disabled, or their developmental and school difficulties showed undiagnosed deficits.

In the present study testing methods were developed that could be used with groups even in the school environment. The purpose was to find tasks that can identify learning disabled gifted children by their strengths and that can also indicate their weak points. A total of 280 third graders were examined and divided into four groups by school achievement and the special experimental tests (see Figure 6.2).

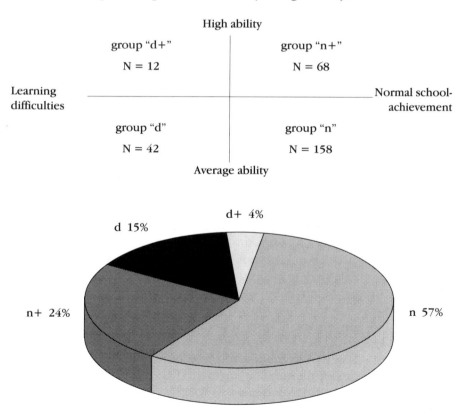

Figure 6.2: Groups formed by test results and learning difficulties

The school achievement of the children was assessed by a structured interview with their teachers. Those pupils who showed some signs of learning disability from their teachers' report were put into the difficulties group. Those children who scored in the upper 10% on at least two tests were considered excellent.

Thus there were four groups: Group 'n' were children with average and below average abilities. Group 'n+' were the group of highly able children. Children who showed signs of learning disability, and who had average or lower than average abilities, were labelled as group 'd'. The most interesting group was group 'd+'. This group showed signs of learning difficulties, yet they achieved far above average in the special tests.

Raven's Progressive Matrices test (Raven, 1988) was used as a standardized method to control for children's intelligence. This test is widely used as a method of assessing nonverbal intelligence. In the normal population scores for verbal and spatial intelligence are usually within a few points of one another. The Similarities and Vocabulary tests on the WISC-R have been shown to be good indicators of high ability and the learning disabled gifted children achieved well on them. Such tests were thus considered appropriate measures of giftedness for the present study. Even in schools, a rich vocabulary and the ability to find similarities with ease are considered markers of high ability. My assumption was that when finding similarities one has to work with simultaneous stimuli, a situation that fits learning disabled gifted children's special abilities.

In the vocabulary test two sets of words were used, where children had to find one real word among meaningless ones. First, easy, everyday words were displayed, and then more difficult ones, even some requiring cultural knowledge. The first set measured correctness of reading, the second measured the knowledge of the child. Another task to measure vocabulary was an anagram task. Children had to form meaningful words from eight given letters. Again stimuli were given simultaneously, and the task required knowledge and motivation to perform. The number and length of the words were measured and a summary score was obtained for the whole number of letters the child had written.

The last task was a memory task. I wished to differentiate between the two types of information, the sequential and the simultaneous. I converted Hagen et al.'s (1975) incidental learning test to a group test. The children's task was to memorize the sequence of animals they were shown on a series of pictures. As incidental learning, they were asked, after they had done the main task, to try to remember the household objects they saw on each card and which were associated with each of the animals, thus putting together the pairs. First, the children had to think in sequences, but in the second task they could perform well if they could remember the whole of the information they had in front of them. Table 6.1 shows the average scores achieved by the different groups and the comparison of the results. The highly able children differed from the rest of the sample on all indices except gender rate.

Most interesting is the comparison of the groups with learning problems. The highly able group was better on most of the indices, but they were not significantly better at those tests that were applied to identify learning disability. Highly able learning disabled children could not do significantly better on the easy vocabulary task, but they were significantly better at the more difficult version. They could find significantly more words in the anagram task, but could not find much longer words than the average learning disabled group. In the memory test the two groups achieved similarly. As can be seen later, they were both poorer in the sequential and stronger in the pair-finding situation. In the school situation the highly able learning disabled pupils can achieve significantly better than their average learning disabled peers.

The third comparison showed that the two highly able groups did not differ in abilities except on the easy vocabulary task, which was more problematic for the learning disabled children. Yet in school work, according to either the teacher or the school marks, the learning disabled children were significantly less successful.

The next comparison showed that learning disabled gifted children were not distinguished from the average students. Although their abilities were significantly better than the average children's abilities, neither the teacher's opinion nor the school marks differ. The more able group could not perform better on the tasks where reading and sequential abilities were measured.

When groups 'n' and 'd' were compared, the lack of abilities in the disabled group (d) could be seen and this appeared in the teacher's rating and the school marks too.

The full range of comparisons showed that group 'n+' and group 'd' differed on all indices except gender. In the simultaneous memory task the high-ability learning disabled group (d+) could do as well as the highly able children with no disabilities (n+).

Summary and conclusions

The results showed that in appropriate learning and testing situations learning disabled gifted children can perform as well as their peers. Most of their problems seem to be rooted in their different information processing and learning style. Their more holistic ways of working can

Table 6.1: The mean scores of all the groups

Holistic learners – Gifted children with learning disabilities

	Gender rate	Teacher rating	Raven Matrices	Stimularities rities	Vocabulary I.	Vocabulary II.	Anagram numb.	Anagram long.	Anagram sum.	Memory sequ.	Memory pair	School marks spell.	School marks litera.	School marks math.	
n	1.57	3.52	32.45	6.06	6.87	3.15	5.96	4.94	20.69	5.43	3.49	3.51	3.99	3.63	n
n+	1.47	4.82	39.31	10.01	8.51	4.22	9.29	5.72	33.37	6.65	4.58	4.37	4.50	4.60	n+
d	1.38	2.79	28.90	5.05	5.78	2.78	5.00	4.65	17.46	4.46	3.78	2.39	3.00	2.54	d
d+	1.25	3.67	42.17	9.33	7.25	4.92	8.83	5.58	29.58	5.83	4.45	3.42	4.00	3.67	d+

prove less effective approaches in school activities, but in some instances they can even be more useful than a sequential approach. Children with learning disabilities tend to think differently and perhaps see the world differently. If we consider this phenomenon as an ability, and some characteristics of giftedness like the ability to abstract, flexibility, inner drive and persistence associate with it, we can identify a possible form of giftedness, instead of a problem group. This is whether or not their ways of working are a cause or an effect of their condition.

Two direct consequences can be drawn. First, we should call learning disabled children 'different learners' and work out appropriate methods of teaching and learning for this population. Second, in the promotion of their high ability and talent we have to be prepared to identify and develop these special abilities and these special students.

Introduction to Part 2

This part of the book sets out to look in more detail at models, strategies and provision for underachievers, and it is interesting to note the commonality of approach arising quite independently in three different continents. This would seem to result from an analysis of learner needs, which do not differ, and is based on 'grounded research' in classrooms.

The provision tends to be consistent with what theoreticians in the field argue is necessary for all gifted and talented individuals. It addresses the cognitive and affective needs and is built on a questioning and problem-solving approach to topics.

Provision for gifted high achievers tends to follow a different model of fast tracking, compacting, setting by ability, acceleration and so on. It will be argued that this is an inappropriate model, especially if education is to be inclusive, and also if it is to be truly educative rather than an indoctrination.

In Chapter 7 Wills and Munro report on a project for underachieving girls at Ruyton School. It is based on the principles of effective learning and has elements in common with the theory of 'multiple intelligences' (Gardner, 1993), on which Sisk in Chapter 8 also draws. She and her colleagues worked in a wide range of schools with non-majority students, using authentic assessment procedures rather than traditional intelligence tests to identify high ability and underfunctioning. These assessments then enabled these researchers to plan appropriate and effective curriculum provision.

In Chapter 9 Montgomery grapples with the issue of inclusion and the need to make provision for the highly able in ordinary classrooms. She recommends that all schools should offer seven levels of provision if they are to meet the needs of all their pupils. Piirto's type of analysis leads inevitably to the question: If the schools system past and present is creating so many disaffected and underachieving learners then surely it must be at fault, not the learners? It is the system that must be reviewed and changed, rather than proffering more 'bolt-on' solutions to something which is fundamentally wrong.

Montgomery identifies the problem with the system, in the pedagogy rather than in the curriculum, and makes recommendations for how schooling and teacher education need to be changed. In Chapter 10 the three main themes leading to underachievement, and which run though the book, are drawn together and translated into further practical teaching examples. These themes deal with the development of cognitive and linguistic competencies through work on oracy, and build on what Freeman identified as disadvantaged learners' needs. The methods proposed have been shown to meet the needs of underachieving boys discussed by Hymer and add to the range of strategies he proposes. The chapter also addresses other widespread problems found in under-achievers – their problems in writing and spelling. Even these are addressed through cognitive and linguistic problem-solving approaches, methods that have been found essential for more able learners but that appeal to all learners. These are thus drawn together to form the central theme of the advocacy of critical theory in education.

The final chapter by Leroux draws on a different type of evidence which is becoming increasingly important in the field. She reports the biographies of those who have been successful, despite the disadvantages, and gives an analysis of how they learned to succeed. In her analysis of these biographies we can see that the proposals made in the rest of the book are endorsed. Leroux emphasizes the role of self-efficacy beliefs in cognitive control, career and academic achievement post school. Education must value learners and help develop resilience, flexibility and the use of multiple strategies. She found that these were major constructs in how the women studied confronted stress and change in their lives.

What we need is an extension of this approach to underachievers in school. We know of a few famous underachievers – Churchill, Einstein, Faraday, Bell, da Vinci. What of the women? What of the ordinary people and the ordinary children? I should be pleased to receive further examples of the successes of ordinary people who were lower attainers at school. Please send them to me at the Learning Difficulties Research Project, 21 Butt Lane, Maldon, Essex CM9 5HD. Please write the 'biopic' in no more than 1000 words.

CHAPTER 7

Changing the teaching for the underachieving able child: the Ruyton School experience

LEE WILLS AND JOHN MUNRO

Introduction

This chapter reports an ongoing study examining the learning characteristics of underachieving, able children, together with their monitoring and suggestions for appropriate teaching and learning procedures. These children need teachers who understand the reasons why some children underachieve, so that they can encourage the children to share their feelings and to look on achievement in the most positive manner.

The sobering thought is that most observers believe that this group comprises at least 10–15% of the intellectually able: ' ... one would think that there would be a major focus upon this by professionals in the field. Nothing could be further from the truth. Instead the gifted underachievers largely have been ignored since 1965 or thereabouts' (Gallagher, 1995: 414–15). Changes in classroom practices are at the hub of reform for these children; however, changes that are made can be achieved only when the child understands the need for such change and indeed wishes to support these changes.

A major issue for schools in this time of rapid change in education is how:

- to help teachers keep up to date with changes in thinking,
- to develop an understanding of how children best learn, and
- to recognize methods of teaching in order to accommodate these changes.

Theories relating to 'how children learn most effectively' are changing. Teachers need to be aware of changes and how to develop the ideas in their teaching. Schools in Victoria, Australia, have recently needed to accommodate new thinking in relation to the curriculum – the Curriculum

Standards Framework (CSF). How schools approach these tasks so that staff can most easily include the new ideas in their teaching is an ongoing problem.

One area that is central to good teaching is how best to enrich the learning of all students. Recent newspaper and journal articles describe how some schools accelerate their most able students. An alternative perspective is to believe that all students have talents in some areas and that the learning of all of them can be enriched. Schools that accept this second perspective will put in place a broadly based approach to teaching that takes account of individual ways of learning and that encourages the acceleration of all students. There will be a number of 'spin-offs', particularly for the group of 'underachieving able' children.

Ruyton Girls' School accepts this second perspective and has, over the past 12 months, been involved in an on-going professional development activity that familiarizes all of its Junior School staff with recent developments in learning and how these developments can be put into practice in their teaching.

The approach, based on 'Facilitating Effective Learning and Teaching', is a programme developed by Dr John Munro at the University of Melbourne. The programme began with four sessions each of two hours facilitated by Dr Munro. Prior to the first session in Term 2, 1997, teachers selected a CSF topic that they intended to teach during Term 3. Throughout the course of the activity, teachers applied the ideas discussed to the development of their chosen topic. In this way they were able to implement the ideas in their teaching immediately and could see how they needed to fine-tune them. This was important for teacher change, because research shows that the longer teachers delay before using new ideas in their teaching, the less likely they are ever to use them.

Retraining the teachers

During the first session the teachers examined:

- what they do when they themselves learn,
- the structure of an ideal lesson,
- recent research on how students can be motivated or challenged to learn, and
- the different ways in which students store and use knowledge.

The second session examined:

- how students use their thinking spaces while learning,
- the different ways of learning, and
- a structure for assisting students to learn by reading.

The teachers worked on developing an understanding of the different ways in which students learn and how they could design activities that match these different ways of learning.

The third session had the teachers examine how students could work on and update what they had learnt by questioning what had been learnt in different ways and by applying and transferring the knowledge. They worked on activities in which students:

- would use the ideas in new situations,
- take the ideas apart,
- use the ideas to help them think ahead,
- forecast and infer,
- synthesize the ideas with other ideas in different ways,
- evaluate the ideas,
- organize the ideas to achieve a specific outcome or solution, and
- use the ideas in creative ways.

Important considerations were for teachers to use open-ended tasks that encourage further learning and explicitly to teach students to ask various types of questions that would extend their knowledge.

The teachers also examined the different ways in which students could show what they know and how they could communicate ideas both verbally and nonverbally. Students who prefer to learn in different ways work on their knowledge differently, by being able to describe in words, pictures or actions how their knowledge is changing. This has strong motivational value for the students.

During the fourth session, the teachers worked on ways of helping students:

- to remember ideas,
- with how they could store what they had learnt in memory,
- learn in different formats, for example cooperatively, and
- learn how to organize themselves as learners.

Finally, the teachers described the teaching units they had developed with colleagues.

This particular format of the professional development had been chosen to overcome many of the limitations of the more traditional 'one-off' activity. First, it is firmly based on what is known about the most effective ways in which adults can be helped to learn to change their practice. Second, it encourages ownership of ideas and, third, it provides teachers with time for linking their existing knowledge with contemporary theories of learning. Before each session, the teachers worked through guided reading that gave them a background to the ideas to be discussed and how they could be applied to their teaching.

The teachers then apply the ideas practically in their teaching and share the outcomes with the group at the next meeting. Ongoing contact with Dr Munro enables Ruyton staff to discuss ways in which the learning programme can be continued for the children. This also helps give support to new members of staff. The objective was to link the most effective combinations of learning and teaching procedures. We believe that this must benefit all children.

The teachers continue to work in collegiate groups and these provide the forum for discussing and sharing ideas and also provide mutual support. This has also been shown to be important if teachers are to be up to date in their teaching.

Characteristics of underachieving students

First the characteristics of 'gifted children' need to be identified: ' ... these students usually learn quickly and readily and see connections between existing and new ideas faster than their peers' (Munro, 1996a: 3). These characteristics will be examined under six major headings. The list (Munro, 1996c) provides us with insight as to the reasons why many able children become underachievers.

It is of major significance that gifted children prefer to work alone. They may avoid group learning situations and develop behavioural problems if directed towards closed learning situations or repetitive tasks.

Superior learning processes

Gifted children's superior learning processes enable them to:

- make decisions quickly,
- keep track of several ideas at once,
- think in larger increments, skipping steps in their thinking,
- require fewer repetitions of, and less exposure to, an idea in order to learn it
- use imagination, fantasy and humour at a high level, and
- have a well-developed memory, particularly for the areas of interest. However, they:
- may have difficulty learning in particular areas, for example rote learning, spelling, handwriting, rote recall of arithmetical information,
- may show carelessness in handwriting and other routine tasks,
- may ignore details in some areas,

- may become bored and frustrated if the learning pace is too slow, and
- they may have difficulty putting into words how they thought or solved problems because (a) they are thinking faster than they can vocalize, or (b) they do not believe they need to communicate to others how they think.

Learning outcomes

These students:

- have a wide general knowledge, and an extreme knowledge in areas of interest which is commensurate with that expected of older pupils,
- know about things of which other pupils seem unaware, and
- may demonstrate advanced vocabulary – particularly in areas of interest – and communicate ideas fluently.

Motivation to learn and learning style

These students:

- are 'self-driven' and motivated to want to know, learning spontaneously without direct teaching,
- frequently learn independently, preferring to direct their own learning, and may have difficulty in situations in which their learning is directed (authoritarian teaching contexts) and those in which their curiosity is not challenged,
- may question group learning situations and may even develop behaviour and discipline problems in more directed, closed learning contexts or in repetitive tasks,
- may rebel against conformity, and
- can concentrate for prolonged periods and show high levels of perseverance.

However, this high level of energy expenditure may lead to complications in other areas.

Interpersonal interactions

They may feel different from peers and alienated because they do not see themselves as getting the necessary positive affirmation from their peers and teachers, but do not understand why. They:

- may not see their exceptional abilities as worth valuing – and may not get affirmation because they do not know how to show what they know so that it fits with the group expectations,

- may have difficulty identifying with a peer group, feeling that they have little in common with peers – that their peers may not comprehend their ideas and/or will feel that there is something wrong with them,
- have difficulty communicating with same-age peers because of interest difficulties, and with older children, who may find them emotionally immature. Often they seem 'the odd one out', and experience loneliness and isolation and do not feel part of any group,
- may not find suitable role models in the peer group,
- may 'over-conform' in the peer group situation when they find social acceptance difficult. They are often sensitive to rejection by others and try to conform so that they do not seem different
- may display heightened perceptions and sensitivities,
- may not be as carefree and easy-going as class peers, but instead are more serious,
- may be irritated by class peers who do not understand their ideas at the same depth,
- may seem to lack confidence in their interaction with their peers,
- may have difficulty understanding and valuing the learning of others,
- may have difficulty trusting others, and
- may feel for others and for events in the world, worry about children whom they see being unfairly treated, take on the problems of others and world problems as personally affecting them, and have a heightened awareness of moral values. They and their peer group need to learn to accept and value individual strengths and differences.

Self-perceptions and affective aspects of talented children learning

These children often:

- have low self-esteem that restricts their preparedness to produce academically. Their self-talk is frequently more pessimistic than optimistic and they need to learn more optimistic scripts as options,
- set high (often unrealistically high) standards and goals for themselves and judge themselves harshly, and
- worry about expectations that they should be 'perfect' and yet know that they are not.

If their giftedness or creativity is perceived to be threatened they withdraw – frequently they lack the analytic strategies necessary for dealing with the threat more constructively. They may also:

- have difficulty understanding the importance of 'risk-taking' in learning,

- have a real sense of failure and may become school refusers,
- be more anxious than other students, putting stress on themselves and feeling stress from others owing to unrealistic expectations,
- be interested in consequences, the future, and so on, but may see consequences that peers do not, and
- tend to worry, seem less self-confident, be unsure of themselves and may have difficulty resolving inner conflicts.

Uneven rates of development

These students often show uneven rates of development, with aspects of their overall functioning developing at different rates. They show 'asynchrony' in development so that they may:

- present as emotionally or physically immature, and
- show specific learning disabilities in particular areas, for example rote learning, spelling, handwriting and rote recall of arithmetic information.

It is therefore essential to identify a model of learning that can explain these types of characteristics and that will enable teachers to make decisions and develop strategies to deal with a broad range of issues related to the teaching of gifted students.

For example, contemporary teachers need to develop strategies that will equip them to implement effective teaching, assessment, management and discipline procedures that reflect the diversity of learning approaches in the class and that encompass the directions and constraints which society imposes on education.

Teaching strategies need to be student-inclusive and provide students with the opportunity to see themselves making optimal progress. As discussed earlier, gifted and talented students display learning characteristics different from those of their peers and often do not match the 'gifted stereotype'. Their learning characteristics can be perplexing and frustrating to teachers. They frequently need assistance and counselling in forming functional peer interactions.

To do maximum justice to these students, teacher decisions need to be based on a sound model of learning. Helping students to acquire an understanding of learning and the ability to manage themselves as learner, which are usually seen as essential outcomes for schools as we move into the next century, can best be achieved when school staff have explicated their personal theory of learning.

Many of the problems that arise with gifted children in classes originate in teaching practices that do not take account of how these students learn. The unrealistic expectations that teachers frequently have of them, for example, are reflected in the expectation that they will be 'good at academic learning across the board'.

In many school situations it is easy to overlook the needs of some gifted and talented students and to make decisions that do not take account of how they learn. This is the perfect breeding ground to promote under-achievement.

General underachievement traits

The parallels that can be drawn between this list and the earlier list for gifted and talented children must give rise to concern if we are to prevent the number of underachieving children from growing. The traits identified are as follows:

- low self-esteem,
- poor performance in one or more basic skills areas: reading, writing, mathematics,
- daily work often incomplete or poorly done,
- pursues projects or shows initiative in the non-school environment,
- superior understanding and retention of concepts when interested,
- dislikes drill work or practice exercises,
- significant quality gap between oral and written work,
- perfectionist, often unhappy with own work,
- fear of failure, avoids trying new activities,
- wide range of interests and possibly special expertise in an area of investigation and research,
- tends to withdraw or be aggressive in the classroom,
- exceptional memory for factual knowledge,
- creative imagination,
- does not work well in groups,
- sensitive, both in perception and defensiveness,
- tends to set unrealistic self-expectations,
- daydreams, finds it hard to concentrate on tasks as directed by others,
- negative school attitude,
- resists teacher efforts to motivate or discipline behaviour in class,
- difficulty in making or maintaining friendships.

Underachievers with spatial strengths

The following additional traits may indicate high spatial strengths:

- early ability in puzzles and mazes,
- sophisticated sense of humour,

- elaborate doodler,
- daydreamer – rich fantasy life,
- creative thinker,
- high abstract reasoning ability,
- keen visual memory,
- avid TV fan,
- loves computers – especially computer graphics,
- highly capable in science,
- excels in geometry,
- grasps metaphors and analogies,
- enjoys music.

As with all checklists, not every item applies to each individual. Underachievers, like other children, will all have an individual profile of talents and difficulties. However, they will present a pattern which includes many of these key indicants. The above checklists were developed from various sources, mostly unnamed, which were collected and edited by Farmer (1993) for the New South Wales Association for Gifted and Talented Children.

Characteristics of a useful model of learning

Having shown the need for a foundation model of learning, what might be its characteristics? One aim of this chapter is to synthesize the learning needs of gifted and talented children with a useful model of learning.

Earlier theories of learning include:

Behaviourist theories, which see learners as passive organisms who during learning are programmed in different ways (Skinner, 1967);
Developmental theories, such as Piaget's (1952), which see learners as actively rearranging their knowledge in a predictable, predetermined way as they move along the same path;
Network-type schema models, which see learning in terms of how knowledge is organized (Norman, 1977);
Information processing models, which explain learning in terms of how information is processed (Newell et al., 1972);
Socio-cultural interaction models and transaction models, which explain learning in terms of the internalization of socio-cultural knowledge (Bandura, 1986);
Constructivist models, which explain learning in terms of the building of subjective models of the world (Desforges, 1998).

None of these has had a lasting effect either on general teaching and educational processes or, more particularly, on the education of the gifted and talented learners, for a number of reasons, not least because they were not classroom or teacher friendly.

A 'user friendly' model of learning

A 'user friendly' model of learning explains gifted learning. It needs to do more than simply describe it; it needs to account for the types of learning behaviours that gifted and talented children exhibit. It explains as much as possible the 'whole-child' operation, explaining both positive and negative aspects of gifted students' learning. It should also predict particular areas of learning behaviours, and map into useful teaching strategies.

What do we mean by learning? (Munro, 1996c)

Learning involves a change or reorganization of an individual's knowledge base. It is more likely to happen when learners construct challenges or purposes for which they judge their existing knowledge to be insufficient in some way, and when they expect to achieve a level of success in the future. The goal of the learning is to deal more effectively with the challenge in the future. In other words, learning is purposeful or goal-orientated; learners learn when they are motivated or have a goal for learning. The goal can range from satisfying curiosity and responding to one's own interests, to attaining a temporary goal (reaching an object in a novel way), or from solving a problem to being valued by others.

Learning can be individually or socially orientated. In looking at the learning of gifted and talented students in the present context, we are focusing more on school-based, institutional learning – that is, the learners internalizing socially or culturally determined ideas. The model of learning that we are using is developed more fully in Munro (1996a, b). It comprises two main dimensions: a sociocultural dimension and an intra-learner dimension.

The social basis of learning

Learning is an interaction between the learner and the cultural-social groups in which it occurs. We are thus proposing a social-constructivist model; an individual's knowledge base changes within a sociocultural context. Social processes influence people's learning in formal educational contexts in several ways. Students learn culturally determined and valued ideas and often need to think in socially valued ways. Given the cultural origin of the ideas, the culture initiates the purpose for learning and needs to challenge the learner to 'know'. Gifted children, however, may prefer not to be 'programmed' by their culture.

In formal learning, learners need to align their experiences and interpretations with the culturally valued meanings. They need to engage in a meaning or understanding negotiation process (Voigt, 1994). They interpret ideas using their existing knowledge, try out their guesses and receive feedback for this trialling. The environment evaluates what learners display by discussing, challenging, validating or extending ideas. Learners learn to use how others respond to their displays.

The cultural-social dimension of the model of learning explains some of the difficulties many gifted students have in formal learning contexts. They construct impressions of an idea that are often qualitatively different from those of their peers. When they negotiate meaning, their peers frequently do not understand the ideas which they communicate. The feedback that gifted children receive may be distorted due to misunderstanding of the quality of the ideas by peers, who often communicate a lack of acceptance of them.

Communication, then, may lead to rejection by the group. This can lead in turn to a tension for them between how they think naturally and what they believe they are permitted to think and learn by the social group if they are to receive positive group valuing.

Some gifted students prefer not to engage in meaning negotiation. They are less prepared to engage in group learning activities and show the outcomes of their guessing. Their earlier learning displays were not valued by the group, leading to their mistrusting it. They may see that the group does not value what they know, but they do not know how to go about getting more positive feedback. They frequently need to learn how to learn in groups and to understand how others learn.

A second aspect of the sociocultural influence relates to the preparedness of these students to be programmed by their culture. Formal academic learning involves students learning culturally determined ideas. Students differ in their preparedness to be programmed in this way. Some expect to be programmed at school, whereas others seek to impose their own ideas on the culture. Gifted students are more likely to be in the latter group.

Students differ in their preparedness to be organized as learners. Gifted students are frequently less prepared to be organized. In addition, because their learning is more idiosyncratically orientated, they do not spontaneously encode in words what they do to learn, and often have difficulty describing how they went about learning an idea or solving a problem.

They often develop a greater susceptibility to group valuing than their peers. This is because they are more likely to receive negative feedback from peers and they have a well-developed ability to perceive consequences a relatively long way down the line. Alternatively, they may simply withdraw from the social group and become, for a good deal of their time at school, a social isolate or 'oddity'.

These issues affect directly how we teach classes in which these students are members. It affects the opportunities we give them to negotiate meaning and their learning to give, receive and use feedback. It influences how different children perceive themselves as successful and how learners frame up challenges for learning in different ways.

Our teaching needs to balance the learning of culturally valued ideas with individually valued ideas and more open-ended learning opportunities. Allowing some students to modify their ideas to match culturally defined ideas, as well as expecting others to internalize the culturally defined version, needs a broader range of teaching strategies. Providing greater opportunity for self-directed learning – in parallel with the opportunity to learn how to learn successfully in groups – is necessary. Helping these students create opportunities to show what they know – in ways that match their ways of learning and that increase the likelihood of group valuing – is also necessary.

Within-learner differences

In the social negotiation of meaning, different learners negotiate learning differently. Individual difference can arise in a range of ways. Students may represent their existing knowledge differently or engage in the reorganizing process in different ways. Some can communicate their ideas more easily than others. Learners may differ in their preparedness to construct challenges or to show that their existing knowledge is insufficient. In terms of a metaphor for learning at any time (see Figure 7.1 below), it may be proposed that:

1. Learners have one or more sites for learning, in which the reorganization of existing knowledge occurs. Terms used to refer to these sites include 'thinking space' and 'short term working memory' (Baddeley, 1990).
2. The total amount of data that can be accommodated at any time in the learning sites is limited. This restriction can be interpreted in terms of thinking space and the allocation of attentional resources.
3. New ideas are learnt in terms of the learners' existing knowledge. Learners interpret information during learning in idiosyncratic ways.
4. The ideas the learner is thinking about can be coded or represented in these 'sites' in different ways; we can look at ideas in different ways. Each code links the new ideas with what is already known in particular ways, is associated with thinking about the ideas in a particular way, and delivers a different perspective on the same ideas.

5. Ideas can be 'moved' between codes via a recoding process that brings the new code to bear on the ideas. The meanings they had in earlier codes can be retained.

6. Learners differ in how they act on the ideas during learning: some learners operate more analytically whereas others may operate synthetically.

7. In any particular learning act, learners manage, control and direct their learning; they can, for example, monitor progress being made during the learning, ask themselves questions about what they are learning, and so on. Our knowledge as learners affects how we learn. We tell ourselves early in learning how we will feel about learning the idea.

8. The opportunity to display what has been learnt is necessary for a variety of reasons, as is the need to recognize that learners prefer to do this in different ways. We may ensure that the change in knowledge is retained, and we act on an idea in various ways to retain it.

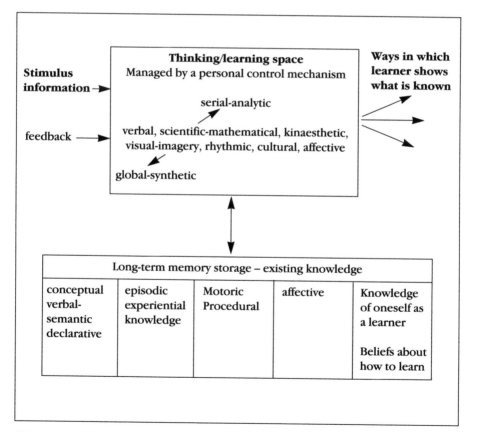

Figure 7.1: Diagrammatic representation of the metaphor of learning (Munro, 1996b)

Differences in how ideas are coded during learning

The ideas manipulated during learning need to be coded or represented in the 'sites', in forms that allow learners to think about them. Whenever we think about an idea we need to link it with other ideas, using what we already know. Our existing knowledge gives us these ways of thinking or 'thinking codes'. These codes represent what we already know about how ideas can be related or linked. Ideas can be coded or represented in different ways.

Each code involves organizing or relating the ideas in particular ways – that is, it draws attention to particular aspects of an idea. Contemporary models of cognitive processing propose two main encoding systems: verbal propositional and nonverbal imagery knowledge (Halford, 1993). Preferences in how learners use particular thinking codes lead to cognitive styles which are dispositions in how we think.

The model presented above (Munro, 1996b) proposes that students have access to several alternative codes in which they can learn, as follows:

- *Verbal/linguistic* – knowing by using one's understanding of words and properties of language (thinking by using words, sentences and verbal propositions). This allows students to think at an advanced level using linguistic templates. They have a rich vocabulary, read and comprehend sophisticated text, engage in complex verbal discussions and debates, and reason about verbal concepts at an advanced level. They readily learn verbally referenced ideas in linguistic context, and think about ideas by discussing, arguing and debating. They may have difficulty using what they know to solve real-life problems and translating their ideas into action.
- *Scientific/mathematical code* – understanding by using abstract mathematical or scientific concepts, logic and symbols, to link ideas. This code allows students to build ideas by reasoning inductively and deductively; to look for organization and logic, analyse complex patterns, and recognize order and consistency at a high level; and to make objective observations, draw conclusions and formulate sophisticated hypotheses, as well as applying general rules to particular situations.
- *Episodic/spatial or visual-imagery code* – understanding by making nonverbal images of ideas, either by processing earlier episodes or by constructing icons/templates that operate as prototypes for concepts that we have learnt. This code allows students to relate ideas using spatial or temporal properties. When used most efficiently, some students can manipulate a comparatively large number of spatial relationships – or images of episodes – at once, allowing them to

synthesize high levels of previously unrelated ideas. They 'slot' several specific pieces of information into a mental picture in unique ways. They can manipulate images by moving them around, imagining how they can change over time. This leads to high-level creative and lateral thinking.

- *Body/kinaesthetic code* – understanding by using actions to represent ideas. Learners using this code think in terms of action sequences or procedures. Some students think about action sequences in complex and sophisticated ways. They solve complex problems efficiently and elegantly using action-based comprehension.
- *Rhythmic code* – knowing by using rhythm, repetitive patterns and rhymes; learning ideas by rote or chanting. Some students develop an elaborate rhythmic knowledge that they use to identify and produce intricate and creative rhythmic patter in music, movement and in other conceptual areas.
- *Affective/mood representation* – understanding in terms of affect, emotion, feeling or mood. Some students develop a highly differentiated and integrated mood representational system that they use to learn and understand ideas. They can recognize and respond to find discriminations in affect or mood, can display differences in mood in a range of ways and can 'read' and respond effectively and rapidly to emotional characteristics of a context (a painting, a novel, a social interaction and so on). They can understand the factors that manage emotion (the attribution of success and failure, level of persistence and so on).
- *Interpersonal representation* – understanding in terms of historical, social, cultural or religious knowledge. This involves ideas referenced against a network that is defined by historical, cultural or religious relationships. Cultural and religious 'logic' refers to the linking of ideas on the basis of cultural and religious belief systems. These beliefs achieve the status of propositions. These logics meet criteria that differ from those for mathematical-scientific logic, verbal-linguistic logic and episodic logic. Students from different cultures can interpret the same teaching differently. One cultural perspective may encourage unquestioning construction of the ideas as accurately as possible, whereas another may encourage questioning of the ideas as accurately as possible, and another may encourage questioning and successive approximations. Learning from a perspective that sees no gender differences in access to mathematics learning will be different from one that believes that males have a greater right to learn mathematics.

Moving ideas between codes

Learners need to learn how to move ideas between codes, to switch an idea from one code to another by a recoding process. This is important for gifted students. Learning situations usually provide a limited range of options for showing what one knows. Gifted students can learn how to show what they know, both in ways that fit within the constraints of the learning situation and in ways that their peers will be more likely to value.

This does not involve 'scaling down' the complexity of the idea, but rather recoding it to a form that takes account of the audience. Gradually learners need to build an idea in one code (probably one of their preferred codes) and then switch it to another in order to show what they know in acceptable ways (Munro, 1996a, b).

Relating the ideas represented: Analytic or holistic strategies

A second dimension is how the ideas are manipulated within each code; either (a) analysed into parts that are then linked up, or (b) integrated with other ideas, with each idea being treated as a whole rather than being analysed into parts. The first type of strategy is described as 'analytic', and the second is 'synthetic' or 'holistic'. Although most learners use these strategies selectively, some use one excessively.

Gifted and talented students are more likely to use holistic than analytic-sequential strategies. They are more flexible in their thinking and can often tolerate ambiguity and unanswered questions. Because they are often more likely to ignore or miss specific details unless these are integrated in a larger conceptual structure, they are more likely to have difficulty learning ideas taught in a sequential, rote way. They are often more able at reading comprehension than at reading words accurately, because they have the verbal reasoning knowledge necessary for high-level thinking but are less likely to engage in the analytic activities needed for learning to recognize written word patterns.

Formal teaching often assumes that students learn best by being presented with small parts of an idea at a time arranged sequentially. It supports learners using strategies that analyse ideas using criteria prescribed by the social group or culture.

Students can, of course, analyse ideas in idiosyncratic ways. When they do this, the criterion for the analysis is known only to them. Often when gifted students analyse an idea into parts subjectively, and manipulate it in a novel, creative way, they have difficulty describing what they did; they did not encode what they did in words.

When students analyse ideas into parts in the culturally recognized ways they also learn the ways of talking about the analysis and can tell people more easily what they did. Those who prefer to use global holistic strategies are less likely to do this, do not get positive regard for what they have learnt, and often become alienated from effective learning.

Just as each of the codes is linked with a set of thinking strategies, so the two types of manipulation or processing strategies are managed by self-instruction sequences. These are described more fully in Munro (1996a, b).

A management/control mechanism

This is how learners manage or regulate their learning – that is, their metacognitive knowledge. They use this to plan how they will learn, to monitor their learning, to evaluate its effectiveness in terms of some goal or purpose, to take further strategic action if necessary, and to review their change in knowledge.

Gifted students use aspects of this control mechanism extremely effectively. Their ability to direct and regulate their learning, to plan and monitor their learning progress and to take further strategic action if necessary is obviously well developed. In fact, much of this activity by these students seems to be automatic.

Their knowledge as learners, on the other hand, and their lack of self-confidence in the group learning context can mean that on occasions they opt not to engage in learning. They perceive consequences but do not have the experience necessary to deal with this.

In summary, in this learning model, gifted learning is associated with the extremely efficient use of two or three of the codes, particularly in parallel with the use of global-synthetic strategies. Other codes may not be as well developed, and students may display gifted learning in some areas and immaturity in others. In the favoured codes, they can deal with several ideas at once because they have automatic response to these codes and give the impression of thinking synthetically or 'simultaneously' rather than sequentially.

Armed with the knowledge of the Model of Learning the teachers at Ruyton Girls' School presented ideas in the range of codes discussed with Dr Munro. They designed activities that would develop an idea in each of the codes. They began with episodic knowledge of the idea and then recoded it in a verbal-linguistic way and then in a decontextualized-action way. The example of evaporation which follows shows how it is possible to build ideas associated with evaporation in each of the codes.

WAYS OF LEARNING USING THE SUBJECT OF EVAPORATION

Code ideas culturally, socially, historically: How has evaporation been used in history (to obtain drinking water, for refrigeration)? How is evaporation used in different communities? What are the problems? How can communities control it?

Code ideas logico-mathematically: Is there the same amount of water in a room when a dish of water evaporates? How has it changed? – same amount; change of state. What matches evaporation for solids? Why/when do things evaporate?

Code ideas verbal-linguistically: Brainstorm ideas; a conceptual map; a network map. Paraphrase, summarize text that explains evaporation. An evaporating liquid is interviewed. What would it say? Ask six hard questions about evaporation. Write a story/play about evaporation. 'Adventures of ...' When else would you use the word evaporate? Discuss situations involving evaporation – what happens?

Code ideas affectively: What feelings would you have if you evaporated (light-headed, strung out)? How might liquids that are evaporating feel?

Code ideas visuo-spatially in episodes: Imagine, draw, collect situations in which evaporation occurs (water on a dish; clothes drying; petrol on the body of a car; vapour rising from the sea; dry ice foaming). Draw a comic strip of petrol evaporating from the body of a car. Invent useful icons for evaporation. Classify pictures of instances of evaporation.

Code ideas in actions: Make an action model of evaporation (for example, corks flying out of a jar). Small groups of children act out gas evaporation (rising up, stretching, spreading out). Is there a reverse action to evaporation which can be enacted?

Teachers can use this type of structure:

* for developing lesson plans that encourage students to encode ideas in different ways,
* to help students review the different types of activities and note how they can learn these different types of questions.

Presenting key ideas in this variety of ways allows students to learn in 'learner-friendly' contexts that take account of preferred ways of learning. Individual learning characteristics are acknowledged and accepted. It also encourages the valuing of others.

Cueing students to think about the idea in different ways

Teachers cannot control how students think about the ideas being learnt. Even if ideas are presented visually, this does not mean that the students will visualize them. Thus one strategy is to cue them to think about an idea in particular ways.

Teaching the thinking or learning strategies associated with each code

Each code involves thinking about the ideas in particular ways and teachers can make these explicit. Students can learn to ask the various types of question for the different codes.

Using codes selectively to achieve particular outcomes

Students can learn when it is useful to use each type of thinking and how the different ways of thinking lead to different outcomes. They learn to match the desired outcomes of a context or task with the ways in which they need to think about it.

Switching ways of thinking about ideas

Learners need to learn how to move ideas between codes themselves, to switch an idea from one code to another. Gradually they need to learn:

- to build an idea in one code (probably one of their preferred codes) and then switch it to another in order to show what they know in acceptable ways,
- to understand ideas better by building them in a preferred code and then converting them to the code in which they were presented.

Learning to look at an idea from different perspectives

Once learners have explored some core ideas in different codes, and have learnt some of the thinking strategies linked with each code and practised recoding ideas, they can practise looking at an idea from different angles. This will provide a richness and complexity to their understanding of an idea that it otherwise would not have. In the next example the topic of 'Flight' was undertaken by Year 4 at Ruyton Girls' School.

The class teachers worked in teams creating a learning environment that encouraged all the children to become involved. They were aware of the difficulty in learning caused by a mismatch between teaching and preferred ways of learning.

Example: flight – ways of learning

Culturally, socially, historically

- Key milestones in history.

- Time lines from Zeppelin balloons to Mir space station.
- Guest speaker aviators of importance.
- Excursion to the Royal Australian Air Force (RAAF) museum.

Logico-mathematically

- Logo writer.
- Graphing Mach speed of various planes.
- Calculating differences in flight speeds over varying distances.
- Comparing speeds of various aircraft.

Verbally-linguistically

- Brainstorm interest words to produce concept maps.
- Read and write related poems and stories.
- Examine journal records of the RAAF museum and knowledge gained.
- Undertake 'jigsaw' activity (Lerner, 1971) on five pilots.
- Read stories about the Wright brothers, Amelia Ehrhart, for example (Lerner, 1971).

Affectively

- Why has man always wanted to fly?
- How do you feel about flying?
- What have we learnt?

Visuo-spatially

- Imagine – draw situations of flight.
- Drama – flight machines; fighter planes.
- See video on flight.
- Make models of spacecraft, early aircraft.

Actions

- Design and make planes, gliders, whirligigs, aerofoils.
- Make balloons and test.
- Make and test planes and gliders using a variety of materials.

Mismatches

Mismatches can lead to:

- difficulty in learning
- high levels of frustration and anxiety
- behavioural and discipline problems, and
- ultimately alienation from school.

Teachers too can explore the links between their learning styles and teaching styles and the learning styles of students who learn most or easily with them, and use this to broaden their teaching styles. Students can also be encouraged to recognize mismatches between teaching and learning styles and explore ways of managing constructively.

Give a range of ways of showing what students know

Students who prefer to learn *visually* can record ideas in pictures and then convert them to symbols or words; those who prefer to learn *linguistically* can talk to themselves about ideas before they convert them to symbols; and those who prefer to learn *kinaesthetically* can act out ideas before they write or speak about them. (They may try to avoid being seen to do the actions but they need to see that they are acceptable and will help learning.)

Help students monitor how they learn best and to understand and broaden their range of learning strategies

Key ways include:

- Encouraging them to focus on what they do when they are solving tasks and to talk about what they say to themselves, and so on.
- Students can be reminded to use their preferred strategy.
- Making them aware of additional strategies.
- Having them try out new strategies, observe their effectiveness, and consciously add them to their set of learning strategies.
- Having them decide whether and when they might use the strategy in the future. They can keep a list of 'Things to tell myself when I do ...', writing down the strategies that have worked, and adding to it.

Verbalizing 'mental actions' makes them more 'concrete' and easier to recall, analyse and modify.

Storing information in long-term memory

Remembering ideas long term involves:

- storing information in memory by linking it to knowledge already there, and
- retrieving it by gradually reconstructing information.

Types of long-term memory and different forms of storage involve storing ideas in terms of their meaningful relationships to other ideas, and storing ideas in nonverbal ways (episodic memory), in action sequences and in emotions.

A sequence of self-instructional strategies for storing an idea in long-term verbal-semantic memory

1. Describe the main ideas as concisely as possible.
2. Relate these ideas to the existing knowledge base. What do these ideas remind me of? How are they like/different from things I have already learnt?
3. Draw a picture of the main ideas, or use a concrete model of them, showing how ideas are related.
4. Draw a semantic map of these ideas.
5. Describe when the ideas might be used in the future.

Summary and conclusions

There are clear implications for learning in the content areas and in displaying what one knows. In writing an essay, for example, learners using analytic-sequential strategies are more likely to sequence the ideas in predictable, conventional ways that they have learnt. Those using global-holistic strategies are more likely to sequence the ideas in less predictable ways. An English teacher whose preference is for the analytic is more likely to find sequential organization easier to read. However, a teacher whose preference is for the sequencing of ideas in ways that have not previously been taught is more likely to value the organization displayed by the students using global-holistic strategies. Generally, teachers and students operate from their perspective unconsciously.

The theme of this chapter is the need for the inclusion of learning criteria in the implementation of teaching activities for all students and a 'learning dimension' in the curriculum.

This is not about adding to the curriculum but rather is about examining ways of implementing it according to demonstrably sound learning principles.

Twelve months on since the implementation of the project, it is encouraging to report that teachers at Ruyton Girls' School continue to pursue the programme with their initial enthusiasm intact. Involvement of the students in their own and their groups' exploration across the core study areas, together with the way in which they have grown to value the participation and successes of their peers, has created an inspirational learning environment

CHAPTER 8

Overcoming underachievement of gifted and talented students

DOROTHY SISK

Introduction

When the demographics of many programmes for gifted students in the United States are examined, they indicate that special populations are not proportionately represented (Ross, 1993). Children and young adults from all non-majority groups, as well as learning disabled individuals from all populations, are often labelled as underachievers because they do not perform well on standardized ability and achievement tests (Cromer, 1990; McCalope, 1991; Wayman, 1991; Steele, 1992; Ford, 1995). As a result they are seldom included in screening or identification procedures for programmes for the gifted.

In a recent study with non-majority populations, Sisk (1999a, b) used authentic assessment procedures including a variety of means, strengths, interests, cognitive and affective needs, learning styles, disabilities and other critical data. With this information, appropriate teaching objectives, strategies and evaluation techniques were developed to assess more accurately the students' potential and to address their educational needs.

Many gifted students become reluctant learners when they do not understand the relevance of daily teaching activities (Arter and Spandel, 1992; Coil 1992a, b). They intuitively recognize that many assessment procedures used in the classrooms portend failure, and a cycle of under-achievement is inevitable in such an educational situation. Portfolios, real world assessment and authentic assessment are terms used interchangeably to describe alternatives to paper and pencil tests.

Using this type of assessment provides a means for evaluation of student achievement rather than just a 'collection of stuff' (Knight, 1992). Sisk (1999a, b) found that by providing underachieving students

111

of high potential with an opportunity to help plan their educational experiences and the assessment of those experiences, underachieving students can function as collaborators in their education. The students in the study helped to determine the content of their achievement portfolio and this involvement helped further empower them to learn. They began to recognize that some aspects of education are non-negotiable, such as state-required tests, but they were convinced that their input was important.

Over the past 10 years, Sisk and research associates June Maker, Roberta Daniels, Robert Seney, Pamela Gilbert, Gillian Erickson and Charles Whaley have conducted research on the underachievement of gifted and talented students from special populations (Maker, 1992). Several research questions directed their efforts.

Research questions concerning underachievement

Using federal funding (Jacob Javits grant) five research questions were examined:

1. Is underachievement situational, temporary or chronic?
2. Is underachievement general or related to specific subjects?
3. What factors contribute to underachievement, including motivation, academic self-esteem, peer pressure, family support, student–teacher relationships and teacher expectation?
4. Can these factors be used to design counselling and educational programmes for underachieving students?
5. Can underachievement patterns be turned round?

These questions were pursued through five projects over the period of a decade – Project Step Up: Systematic Training of Educational Programs for Underachieving Pupils (1991–94) funded through the United States programme office for gifted and talented; two federally funded early childhood family-centred Even Start projects (Step Up/Even Start 1994–98) and Step Up/Even Start II (1998–2001); and a family literacy project (Project 100: Mothers Read) sponsored by the Texas Governor's office.

Principles guiding Project Step-Up

The following principles guided Project Step-Up:

- develop and implement a philosophy that children from all ethnic and socioeconomic groups have gifts and talents,

- develop and implement a practice of flexible grouping to provide opportunities for high-potential minority economically disadvantaged students to be grouped for appropriately differentiated curriculum,
- develop a cadre of teachers, mentors and community members willing to nurture talent in all ethnic and socioeconomic groups,
- provide professional training and time for Project Step-Up teachers to collaborate, plan and share information with other teachers,
- provide after-school and summer programmes for Project Step-Up students,
- use technology and telecommunications to link Project Step-Up students and teachers, and
- develop community and business partnerships to provide real-world involvement and fiscal and human resources for Project Step-Up schools.

These seven principles were introduced by the Project Step-Up staff, discussed during summer institutes at Lamar University and reiterated at local and regional meetings. The principles were placed on a Likert scale of 1–5 (low being 1 and 5 being high) and supervisors of the gifted programmes, principals and Project Step-Up staff used the checklist to evaluate each site. Implementation of the principles was found to be positively related to successful performance of the students.

Suggested strategies for preventing and overcoming underachievement

One effective strategy was the ongoing involvement of administrators, teachers and parents in open dialogues concerning the underachievement of the students designated as high potential students. Traditional district school tests were supplemented with alternative tests, including Raven's progressive matrices, the Guilford Structure of Intellect (SOI) battery, and selected problem-solving tasks based on the Howard Gardner Multiple Intelligence Model (MI) developed by June Maker (Maker, 1992).

Qualitative as well as quantitative measures ensured that the measures were valid and reliable, and all information was considered by teachers, principals, gifted and talented supervisors and the Project Step-Up staff. These data served as baseline data for the participating students in Project Step-Up classes. None of the children selected for the original high potential classes would have been considered for either screening or identification for gifted programmes because they were underachieving on standardized tests, many of them scoring well below average. However, when all the students were administered the Structure of Intellect battery

(SOI), all of them achieved a level of giftedness in one or more of the processing activities. The Project Step-Up 'Child Find' assessment and selection procedures are in Figure 8.1. According to Meeker (personal communication 1991), this level of performance qualifies students for consideration as potentially gifted students.

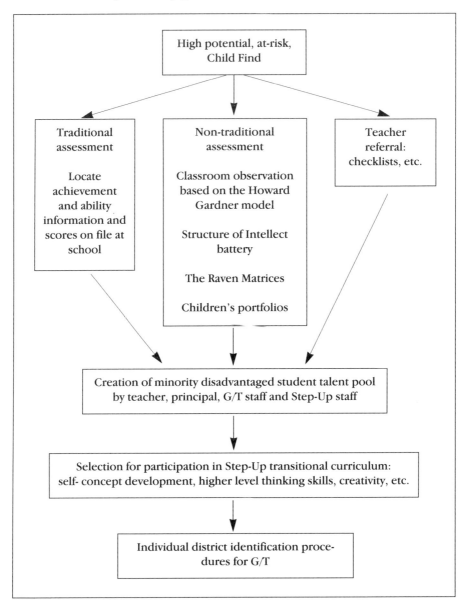

Figure 8.1: Project Step-Up 'Child Find': assessment and selection process and procedures

Approaches to teacher training

A new approach to teacher training was implemented that concentrated on five skills: focusing, empowering, facilitating, transforming and coaching.

Focusing was defined as the ability to centre one's attention and energies to maximize time and resources. The skill of focusing helped the teachers achieve focus not only in themselves, but in their students. They used their creative energy to maintain a balance between the project's goals and school demands. Successful Step-Up teachers were able to focus on the project's singular purpose, that of developing each student's potential.

Empowering was defined as developing strong, trusting relationships with the teachers. Discussions were held to develop shared purpose and to clarify mutual values concerning the students. Teachers were provided opportunities to present the Step-Up curriculum at local, state and international meetings. As they experienced empowerment, they were able to help their students be more successful by emphasizing a 'can do' philosophy.

Facilitating was defined as supporting the teachers with positive feedback, as they moved from traditional teaching styles to child-centred facilitating styles. A taxonomy of teacher change identifies their progress (see Table 8.1, pages 118–19). Opportunities were provided for the teachers to experience a free flow of information and ideas in numerous formal and informal discussions. Facilitating the project teachers enabled them to create a classroom learning environment that enhanced self-perception, self-esteem, self-concept (academic and social) and to build and strengthen racial pride and identity.

Transformation was defined as providing opportunities for administrators and Step-Up staff to remove and surmount a number of barriers to provide educational change. Barriers addressed included stereotypes of special population students and their parents, such as 'they won't arrive on time', 'they aren't interested in their children's work' or 'the students are lazy, slow and underachievers'. Education was transformed for the students by adding specific training in study skills, time management, organization and test-taking skills (Coil, 1992b). Another example of transformation was the identification of gifted students in schools where none had been previously identified. Transformation also included change in the teachers and administrators' perceptions of the students. In these economically disadvantaged schools, students were regularly identified as emotionally disturbed, learning disabled, delinquent and developmentally delayed, but not as gifted. In addition, the teachers at these schools were seldom viewed as innovative, effective or creative. The project transformed these attitudes by demonstrating that the students and the teachers were able to achieve excellence.

Coaching was defined as encouraging the teachers to identify effective strategies that they were currently using. The project staff served as role models for the teachers by coaching and demonstrating effective teaching to modify and influence teacher behaviour. As coaches, the staff praised and supported the teachers by giving individual help with instruction, strategy options and resources.

Project Step-Up hypothesized that 60% of the children would be identified as gifted and talented using standard and state criteria. This project goal was realized as the overall percentage in the 14 sites where the project operated. The identification rate within the group of sites was variable, ranging from 10% to 100%.

The Step-Up formative and summative evaluation identified 10 programme variables that were essential for programme success. These were as follows:

1. Positive classroom climate.
2. Use of positive language.
3. Direct instruction of thinking skills.
4. Visual reinforcement.
5. Teacher flexibility and creativity.
6. Teacher training to integrate multicultural education and counselling.
7. Emphasis on content and process.
8. Integration of language arts and arts.
9. Use of Step-Up teacher materials specifically designed for the students.
10. Involvement of family members as partners in the educational process.

New and appropriate curriculum project

Step-Up teachers differentiated the curriculum through direct teaching of thinking skills (daily for 45 minutes), engaging the students in identifying, observing, judging, sequencing, comparing, contrasting, making decisions, justifying choices, predicting, forecasting, estimating and problem-solving. A Communications and Arts National Diffusion Network (NDN) programme was used to focus on comprehending meaning and understanding (Bronson, 1992). Literature, music and art from the students' cultures, together with biographies of leaders who had made contributions to society, were integrated into the regular curriculum. Students learned to communicate important ideas, and routine skill learning was balanced with novel and complex tasks. Drill and practice were accomplished through challenging games and group work. Students were encouraged to discuss reasons for learning and they were provided with choices based on their interests, as suggested by Hendryx (1993). Emphasis was placed on building self-confidence, goal-setting, motivating oneself, study skills and dealing with 'the system' (Coil, 1992b). Teachers were encouraged to hold high expectations for the students and to encourage the use of problem-solving based on the Gardner Multiple Intelligence model (Gardner, 1983). Students learned to use the correct terms of the MI model with one another and their parents, and through this process they were able to 'think about their thinking'. Project staff made a conscious effort to influence attitudes and beliefs towards various subjects and topics of study, and teachers were encouraged to go beyond dispensing knowledge. To facilitate this, time was made available for the students to discuss concerns with teachers and counsellors.

In teaching thinking skills, the teachers and project staff modelled the cognitive processes. For example, when they read to the children, under-standing the author's point of view was encouraged and students were engaged in discussions addressing higher-level thinking. The students learned to use one another as resources in classroom discussions and to appreciate group work. On a regular basis, the Step-Up second-, third- and fourth-grade students assisted younger students by reading stories, intro-ducing educational centres and helping with skill development in mathe-matics and spelling. Teachers placed a high priority on establishing a positive student-centred classroom environment to accommodate a variety of learning styles. They also modelled flexibility and creativity by using a variety of materials and teaching strategies to help the students experience the importance of self-perception and to feel self-satisfaction with their learning.

Curriculum for the project concentrated on providing complex tasks, sophisticated products and higher-order thinking. Students were exposed to multiple perspectives through seminars given by a number of speakers from various cultures and they participated in field trips to broaden their scope of information. The Step-Up teachers taught to mastery level, emphasizing understanding knowledge, retaining knowledge and using knowledge in simulations, role playing, case studies, projects and intern-ships. This focus helped to personalize the students' learning and to give it a purpose.

The teachers used a checklist of behaviours, including responsiveness, creativity, flexibility, empathy, communication skills, sense of humour, problem solving, leadership and autonomy, to appraise student perfor-mance. Emphasis was placed on positive reinforcement and constructive and consistent feedback.

The Step-Up programme was successfully implemented in 15 schools in Texas, Arkansas, Florida and Arizona. In these schools, Step-Up teachers were released from their classrooms to teach thinking skills to other classes. Most Step-Up schools had positive school involvement and expanded their programmes to additional classes. Each school started with one second-grade class and, as the students moved up a grade, another class of second graders was added. At the end of the third year, the schools thus had three Step-Up classes.

Table 8.1: Project Step-Up teacher training

What follows is an outline taxonomy of the Step-Up training for coaching, empowering, focusing, facilitating and transforming teacher training skills:

Teacher behaviour	Project support strategies
A. Hesitant, reluctant, fearful of change. Traditional teaching style. Full group lecture Q&A.	1. Provide role models to modify or influence teacher behaviour (focusing/coaching/facilitating). 2. Work with principal and secretarial support for change (focusing/facilitating). 3. Conduct on-site seminar focusing on questioning skills, learning centres and so on (focusing). 4. Provide instructional resource manual (focusing/facilitating). 5. Identify effective strategies used by the teacher, praise their use and build on them (focusing/coaching/facilitating).
B. Aware and sensitive to the special needs of individual students.	1. Provide further awareness training (focusing/facilitating). 2. Provide teaching curriculum materials and background research information on children with special needs (focusing/facilitating). 3. Make site/classroom visits to help assess learning environment and clarify/suggest appropriate strategies (focusing/coaching/facilitating).
C. Seeks knowledge and information.	1. Encourage and implement networking/exchange between Step-Up classrooms (facilitating/coaching). 2. Invite teachers to visit other Step-Up sites (coaching/empowering). 3. Establish computer/email link between sites (coaching/empowering).

Table 8.1: (contd)

Teacher behaviour	Project support strategies
	4. Provide informal discussion groups, identify resources (focusing/facilitating). 5. Encourage information sharing through network (empowering). 6. Offer advice/training on specific strategies such as higher-level thinking skills and creativity development (focusing/coaching/facilitating).
D. Seeks to accommodate and adapt curriculum to special needs of individual students.	1. Provide external motivation through on-site seminars and attendance at state/national conference (empowering). 2. Provide on-site or videotaped classroom demonstrations (empowering/facilitating). 3. Continue process of building positive communication with principal (empowering). 4. Provide newsletters and Step-Up Grams for teachers (facilitating). 5. Provide process sharing in on-site seminars (empowering/transforming).
E. Understands and is committed to meeting the special needs of individual students.	1. Assist teachers in making appropriate adaptations in curriculum (facilitating/focusing/empowering).

Methods and materials for parental involvement

The parental component of the project was a vital part of the total change process. Family members were involved in planning and implementing educational programmes. Constance Shannon (1993) worked with the parents to provide information on how children learn and how to assess and use learning styles to modify teaching (for example, abstract, concrete, visual and auditory). She demonstrated a variety of ways to support critical and creative thinking through six interactive seminars. Shannon's goal was to enable parents and children to learn and work together. By conducting individual interviews with the parents, she found that the parents' increased self-esteem and confidence in helping their children learn were positive benefits of the parent's component.

Locating and involving community members as mentors, role models and instructors

Working with the various local chambers of commerce and a variety of professional groups, including university and college personnel, the project staff provided the students with minority role models, mentors and speakers. One major emphasis was to integrate multicultural education and counselling strategies. The participating school was encouraged to involve business partners, and successful school-wide activities included toy making, creative writing, storytelling, computer and mathematics games and contests. These activities focused on the importance of developing the students' passion for learning and increasing interest in artistic impression, particularly emphasizing traditional cultural art and music.

One site: up close and in detail

Worsham Elementary School, located in Houston, Texas, has 940 Hispanic students of whom 80% receive free lunches. Two teachers and the assistant principal attended a summer institute at Lamar University in 1994 and they decided to plan and develop two Step-Up classes to provide a nurturing, affective and innovative individual curriculum. Prior to establishing the Step-Up classes, the school reported considerable difficulty in locating gifted students using traditional measures.

Using the Step-Up identification process, a pool of talented students was established at the second-grade level based on Structure of Intellect (SOI) scores, available achievement and ability test scores, and teacher recommendations using the Minority Strength Checklist developed by Sisk (1991). Two classes comprising 20 students were taught by Susan Birkitt and Norma Leza. In Ms Leza's bilingual class, the children were primarily Spanish-speaking and the test scores reflected the students' difficulty with English. La Prueba, a Spanish version of the Illinois Test of Basic Skills, was administered to the students and, using Developmental Cognitive Abilities Test (DCAT) scores, teacher recommendation and SOI scores, 10 of Ms Leza's students were identified as gifted, as were 14 children in Ms Birkitt's class.

Two case studies of gifted students

Miguel, a Hispanic, underachieving student was in the second grade when he began the Step-Up programme. He is a small, wiry boy with a certain amount of charm and is well accepted by his peers. At the beginning of the programme, he was having a good deal of trouble in his classroom because he could not complete his work or take responsibility for it. His response to failure was a shrug. In a group he tended to be a complainer. His teacher reported that she could get Miguel to do the minimum and that was all. He felt that he was being pushed and that the teacher's demands were unreasonable. His mother wanted him to do better, but she was very busy with three children younger than Miguel and she was somewhat apathetic about his schooling.

In the Step-Up programme, the teacher gave Miguel opportunities to work with younger students, reading simple books to the kindergarten children, and this experience reinforced his self-concept. He loved the 'Stories with Holes' riddles that call for creative thinking and was often the first one to come up with the correct answer. As he became more successful he also became more motivated to learn. The Step-Up teacher continued to give him more and more responsibility, and Miguel went from a lackadaisical student to an enthusiastic student. His class participated in a group project involving planning and planting a vegetable garden. Each day the children watered the young plants. Miguel asked to take the responsibility of bringing the jugs for the daily watering. When the carrots, beans and potatoes grew to maturity, the children made some soup, which they proudly shared with their parents. Miguel wrote a poem that he read to the group:

> I see the tiny green shoots,
> I hear the birds calling in the trees,
> I touch the soft ground around our plants
> I smell the coolness of the morning air,
> I feel happy about our plants.
>
> I see cut carrots, beans and potatoes,
> I hear the sound of chop, chop, chop as
> the pieces fall in the bowl,
> I touch the smooth green peppers,
> I smell the good soup,
> I feel proud!

As Miguel read his poem to the group, it was quite apparent that he was learning how to use his talent to his advantage and was able to contribute to the class. At the end of the third grade, he passed both the reading and math assessment of academic skills. Miguel progressed from a child 'at risk' to a child with high potential.

Shamir is an African-American girl who was seven years old when she enrolled in the Step-Up programme. She loved to write stories and her favourite part of class was when they were 'making things'. If there were no art activities offered, she would make tiny sculptures from pieces of construction paper and place them on her desk for the rest of the students to admire. In her regular classroom work, she was careless and seldom turned in homework. Her single-parent mother was frustrated with her and tended to be stern in her discipline and criticism of Shamir. Shamir was sensitive, spoke in a soft voice and her reaction to any criticism in the classroom was to softly cry. This upset other children in the class and they began to pull away from her.

Her Step-Up teacher began calling Shamir 'our creative girl' and when the class was engaged in creative activities in the classroom, she would call on her for ideas. Shamir never let the class down – she always had a creative idea, and the teacher openly praised her. She asked her to compile the stories for their class book and happily she rose to the occasion, making a clever three-dimensional cover.

To help her with getting homework assignments completed, the teacher was able to encourage a local bookstore to donate small notebooks and she asked a middle-school student (sixth grade) to show the class how to use the notebook to keep track of assignments. Shamir and the rest of the class were impressed with the student's favourable comments about the importance of 'organization'.

Shamir's mother reported that Shamir began to bring her work home and was very proud of her 'organization'.

The Step-Up teacher also encouraged Shamir to work in small groups to create a paper sculpture display for the holidays. This completed paper sculpture was placed in the library for all the students in the school to share. Shamir began to stand taller, talk more freely and openly and it was apparent that school was a happier place for her. She was tested for the gifted programme in third grade and identified as a gifted student. She has successfully continued in that programme. Her school won first prize in a creative thinking competition recently and she was team leader.

Examples of the Step-Up programme lessons

Warm-up thinking lessons

1. *What am I?* This is a large group activity, where one student thinks of an object or animal, then gives oral cues about its physical characteristics. Other students try to identify the mystery object or animal in the riddle based on the clues. For example, 'Most people like me for about one day, then they cast me aside. I am black and white and "read", although sometimes I might have a touch of other colours on special days. Even though I don't hang around long, you might see me again as something entirely different. What am I?' (A newspaper.)

2. *Category activity* This activity is a favourite of students. Choose a category, such as things that begin with 's', without divulging it to the students. Then say, 'Finicky Fred likes the sun, but he doesn't like the water.' Students do not tell the rule, but they must give an example of what he likes and doesn't like.

A creative/critical thinking lesson

This lesson asked the children to determine the guilt of the Wolf in the story of the *Three Little Pigs*. First, they divided into three groups: the jury, the pigs and the wolves. (The jury on the wolf or pig side can help prepare the case as long as they remain impartial when they serve as the jury.) Each student has a part in the court case.

1. The true story as Mother Goose told it the first time. (The children read the story and discussed it for content.) (Cognition and memory.)
2. The witnesses. The witnesses were identified by each group to prepare their case. (Creativity, decision-making.)
3. The crime. The prosecution determined what the charges were against Mr Wolf as the defence worked with these charges. (Analysis and decision-making.)
4. The case. Each group prepared a set of evidence. The students determined what they would need – documents of death, police reports, fingerprints and so on. (Decision-making/analysis.)
   A. The prosecution arrests Mr Wolf. (With proper warrants.)
   B. The prosecution registers the charges.
   C. The prosecution enters the first set of evidence.
   D. The defence enters the first set of evidence. All information up to this point is public knowledge, i.e. no hidden evidence.
   E. Both the prosecution and the defence enter any additional evidence that will not be made public until the trial.
   F. Both the prosecution and the defence were allowed one piece of evidence that had not been registered, but had to be supported by appropriately signed documents.
5. The trial. The courtroom had:
   A. A bailiff.
   B. A clerk reporter (who actually recorded what took place as closely as possible).
   C. Lawyers for the prosecution and the defence. (Assistant lawyers were used as well.) (Critical/creative thinking.)
   D. A judge. (Decision-making.)
   E. A six-person jury. (Analysis/decision-making.)

6. The verdict. In order for the verdict to be guilty there had to be a 4–2 or better vote. (Decision-making/analysis.)

A collection of thinking problems for gifted students to solve

When students have learned and practised using different strategies, they are ready to solve problems where they must decide what to do. In many cases, more than one strategy can be used. Gifted students may use different approaches to problems as long as their explanations and answers are logical.

For example, Katie is making a quilt for her doll. She wants her quilt to have three green patches, three red patches and three yellow patches. How can she sew the patches so that she has a green, a red and a yellow patch in each row and each column of her quilt?

Strategy: Draw a picture or use real objects.
Sample solution
G Y R
R G Y
Y R G

Thinking skill lesson with fourth-grade students

The teacher read Carl Sandburg's poem *Fog* and engaged the students in a discussion on how Sandburg used a cat to describe fog. This was followed by completing a chart on understanding metaphors.

First, the students brainstormed the characteristics of a cat and then the characteristics of fog, and they examined a number of ways that the cat and fog were alike, such as sound, attitude and behaviour. The cat is noiseless and soundless and the fog is soundless and hushed. Cats are aloof and impersonal and the fog is impersonal. Cats are low-lying and they sprawl, and fog sprawls and is overlying.

Fifth-grade students worked on metaphors of dinosaurs using the same 'mapping chart' format derived from Black and Black (1990).

Logic problems

Logic problems are generally favourites of gifted students. After they have worked through several deductive thinking problems, they write their own. The following is an example of a third-grader's deductive thinking problem (she loves dogs).

Ronald Retriever, Harry Hound, Billy Beagle, Sammy Setter and David Dalmatian all have different breeds of dogs. One has a golden retriever, one has a basset hound, one has a beagle, one has a setter and one has a dalmatian.

A. David Dalmatian and Ronald Retriever have doga with no black.
B. Sammy Setter and Billy Beagle have dogs that are afraid of engines.
C. Sammy Setter and Ronald Retriever have dogs with no red colouring.
D. Billy Beagle has a dog with *huge* ears.
Who has which kind of dog?
Answers: RR – golden retriever; HH – dalmatian; BB – basset; SS – beagle; DD – setter.

Understanding metaphors

CAT   FOG

How alike?

Aloof, impersonal, disinterested, watchful	← With regard to ATTITUDE →	Impersonal, relentless
Stealthy, padded, calm, noiseless, soundless	← With regard to SOUND →	Muted, hushed, muffled, soundless dampening

and so on.

Figure 8.2: To show mapping technique for metaphors

Expansion of project Step-Up

Sisk and her staff at Lamar University received two Even Start Grants in collaboration with Beaumont Independent School District to provide expansion of the Step-Up programme to grades K-2 in five low-income elementary schools (Blanchette, Fehl, Fletcher, Martin and Southerland). In 1999, all of the 4–5-year-old Head Start children were able to progress from the fourth- to the fifth-year level on the Kaplan Learning Scale and were promoted to kindergarten. In addition, these two early childhood grants have provided assistance to the parents of the Step-Up children in securing high-school diplomas and developing parenting and tutoring skills. The Project Even Start Program is depicted in Figure 8.3 (p. 126). The original Beaumont Project Step-Up site has been extended to additional sites in El Paso and McAllen, Texas. In Rockpoint, Arizona, the programme officer, Bobbie Ackley, demonstrated the enthusiasm for the programme by sending three teachers to Lamar University's annual teacher training institute to expand the programme. Maker has expanded the Step-Up project to include students who speak only a limited amount of English, in a project funded through bilingual education called Discover (Schmidt, 1993).

Summary and conclusions

Out of the 287 students identified as capable of or suitable for joining the programme over the 14 sites, the number of gifted and talented individuals

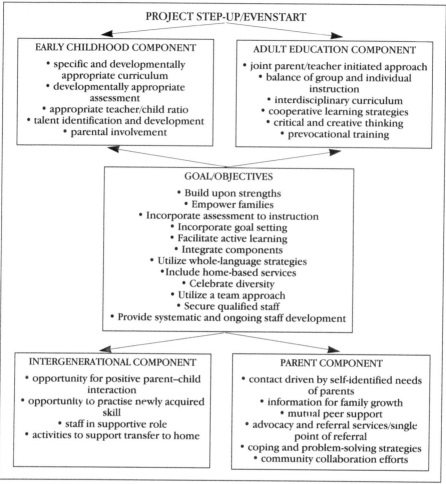

Figure 8.3: Project Step-Up Evenstart

identified by the schools' procedures and tests was only 60% (N=168) of the total group.

Over the programme it was found that the high-potential students' underachievement was situational. They were underachieving specifically in the basic skills of reading and mathematics. Now a significant number have been identified as gifted students and they have the potential to make vital and positive contributions in the future.

Overall this was a remarkable achievement when we consider where the students were on the programme on entrance, since many were below the 50th percentile in ability aand achievement on standardized tests.

The Step-Up framework for identification, counselling and curriculum development presented here offers one successful way to overcome underachievement in these socially and culturally disadvantaged groups.

CHAPTER 9

Inclusive education for able underachievers: changing teaching for learning

DIANE MONTGOMERY

Introduction

In recommending any form of special provision for the more able we need to have regard to the principle of inclusion. Progress is being made on this front in the UK in advance of that in other countries, where identification of high ability leads to some form of segregated provision, whether in the form of pull-out programmes or Olympiads. Yet even now, in the 'Excellence in Cities Project' (Department for Education and Employment, 1999), schools are required to select their top 10% for the able strand provision. So the fight is not won.

Over time it has become clear that differentiation in the form of modified materials, methods, inputs and outcomes has served only to segregate the pupils receiving them in the classroom. This is because in integrated education the learner is helped to adapt to meet the needs of the school whereas in inclusive education the school adapts to meet the needs of the learner. Inclusive education can be the key to meeting the needs of the underachiever. It will be argued in this chapter that because it is the teaching methods by which the curriculum is delivered which are predisposing children to fail and to underachieve, it is the schools that must be made to change. Those children who arrive at school with difficulties and disadvantages can be doubly handicapped by the style or type of schooling they receive.

At this time we are seeing a significant rise in disaffection among pupils and a rapid increase in exclusions from school over the past five years (Department for Education and Employment, 1999). Pupils in primary and secondary schools say their major worries are about passing exams (Visser and Rayner, 1999). This should not be the case.

All of this raises major questions for education of the gifted and talented. If inclusive education is the most appropriate form of education for all our children, how can this be compatible with any form of acceleration, enrichment, selection, ability grouping or special provision for a more able group – however they are defined?

If we are to operate on the basis of inclusion, how can those at the extremes be catered for? How can teachers possibly cope? Should the principle of inclusion also be one of those precepts in gifted education that Piirto in Chapter 1 says we should question and even perhaps reject?

Identification of underachievement

Because high ability and talent are a more widespread phenomenon than has generally been believed (Goldberg, 1965) and because IQ tests and teacher assessments frequently fail to identify many gifted individuals (Montgomery, 1996), different models for identification and provision are needed other than those narrowly based on tests and checklists.

Identifying the able has been shown not always to be simple and straightforward, but identifying the underfunctioning able can be even more problematic. In a family one child may be of average ability and attainment, another may be of high ability and doing well in school, and the third may be of even higher ability but functioning in school at a level lower than the average one. Parents often know that such a child is underfunctioning, but the school sees only the poor attainment and concludes that the pupil is of low ability or lazy and may refuse to investigate further. It can be difficult for parents to secure an assessment through the school as there are often many other children whose special needs seem more severe. Even if an independent psychological assessment is obtained there is no guarantee that it will show the high ability or, if it does, that any provision will be made. Parents are on hand to observe the challenging questions raised and the ingenious ways their children may solve problems and how quickly they 'catch on' when being given an explanation or demonstration. They can note the different profiles of development. Teachers with large classes do not always have the time to observe these nuances. Teacher judgement can be facilitated, however, where there has been in-service training in identification strategies (Denton and Postlethwaite, 1985; Hany, 1997).

In test conditions some highly able children work slowly, whereas others see uniquely different answers to items and problems and so their scores may seem artificially low until their performance and rationales are explored. A few children will deliberately exploit the tests and give wrong answers so as to remain with their friends or not seem to be noticeably different. If pupils fail to shine in school subjects there is a tendency to perceive this as laziness and a failure to pursue school goals. Pupils' reports read 'could do better', 'has good ability but ...', 'must work harder' and so on. This negative stance adopted by the school can be frustrating for the pupil who may not know why nothing seems to satisfy them – a scene set up to create an alienated able misfit.

In order to offer identification to all children, the principles of *open access* and *self-referral* need to be applied. This does not prevent tutors and mentors from suggesting to pupils that they should try a programme, nor does it prevent them from recommending them for, for example, masterclasses and special enrichment, but it also means that every pupil needs a mentor, someone who will promote their best interests.

If we must identify more able pupils for some reason then we need to engage in a process of triangulation, as illustrated by Sisk in Chapter 8. This means that in addition to standardized abilities tests in IQ, school attainment results such as SATs in curriculum subject areas and basic skills tests of reading, spelling and number, we need to add results of teacher assessments supported by checklists. To these results should be added the pupils' performance on the Cognitive Curriculum. It is in this curriculum that performance-based assessment (Shore and Tsiamis, 1986) or authentic assessment (Gardner, 1993) can be operated and can identify many of those pupils missed by the other methods. The implications of performance-based assessment and the nature of the cognitive curriculum are spelled out in later sections. It is also important, as Gyarmathy and Sisk have pointed out, to use a test such as Raven's Progressive Matrices (Raven, 1988) in order to overcome literacy, oracy and cultural biases. This tests a different and more right hemisphere-orientated problem-solving ability. It has proved particularly useful with deaf children, new immigrants, dyslexics and refugee children. Tests of any kind should, however, be regarded only as a small sample of behaviours and therefore can give only an estimate or indication of ability and potential which needs to be supported by performance-based assessment.

Characteristics of effective provision for the highly able

Since almost everyone has been to school, there is an assumption that they therefore know all about teaching and learning and teacher education. Even the pupils hold views that 'what they want is facts'. Highly able eight year olds may learn all the names of the seas of the world and of the rivers of their own country to fill their want for knowledge, and will enjoy doing so. But this does not mean that rote learning all aspects of the curriculum is a valid exercise in education now, although at the turn of the last century it was a common method.

There is also a distinct mismatch between what employers and governments say is required of workers of the new millennium and what is intrinsic to school learning. The people and workers in this new age, it is frequently said by government ministers and employers, will need to have the necessary skills and abilities for their countries to compete in world markets. If we can believe them, workers will need good communication skills, problem-solving skills, creative thinking abilities, flexibility, good listening skills, ability to learn from experience, ability to learn from others and cooperative abilities. The main vehicle for the development of these skills and abilities or competencies in young people is designed to be the school curriculum. In the UK this consists of the National Curriculum (Education Reform Act 1988, revised 1995), a highly specified content-specific curriculum in most subjects with Standard Assessment Tasks at ages 7, 11 and 14 to ensure that teachers have taught it and the children have 'learned' it. The objectives implicit in the National Curriculum are fundamentally different from those of the new millennium. We also need to bear in mind, as Piirto might argue, that both are built on propaganda.

Teacher education has also been changed in the UK for the National Curriculum. It has become a school subject-based system and education theory has been removed from the courses. Much subject learning and teaching practice now takes place in schools supervised and mentored by teachers. That is, new teachers are trained by those who have been designated (current propaganda) as not well enough trained themselves in earlier decades. The National Curriculum itself has been specified in such detail that the assumptions seem to be that it is simply the job of the 'teacher' to read it up and then tell it in a lively manner to the pupils.

What we do know is that boredom and lack of cognitive challenge in the daily curriculum is playing a more significant role in causing pupils across the ability range to become disaffected than was originally suspected. Where there is pressure for so-called academic standards, to the exclusion of a concern for individuals and their needs (Hargreaves, 1984; Galloway and Goodwin, 1987), then this will predispose many children to feel alienated from school work.

The all-important principle that has been overlooked by those enforcing these changes is that teachers do not 'teach subjects', but they teach pupils how to learn subjects. This is a much higher order set of social and cognitive skills and not as easily acquired as a straightforward subject degree.

Ten years on in the UK we have a cadre of teachers who are educationally illiterate and pupils who are becoming repositories of fact but who lack the ability to put their knowledge to any useful real-world purpose. In addition, more pupils, including the highly able and the more creative, are rejecting such 'schooling' and are switching off. We now have the situation where the National Curriculum and the methods by which it is taught have especially not led to a stimulating and educative experience for the gifted and talented. The UK government has now set up an advisory group to help solve this problem. In terms of the general school population, more of the same will not lead, and has not led, to the creation of workers with the competencies to be successful in the new millennium. Nor did the selective system work, which was implemented after the 1944 Education Act, whereby 20% of the 'most able' of the school population went to grammar schools.

Most of these students arrived, and still do, in higher education lacking the critical capabilities, study skills and self-organizing abilities to profit from their advanced education (Thomas and Augstein, 1975; Gibbs, 1990, 1994; Montgomery, 1993). But in higher education these competencies are still seldom taught – the assumption is made that they already exist or that students will somehow learn them.

The content-based curriculum and approaches in most degree programmes are also not capable of inducing critical and creative thinking, according to Stephenson and Weil (1988) and Gibbs (1994, 1995). These writers launched programmes of staff development in the universities to try to counteract the problems in the belief that if they could change higher education then this would filter down into schools and companies.

Research has shown that methods of teaching, in 90% of classrooms worldwide, are formal and didactic (Skilbeck, 1989; Rogers and Span, 1993). Paul (1990) has described the didactic theory of education as a system in which the student is taught what, but not how, to think. Students are said to know when they can repeat what they have been told and are given the products of other people's thinking. In this model the educated person is merely a data bank and this is characteristic of 19th-century learning, when what is required is 21st-century learning. What Paul shows that is conspicuously absent from school learning is some systematic and programmed attention to thinking and problem-solving in relation to 'messy' problems, in other words a 'cognitive curriculum' which develops multilogical not monological thinking. It is these thinking-orientated programmes that a range of researchers has found to be essential to help the gifted and talented realize their potential (Tannenbaum, 1983, 1997; Passow, 1990; Poorthuis et al., 1990; de Alencar, 1990, 1999). However, the benefits of this approach are not confined to the gifted, as evidence shows that all children benefit from such cognitively engaging work (Tannenbaum, 1983; Montgomery, 1990, 1998; Watson, 1996).

In an age when there are vast stores of knowledge available through a computer terminal, although some knowledge is essential we do not now have to be encyclopaedic. Instead, we need to learn how to manage and use the information we gain. We also know that where subjects are taught in integrated themes rather than separately, then pupils are able to reach higher levels of understanding and competence. In computer terminology we have set up a system without an appropriate set of 'applications menus'.

Passow (1990) concluded that the gifted needed: a curriculum which provided additional depth and breadth of coverage; a speeded-up coverage tailored to individual needs; modification of the material to take account of needs and interests; and the development of critical and creative thinking, heuristics and problem-solving, and effective interpersonal communication and social skills.

In analysing whether provision was effective, Poorthuis et al. (1990) concluded that enrichment materials should meet a number of criteria. They produced a curriculum analysis tool for this purpose, as follows. The materials:

- should be beneficial to the development and use of higher-order thinking abilities;
- ought to provide the possibility to explore continually new knowledge and new information;
- should teach and encourage students to select and use sources of information;
- should have content that aims at complex, enriching and in-depth study of important ideas, problems and subjects, and integrating knowledge between and within subject areas;
- should offer the opportunity to increasingly autonomous learning activities.

In any consideration of effective teaching there needs also to be a consideration of what makes for effective learning. De Corte (1995) in an extensive review of the literature summarizes the nature of effective learning. His main points are that effective learning is to be found where the following conditions apply:

- learning is constructive,
- learning is cumulative,
- learning is best when self-organized,
- learning is generally goal-orientated,
- learning is situated,

- learning is individually different,
- learning is usually best when collaborative.

Learning in classrooms seldom complies with these conditions. Learning may often be assumed to be cumulative in the teaching sequence that is prepared, but there may be omissions and jumps with which the learner cannot cope. Individuals are seldom given opportunities to construct their own learning or organize it themselves. They rarely have opportunities to set their own goals or to make learning individually different and situated. Classroom learning is situated in the same place, but at times the emotional climate varies and embeds the learning to make it more memorable. Learning may take place in groups but it is usually the case that students sit together but are doing individual work rather than collaborating (Bennett, 1986).

It can be seen that there is overlap between the conditions for effective learning and the curriculum needs of the gifted. In addition there is overlap between both of these and what Gibbs (1990) has identified as key elements of 'good teaching':

- intrinsic motivation, a need to know and have ownership of knowing;
- learner activity rather than passivity although doing is not enough – we need to reflect and connect present to past learning;
- interaction with others so that ideas can be discussed and negotiated or 'taught' by students, for the best way of learning something is to teach it to someone else;
- a well-structured knowledge base where knowledge is displayed and integrated into meaningful wholes not disparate units. This is best seen in interdisciplinary studies.

A key concept here is intrinsic motivation. It is not easily induced in ordinary classrooms. Passow (1990) in a survey of research concluded that there was a lack of knowledge about how to induce such love of learning for its own sake among the gifted. According to Deci (1988), intrinsic motivation is fostered by a consistent, positive, supportive climate and positive constructive feedback. It is destroyed under a pressure to reach and maintain 'standards', a fate often assigned to many gifted children. When pupils are exposed to the pressures of extrinsic motivation, and have to be made to learn, they lose autonomy and self-regulation. It is this effect that we are seeing in many UK classrooms (Montgomery, 1999).

Only recently, a small mixed-ability group of pupils in years 8–10, who had been referred for special education because they were disruptive, were given a lesson comprising a simulation game in geography about conflicting aspects of planning and land use using a problem-solving approach. All of them undertook the task and six of them, the boys, became very involved with it and collaborated well in their small groups and resolved the problem. For once they were highly motivated. The two girls, who reported that they could not see the point of the exercise, did the basic minimum but did not become disruptive or attention-seeking as previously. The general view of the group was that it was not 'real' work, as they had enjoyed it and had not had to write anything down. Most of the group also had literacy difficulties.

It is clear from this and other similar examples collected in the Learning Difficulties Research Project (LDRP) studies[1] that pupils must have explained to them the relevance of what they are doing, why they are doing it and how best they can learn. On its own this would not necessarily enthuse the two disillusioned and alienated girls, but they might listen and note and be more likely on a subsequent occasion to allow themselves to become a little more involved. Typically they would be interested at least in monitoring what was going on. Overt participation would be likely to make them feel too vulnerable at first, but more detail and insight would appear in any written or oral work they undertook.

Self-regulation and self-monitoring activities consist of planning, predicting outcomes, scheduling time and resources, monitoring learning, and evaluating learning outcomes against plans and criteria.

One final distinction needs to be made before looking at methods and models, and that is to clarify the meaning of intellectual versus cognitive skills, which sometimes seem to be used as interchangeable terms. It is not uncommon for teachers to believe that they are developing problem-solving and thinking skills when they are not. The definitions are based on Gagné (1973).

Intellectual skills

These are about knowing 'that' and knowing 'how'. They include converting printed words into meaning, fractions into decimals, knowing about classes, groups and categories, knowing the laws of mechanics and genetics, and forming sentences and pictures. They enable us to deal with the world 'out there'.

Cognitive skills

These are internally organized capabilities which we make use of in guiding our attention, learning, thinking and remembering. They are executive control processes which activate and direct other learning processes. We use them when we think about our learning.

It is clear from this that tests which purport to assess cognitive abilities most frequently do not – they are testing what has been learned in the form of intellectual skills. Sometimes there is a close link between intellectual and cognitive skills, such as when we might argue that sequencing and ordering text is a cognitive skill but when we are sequencing letters in words and numbers in an IQ test we are looking at an intellectual skill.

Models and methods in the education of gifted children

In making more effective provision for the gifted it is necessary to reconsider our models and methods. The evidence which follows is based on extensive work in teacher education and in schools (Montgomery, 1983, 1985, 1990, 1996, 1999). From these studies it was found that if teachers' practices were to be changed, they themselves had to be taught by the methods to which we wished them to change (Montgomery, 1993, 1994). When this was implemented, instead of only a small percentage of the group getting first-class grades in the final degree examinations, the proportion rose to more than 20%, and the whole group's results (n=72) improved significantly in comparison with previous years. The data on effectiveness collected more recently come from multiple case studies conducted in many countries with mixed-ability and high-ability groups of pupils. It is undertaken and reported by teachers as part of their work for one of two distance learning MA programmes with Middlesex University. The teachers in each module evaluate the techniques with pupils in their own classrooms and in different subject areas.

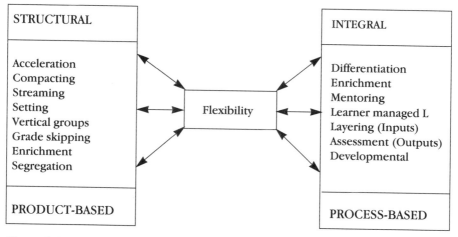

Figure 9.1: A model of types of differentiation

If we look first at models of differentiation, they can be roughly divided into two main approaches. One, which I call 'structural', involves a response by the school and a modification of the system of grouping in the cohorts. The second is called 'integral' and is more a 'way of life within classrooms' model, in which the individual teacher modifies the curriculum or teaching method.

Briefly, the general approach behind most structural methods, even where 'enrichment' appears, is that the able pupils receive accelerated content. That is, content which older students would expect to receive is given to younger students and they are often put through it more quickly (compacting).

The term differentiation in the integral category is often used to symbolize the approach itself. Enrichment here is frequently a bolt-on provision and may consist of extension material. Layering consists of giving the mixed-ability class different levels of the same work after the main introduction. The gifted group receive more of the problem-solving approaches and this can prove divisive as their work may seem to be more enjoyable. In assessment approaches it is the teacher again who decides whose work will be marked more harshly, although all the pupils are set the same task. What has been found over an experimental period of about 20 years in the Learning Difficulties Research Project into which all the results are fed is that the method called developmental provision is the most effective for both mixed-ability classes and selective groups. It can also provide scope for both mentoring and learner-managed or self-regulated learning within it. In essence, developmental differentiation involves the setting of common tasks to which all students can contribute their own inputs and so progress from surface to deep learning, and thus be enabled to achieve more advanced learning outcomes.

Achieving this form of differentiation thus results not from changing the curriculum itself but by making modest changes in the methods by which it is taught across all subjects. It should be the basis of all class teaching by every teacher. This does not mean that no other provision for the gifted will be needed. Therefore it is essential that schools become more flexible and that they do not go in for 'either acceleration or enrichment' but offer the levels of provision shown in Figure 9.2, which illustrates the seven types of curriculum differentiation which should be on offer in every school.

It is being recommended that in the 'new age' we need to be creative and imaginative, to be good communicators and problem-solvers. However, the traditional method used is teaching text or curriculum content with strict adherence to the set book or work sheets. Some teachers use text extension methods but very few use text thinking approaches. The lesson usually consists of teacher exposition and question and answer, followed by 'seat work' involving reading, writing, drawing or performing.

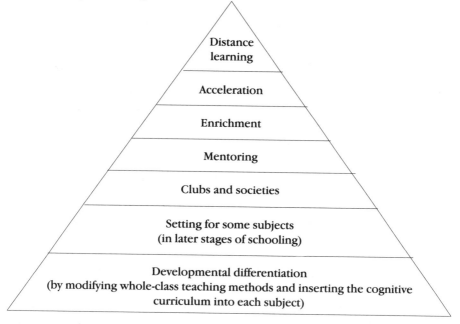

Distance
learning

Acceleration

Enrichment

Mentoring

Clubs and societies

Setting for some subjects
(in later stages of schooling)

Developmental differentiation
(by modifying whole-class teaching methods and inserting the cognitive
curriculum into each subject)

Figure 9.2: The pyramid for potential

If we consider the school curriculum itself in relation to the needs of the new millennium and developmental differentiation we can see that there are some shortcomings. The school curriculum generally comprises:

- the National Curriculum, school subjects,
- the extracurricular activities,
- the hidden curriculum,
- the personal and social curriculum,
- the basic skills curriculum – reading, writing and number,
- the ethical and moral curriculum,
- the cognitive curriculum.

It is the cognitive curriculum that we could usefully focus on to show how it can be linked to the subject and other curricula to achieve differentiation. The cognitive curriculum consists of:

- developmental positive cognitive intervention (PCI),
- cognitively challenging questioning – open and problem posing,

- deliberate teaching of thinking skills and protocols (Swartz and Parks, 1994),
- creativity training (de Alencar, 1999),
- cognitive process teaching methods (Montgomery, 1990, 1996).

Developmental positive cognitive intervention

Developmental PCI (Montgomery, 1984, 1999) consists of the teacher moving around to every individual in the class each lesson and saying something constructive about their work, especially to move it on to a higher level. Cognitive process methods are discussed later.

Deliberate teaching of thinking skills

CBC (Catch Them Being Clever is an important part of PCI. In a recent review of teaching thinking in classrooms, McGuinness (1999) identified several different approaches as follows:

- *Teaching of thinking*: direct instruction in thinking in noncurricular contexts.
- *Bolt-on provision*: this is illustrated by the work of de Bono (1983) in the Cognitive Research Trust (CoRT) Thinking Programme; Feuerstein et al. (1980) in Instrumental Enrichment; and Blagg et al. (1993, revised edition) in the Somerset Thinking Skills Project
- *Teaching for thinking*: use of methods which promote thinking in curricular contexts, for example Adey (1991, 1992) and Adey and Shayer (1994) in Cognitive Acceleration in Science Education (CASE, also Cognitive Acceleration in Mathematics Education (CAME) and Cognitive Acceleration in Geography Education (CAGE)) projects; by Lipman (1991) in Philosophy for Children; and by Renzulli (1995) in the schoolwide enrichment programme and revolving door models.
- *Infusion*: restructuring content lessons for direct instruction in thinking, for example; Swartz and Parks (1994) – infusion techniques and lessons McGuinness (1999) – activating children's thinking skills.

Creativity Training

Teachers who fostered creativity (de Alencar 1995) encouraged pupils to: be independent learners; formulate their own ideas; think & reason; cultivate an interest in new knowledge; asked challenging questions & rewarded them for creative behaviour. They were enthusiastic and respected pupil's ideas.

Cognitive process strategies

These are the core of developmental differentiation and PCI and they enable them to be achieved. Cognitive process teaching methods are based in critical thinking theory and are the means by which higher-order thinking and metacognitive skills can be developed through the ordinary curriculum. They are also powerfully inclusive. The whole class can be introduced to the basic idea and then mixed groups or pairs work on the main ideas or subthemes and then pool their knowledge and experience with the teacher's support. These strategies can be widely used to promote inclusion at primary and secondary level.

Central objectives in teaching need to be redefined as follows:

- to enable students to think efficiently (within curricular areas and the real world), and
- to express those thoughts succinctly.

There are six main types of cognitive process strategies or pedagogies:

1. Games and simulations

In the non-simulation game students work in groups and have to know certain facts, perform skills or demonstrate mastery of specific concepts to win or be successful. The participants agree objectives and there are sets of rules to obey. Typical of this form is the card game which can be adapted to educational purposes, such as 'Phonic Rummy' and Whole Book games. Simulation games contain the elements of real situations and students individually or in groups interact with and become part of the reality. Role-playing is often an important feature of the game.

Characteristic of all games is that they must be followed by a discussion-debriefing session to discuss what transpired so that emotional, educational and metacognitive objectives can be achieved.

2. Cognitive study skills

The examples can apply to textual, visual and performance material. They are higher-order reading and learning skills and include locating the main points and subordinate ones; flow charting; completion and prediction activities; sequencing; comparing and contrasting; drafting and editing; organizing – tabulating, classifying, ordering, diagramming, categorizing; drawing inferences and abstractions; recognizing intent, bias and propaganda; and identifying text schemata.

Cognitive study skills are a form of self-directed learning and some examples are discussed in Chapter 10.

3. Real problem-solving and investigative learning

Human nature is such that if you present a person with an open-ended situation in which the answer is not given, the mind automatically tries to resolve it. Humans are born scientific investigators (Kelly, 1955). Although not everything can be converted into a problem, there is considerable scope for doing so across the curriculum.

Characteristic of the approach is that there needs to be plenty of content material around to research, to help develop ideas and strategies or verify solutions. Because the activities start from the pupil's own ideas and knowledge, each pupil is building up his or her own cognitive structures. Some examples are given in Chapter 10. The teacher is not only a resource but is also the manager and facilitator of learning.

Real problems are essentially 'fuzzy' and time has to be spent in finding the issues. According to Gallagher (1997), there are four elements to 'fuzzy' problems: an ill-structured problem; substantial content; student apprenticeship; self-directed learning. This approach is better than traditional teaching methods for long-term retention, conceptual understanding, self-directed learning and intrinsic motivation. Deci (1988) and Gibbs (1990) have both shown that one thing that is essential to effective learning and good teaching is intrinsic motivation, the desire to learn for its own sake.

The essence of problem-solving is to promote and develop thinking skills and abilities, both intellectual and cognitive (Gagné, 1973). We can identify both lower- and higher-order thinking skills as follows.

Some lower-order thinking skills are:

- sequencing and ordering,
- sorting, classifying and grouping,
- analysing, identifying parts/wholes,
- comparing and contrasting,
- distinguishing fact from opinion,
- identifying bias and checking evidence,
- drawing conclusions and giving reasons,
- making predictions, hypothesizing,
- relating cause and effect,
- designing a fair test, and
- weighing up pros and cons.

Some higher-order thinking skills are:

- defining and clarifying problems,

- thinking up different solutions,
- setting priorities, goals and targets,
- testing solutions and evaluating outcomes,
- planning and monitoring progress towards goals
- revising plans and managing progress,
- making decisions,
- real problem-solving,
- generating new ideas and solutions,
- team building (using emotional and social intelligence), and
- creative problem-solving.

It is in fact difficult to assign some of these to separate categories, but a general principle might be that lower-order thinking is more closely associated with curriculum content typical of intellectual processing. Higher-order skills and cognitive skills are much more to do with running the executive control processes (Gagné, 1973).

4. Experiential learning

Experiential learning involves learning by doing or *action learning*. The learning is not circular, returning the learner to the same point each time. Instead, at each turn, the experience, the talking about the experience, and the reflecting on the learning and doing, add to the sum of knowledge and change the processes and the understanding in an additive way.

The result is a learning spiral (Montgomery, 1994), progressing from surface to deep learning (Marton and Saljo, 1984), often with the mediation of the teacher (Feuerstein, 1995) (see Figure 9.3).

5. Collaborative learning

Collaboration means that students work with one another towards the framing and design of problems and strategies, as well as in their resolution or solution. Each contributes some part to the whole. Quite often the process is called 'cooperative learning'. When pupils sit in groups they may be doing individual rather than collaborative work (Bennett, 1986).

Collaborative learning facilitates extended language use and thinking, as well as assisting in team-building skills. It can be used in both content-free (Rawlings, 1996) and content-dense situations. Examples of content-dense lessons related to specific curriculum subjects are given in section 3 of Chapter 10. An example of content-free work would be to use a well-known story such as *Little Red Riding Hood*, but to tell the story as 'the maligned wolf', a reconstruction from the wolf's point of view. This is then used to raise issues about interpersonal perception and role relationships (Bowers and Wells, 1988; Rawlings, 1996).

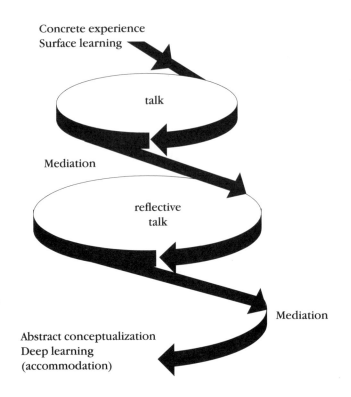

Concrete experience
Surface learning

talk

Mediation

reflective
talk

Mediation

Abstract conceptualization
Deep learning
(accommodation)

Figure 9.3: Cognitive process learning spiral

'Circle time' is a term used to describe a setting when all the pupils sit in a circle or a horseshoe and share in an activity, such as saying something positive about the person sitting to the left or right of them in turn round the circle. They may do a few such ice-breakers or positive supportive warm-up activities and then focus on problems such as 'What are our rights?' or a bullying incident, sharing experiences and deciding what should and could be done about it. 'Brainstorming' and problem-solving and-resolving sessions on human issues are a common feature.

These sessions are widely used in schools and have helped in the management of pupils with behavioural problems and learning needs. They contribute to the language and emotional development of children as well as to problem-solving and creativity development. Conflict management and mediation strategies are also often developments of this type of work.

For underachieving pupils these sessions offer opportunities for affirmation and expression of concerns and needs, as well as guiding them in ways of expressing themselves in reasonable terms. The conflict management and mediation techniques were derived from the crowd-control techniques that were developed after the student and race riots in the USA, and which aimed to keep people safe and focused on their legitimate objectives rather than allowing themselves to be swayed by crowd emotion to riot and loot. The beneficial effects of the techniques were recognized by the Quaker movement and introduced through such groups as the Kingston Workshop Group led by Bowers, Wells and Rawlings during the 1980s. We also introduced it into our teacher education programmes in Kingston with their help as 'Ways and Means Problem-solving Workshops'. Many local schools and local education authorities also found their methods and training techniques helpful throughout the age ranges.

6. Language experience methods

These involve the pupils composing and compiling their own textual and study materials. These methods began as ways of creating reading books for poor readers, in which they would discuss topics and experiences with a tutor and then the tutor would act as a scribe and write down the story that the pupil told. This was then word processed and used as reading material. Now pairs of pupils can compose narrative and other materials on the word processor and gain the same benefits.

In language experience methods students might write and illustrate their own textbooks in a subject area, or they might be asked to write stories or texts for a younger group of students and then try it out with them. Where underachievers have read their own or simple stories to much younger children, this has been found to be a powerful means of enhancing their self-esteem, and of course gives practice in literacy skills.

The teacher or the students might take a chapter or a whole book and base a board game on it in which, when the players land on particular squares, they have to answer a question from a study-skills card. The questions should reflect both comprehension and problem-solving items. Dyslexics, second-language learners and other poor readers have found these games most powerfully motivating. Highly able underachievers can also design games in pairs and try them out on younger children. It increases their interest and skill with text.

These are just a few outline examples of the cognitive process approaches that have been tried out on a wide scale with slow learners, and remedial, gifted and mixed-ability groups. Several more detailed lesson examples can be found in Chapter 10.

What is clear from the studies is that intrinsic motivation is developed by these methods, and children's time on task extends in their enjoyment long after the lessons end. Disaffected children remained at school for these lessons and gifted students recorded such things as 'This is much better than the usual boring stuff we get'. They all began to spend extended periods of time on-task, instead of off-task. The quality of their work frequently exceeded all expectations, as did that of the most modest of learners, and there are sometimes the most surprisingly interesting and creative responses from unsuspected sources. The collaborative nature of the tasks means that mixed-ability groups can easily access the work and all can be included in the same tasks with no diminution of the achievements of the highly able (Zeidner and Scheleyer, 1999).

Enjoyment and legitimized social interaction were not often connected in the children's minds at first with school learning, and so at each stage they had to be shown in explicit ways how much they had learned and how their work was improving. This was done by giving detailed comments on their work and their learning processes, both verbally and in writing couched in constructive terms (Positive Cognitive Intervention (PCI) – Montgomery, 1984, 1989, 1999). At intervals they were helped to reflect on the products and the processes of their learning. Once they began to make these connections, they became avid learners and other teachers began to notice a transformation and comment on complete positive changes in the pupils' behaviour and attitude. It is in these ways that effective teaching methods can also be seen to be making a major contribution to classroom management and behaviour control (Montgomery, 1989, 1999). This is in addition to the general benefits created by a positive and supportive classroom climate and school ethos using what I have elsewhere called CBG (Catch them Being Good) methods (Montgomery, 1989).

According to Gibbs (1990), the characteristics of surface or superficial learning are: a heavy workload; relatively high class contact hours; an excessive amount of course material; a lack of opportunity to pursue subjects in depth; a lack of choice of subjects; a lack of choice over study methods; and a threatening and anxiety-provoking assessment system. Deep learning consists in the reverse of these conditions. Surface learning does not enable the material to be built into the students' internal schemata or constructs and scripts, and so it remains inert and inaccessible. It is often capable of being repeated 'parrot fashion' but without significant understanding. Teachers in their instruction mode give mini-lectures on topics to pupils, and when this is well structured it gives rise to the condition known as reception learning (Ausubel, 1968), which is similar to surface learning. It can be repeated in an examination after revision, but it does not become incorporated into the student's conceptual understanding, and it does not become part of them, or accommodated in the Piagetian sense.

The cognitive learning spiral illustrates the sort of processing that is necessary to move learning to the deep levels. In the first spiral there is discussion about the concrete events in which students explain and expand on what they have just experienced. This may take place with or without mediation from the teacher. In the next cycle they may receive further related input or experience and then go on to reflect and discuss how they learnt and what was their thinking during this activity. This process of thinking about one's thinking is known as metacognition and is a major contributor towards increasing a person's intelligence (Flavell, 1979).

A sample of other inclusive models

Worldwide, there are a number of models for teaching the gifted. Most of them promote segregated provision, Olympiads and so on. However, there are others which can be used in inclusive situations across the subject, age and ability ranges. Three of them are outlined here. What is of interest is their common attributes, even though they developed in isolation from each other. The Multiple Intelligences (MI) approach is not included as it is discussed in Chapter 7. It is sufficient to note here that a two-factor intelligence theory (Spearman, 1927) underpins the cognitive process model. The theory proposes a 'g' factor – a general problem-solving ability – and a range of 's' factors for specific abilities.

STAED: Student-Assisted Education (Roeders, 1995)

According to Roeders (1995), the realization of important pedagogical goals, such as self-reliance, creativity, teamwork abilities and a sense of responsibility, often seems to play a secondary role both in educational policy and in teachers' practical work at school. He says this is because teachers are too busy keeping order and explaining and repeating the prescribed, mainly capacities-based, subject matter, thereby leaving little time to support exceptional children.

STAED is based on a holistic approach, conceptualizing the learner, teacher, learning group, classroom and staff as dynamic interdependent systems composed of several dependent subsystems. STAED tries to optimize these systems' dynamic processes by: (1) creating an optimal learning atmosphere by applying relaxation techniques and promoting mutual assistance as the basis of social relations in school; (2) dealing effectively with individual differences in the classroom by multifaceted methods and materials: and (3) active learning by children in mini-groups, using different constellations, depending on the aims of the activities. By being provided with materials adapted to different learning styles and by fostering every pupil's problem-solving abilities, all of the children can make progress at their own level. As children actively shape the learning processes in interaction with classmates, they learn to feel responsible for their own achievements and to use their creativity.

Teachers are seen as the orchestrators and managers of the learning processes of their pupils, instead of being their direct instructors. Roeders reports that the teachers in the experimental schools experienced more job satisfaction, although they had to invest a considerable amount of time. In comparison with control subjects, the experimental pupils showed more progress in learning achievements both in tests immediately afterwards and in tests after a much longer period, as well as a decrease in learning, social and emotional problems.

After revision and elaboration, STAED is now being used on a wider scale in Dutch primary as well as secondary schools and in several German schools for remediation. These schools are coaching schoolchildren who have difficulties in their daily school life, such as low-ability students, under-achieving gifted pupils, as well as those with personal/personality problems.

As can be seen, this approach moves in the same direction as those already outlined for the highly able underachiever in inclusive contexts. It has, as they all have, arisen independently, based on an analysis of children's learning needs.

Renzulli's Enrichment Triad Model (Renzulli, 1977, 1995)

Renzulli developed this model to enable students to follow their own interests to whatever depth and extent they were able. The primary role of the teacher is to help the students to identify and frame the problem to be studied and then help them in acquiring the necessary skill to carry out an individual or small-group investigation. This may also include finding an appropriate audience or outlet for the products.

The individual does have to be motivated to want to pursue the topic and the environment has to be flexible enough to permit it. This would pose problems for teachers in the UK at present in terms of time allocation. However, the model is based on the same type of theory and practice as others described, showing how researchers and teachers in different countries are all coming to similar conclusions about what is needed in the education of gifted students.

Renzulli's model is composed of three types of activity: Type I – general exploratory activities, such as talks, field trips, films and so on, to generate interest and introduce content; Type II – group training activities, which are focused on teaching processes and skills to expand thinking and feeling development; Type III – individual and small group investigations of real problems.

Clark's Integrative Education Model (Clark, 1986)

Again we have here the influence of the holistic approach to learning, this time based on Jung's work. Clark's model organizes the curriculum through the use of four functions: thinking, intuitive, feeling/emotional, and physical/sensing. The purpose is to integrate whole brain activities into a coherent, total learning experience. The main resource is extra teacher preparation time. Teachers have also to be given special training in establishing 'responsive, flexible classroom environments, use relaxation techniques, provide challenging activities for all four functions, and encourage intuitive activities' (cited in Leroux and McMillan, 1993: 47).

Essentially these last two American models focus on 'pull out' and segregated programmes. However, the contents and methods can be used in inclusive contexts.

Evaluation of materials and methods

It is usual now for teachers preparing curriculum enrichment and extension materials and developmental differentiation to use Bloom's (1956) taxonomy of educational objectives as a guideline. This means they try to produce materials and methods, even for five year olds, which tap into Bloom's higher levels of analysis, synthesis and evaluation. In the LDRP we have examples of mixed-ability groups of five year olds, which include gifted individuals, all working at these higher levels. These higher levels of operation thus need not be reserved until the teenage years when vast bodies of content have been learned. Thinking and study skills by then may have been dimmed.

In addition to these guidelines we can add a composite checklist or seven-point plan for evaluation of materials for the gifted, and indeed for all children at the basic level – developmental differentiation in the curriculum – to be provided by every teacher in elementary and secondary school. Similar methods are appropriate at university level (Gibbs, 1994, 1995; Montgomery, 1995a, 1996). The seven-point plan or checklist for the evaluation of gifted education materials is as follows:

- Are they beneficial to the development and use of higher-order thinking abilities?
- Do they enable the exploration of new knowledge and important ideas in breadth and in depth?
- Can they teach and encourage study and research skills in the selection and use of sources?
- Do they offer opportunities to engage in increasingly autonomous learning and induce intrinsic motivation?

- Do the processes help integrate knowledge between and within subjects?
- Are some problems 'fuzzy' or open-ended and so promote multilogical, innovative and creative responses?
- Do the activities promote real collaborative learning and abilities to work in teams?

If the answers to these questions are in the affirmative by all teachers in a school then we can begin to be assured that we are working out the 'applications programmes' for the curriculum which will prepare students to achieve and nations to succeed in the new millennium, for they are teaching the gifted and all students more effectively.

To effect this change, the principles of effective learning need to be incorporated into our thinking about teaching. This means that teaching methods need to be adapted to make education inclusive, and the curriculum can then stay the same. The revision of the UK curriculum to free up 20% more time should be of benefit if we can persuade schools to cut the curriculum content but not fill the time thus freed by add-on enrichments and extensions. Pupils need more quality time on-task and time to think.

Summary and conclusions

There is a wide range of what have been termed 'at risk' factors operating in the home and school environments which can predispose pupils to underfunction and underachieve. As the risk factors multiply they cause a progressive deterioration in motivation, which can lead to disaffection and alienation from school and learning environments of any kind.

It has been suggested that lack of cognitive challenge in the curriculum is a major cause of underfunctioning. A range of learning difficulties which conceal learning potential, particularly in the literacy area, can also make a contribution to lower achievements. Stereotypic views of the 'good' pupil, gender, ethnicity, culture and the 'able child' can also cause pupils' abilities to be overlooked and lead to underfunctioning as expectations are lowered.

Having considered all these factors, it becomes difficult to understand how anyone ever succeeds at school and avoids the complex mesh of damages and dangers to which they are exposed. It suggests that some pupils' determination to succeed can outweigh the negative effects to which they may be exposed, but with a little support many more might achieve substantially higher levels of attainment than they do.

Even now teachers in the UK are complaining about the excess of content in the National Curriculum and the over-rigid rules for implementing it and the National Literacy Strategy. They complain of lack of opportunity for creativity, time to teach, and of feeling deskilled by prescriptive measures emanating daily from Government agencies.

It is proposed that every elementary, secondary and high school could make available seven levels of provision, the 'pyramid for potential', to meet pupils needs. School provision should include the direct teaching of the cognitive developmental curriculum in every classroom by every teacher within their subject content as this has been observed to be the most fundamental need for all students, but particularly for the most able.

Through this provision, and by the methods of teaching proposed here, teachers can engage in more accurate curriculum-based identification of the highly able and, in a process of triangulation, the gifted and secretly talented can be identified. Through this same process they can be given a curriculum that is appropriately matched to their needs. This form of curriculum and pedagogy addresses both cognitive and emotional intelligence and would offer teachers some personal and professional autonomy and creativity.

Note

[1] The Learning Difficulties Research Project (LDRP) is a non-profit-making foundation established in 1981 by the author with a small grant from the Schools Council to collect and disseminate research and practice, and from which books and projects have arisen.

CHAPTER 10

Combating literacy difficulties in able underachievers

DIANE MONTGOMERY

Introduction

Literate persons are able to read and write, with the same facility and fluency, the words which they speak or are spoken to them. The routes to this literacy are more varied than current teaching methods would indicate and so, despite the National Literacy Strategy (NLS), there are still significant numbers of children who are failing to become literate. Although improvements in reading have been found since the implementation of the strategy, serious concerns are still being expressed over spelling and writing, so much so that a National Writing Strategy is to be developed.

Some highly able children learn to read very early and some are fluent by the time they enter reception classes. The rest learn quickly once at school in a reading environment, unless they have a dyslexic-type difficulty. At about nine years of age some children have a reading ability that is five years in advance of their chronological age, which is an indication of more than just a facility for reading. This ability on the reading test may not always be matched by comprehension if the child's background is culturally and linguistically disadvantaged, and there may be no other signs of high ability or high achievement. Such children's potential gifts may be ignored in busy classrooms, but they need opportunities to develop and exploit their analytical and inductive abilities, which have enabled them to read untaught and frequently understand and speak sentences at six months old. In infant classrooms where there may be a great deal of copy writing and learning by rote, and many repetitions of lesson material for the benefit of other learners, more able children become bored. Whether they react to this boredom by passivity or 'acting out', the lack of cognitive challenge is deleterious so that their capabilities remain dormant. Occasional flashes of what they are capable of might be seen in the difficult questions they ask or in the way they do tasks.

Many able but dyslexic pupils may not have their dyslexia detected for years. Steven is currently studying for 10 GCSEs but is worried about getting less than a C in English. He is well thought of at school and is able to explain anything he has done clearly, and in great detail. But if asked to write any of it down, he produces about six lines with effort and the spelling is 'atrocious'. His reading is adequate but he does very little. The school's advice is to encourage him to do more reading – some hope! He needs immediate help from a dyslexia specialist to change him to cursive writing, and to teach him articulatory phonics and linguistics to sort out his spelling. He will also need the help of an English specialist or help from the dyslexia tutor in writing and structuring essays and engaging in study skills because of lack of experience with text.

In research involving case analyses of 300 dyslexics compared with similar numbers of reading and spelling matched controls (Montgomery, 1995b) it was found that highly able dyslexics, those with IQs on WISC–R of at least 130 (for dyslexics four of the subtests on the ACID profile generally show lower scores on Arithmetic, Coding, Information, Digit Span), made up 10% of the sample. These dyslexic boys and girls were a year ahead of their less able peers (mean IQ 110) on reading and spelling. This means that in many local education authorities they are referred for special tuition later, if at all. If their reading is up to grade level for their age then even though they are severely disabled in spelling they are unlikely to get remedial help.

How schools can permit this, even now since the introduction of the Code of Practice (Department for Education and Employment, 1994), is a mystery. For example, Jonathan has a spelling age of 6.8 years at the age of 15 and has had remedial reading teaching since entering secondary school. He has just been referred for a psychological report and this shows he is well above average in ability, and needs to learn cursive writing and have dyslexia support with study skills for English. Nothing about spelling.

If Jonathan had been disruptive he would most certainly have been referred for something other than reading much earlier, for example in the infant school, and perhaps obtained more help. He has by careful selection just gained five GCSEs but has to have another go at English. Such young people, who have great potential for promising careers, are being denied them for lack of early identification of their 'double disability' – giftedness and dyslexia. Both needs are being systematically ignored.

Some able students do not have dyslexia at all, but do have a residual spelling problem. Ann and John were typical of these. They were both early readers, more or less self-taught but with mild problems in articulation and pronouncing polysyllabic words, plus a handwriting problem – dysgraphia. Over the years both developed a strategy of concealing their spelling errors in their nearly indecipherable writing, and shortening forms of words with squiggles.

Despite learning to read easily and early, many able underachievers do not seem to have the same success with writing, especially handwriting, and this affects the amount of practice they also get with spelling. Although reading is a pattern-recognition task and higher intelligence enables readers to guess (hypothesize) from minimal context cues, the same is not true for spelling, which requires total recall, and handwriting, which requires the development of fluent motor programming.

In addition to these within-child factors there are many other factors that have an equal bearing on the pupil who becomes an underachiever. For example, more girls than boys arrive at school able to sit quietly and learn in a formal setting. This is likely to be due as much to early rearing techniques and attitudes as hormones at this stage.

Boys in five reception classes (Montgomery, 1977) made significantly less progress than girls when they all entered as a large class group in September. Summer entry boys performed as well as girls in reading. This was put down to the greater individual attention boys could receive in a smaller summer entry group of 9 to 12 pupils. Girls' performance remained the same. It was noted that in large, busy September classrooms there was more opportunity for (usually) boys to escape attention and spend time wrestling on the mat, as long as they did so quietly, and they also spent more time 'wandering' than seated at desks engaged with tasks than did girls.

The social context of school and the wider community and media also can exert strong pressures to conform and boys would seem more vulnerable or suffer from stronger pressures at an early age than girls. For example, Harris et al. (1993) analysed the influence of school, community and peer group régimes on gender stereotypes and found that although in one régime such as the school they may be challenged, in another they may be strongly reinforced. They also found that boys tended to have fixed views about when work, especially homework, should be done. These views derived from their upbringing. Their fathers traditionally had clear boundaries between time at work and time spent relaxing. Relaxation time was when they were looked after by 'their' women or were enjoying the company of other men. Boys mirrored this behaviour and wherever possible avoided homework or relegated it as a low-priority activity which should be done at school and in the shortest possible time.

The media strongly stereotype young males (Askew and Ross, 1988).

They depict them as tough, strong, aggressive, independent, brave, sexually active, rational, intelligent and so on. With such conflicting régimes and powerful models (Bandura, 1986), boys can find it hard to kick against these and find themselves. Connell (1989) observed that those boys who failed to achieve power by academic means assumed a different sort of power as the 'cool guys' who used bullying and intimidation to maintain their status. The swots, wimps or 'Cyrils' followed a more academic and therefore 'feminine' route through school and were bullied accordingly.

Holland (1998) found that boys had a false idea of their own abilities and achievements. They felt that they were doing much better than they were, even if they were seriously underachieving. They frequently felt that they should be in a higher grade and that not being in one was responsible for them achieving less. She found, not untypically, that lesson 'style' could be a crucial factor in underachievement. The boys in her sample revealed that they spent 25–70% of the teaching day passively listening to teachers. Flanders observed this in 1970 and his results were confirmed in Learning Difficulties Research Project (LDRP) studies (Montgomery, 1998), when even in one-to-one settings the teacher talk dominated (60–70% of the time) and the questions asked were mainly closed ones requiring one-word answers from the pupil. Holland's boys preferred lessons which had a practical element in them, and which involved personal research and using computers. When asked how they might do better they had little idea but felt that teachers could do a lot more by giving more individual attention, explaining better, going through work more slowly, not shouting so much, giving them more fun things to do and so on (Holland, 1998: 177).

Boys make up a significant proportion of school underachievers and a recent National Foundation for Educational Research (NFER) survey of issues (MacDonald et al., 1999) confirmed what has been outlined above and by Hymer in Chapter 5. MacDonald et al. recommended further research on whether school grouping should be by ability, effort, potential, disruptive potential, gender, subject and so on. In other words, they could not yet find confirming evidence for any of them. They did not, however, question whether it was the inappropriate teaching methods which created underachievement, exclusion and division, forcing schools to organize differently to combat the results rather than the causes.

Under 'support for learning' MacDonald et al. found that the key items were: literacy support across the curriculum; highly structured lessons; more emphasis on teacher-led work; clear objectives and detailed instructions; clear and firm deadlines; short-term targets; positive reinforcement – immediate and credible rewards for good work; increased effort and/or improved behaviour.

Through all of this we can detect the concerns raised by Piirto in Chapter 1 and see management by objectives, teacher in firm control, and the leading, directing didact as favoured model permeating all government publications. Yes, highly structured lessons can be effective, especially in basic skills. It is also easy for researchers/observers to measure their effects, but we should not conclude from this that we must apply the principle to all we do in classrooms. Real problem-solving and simulations are often essentially 'fuzzy' with no set lesson protocol that can be followed. However, even these lessons may have their tactical plans, of which non-teacher researchers may be quite unaware. Even teachers using them may not be able to make them explicit (Montgomery, 1999).

In the previous chapter a framework for effective teaching and learning has been outlined which can promote the learning of all pupils but which is essential for the more able and the able underachiever. In this chapter some of the recommended techniques will be explored to show how, for example, Holland's underachieving boys might be helped to overcome their stereotypes without handicapping the girls and Lee-Corbin et al's (2000) underachievers could be helped by developing fluent writing among all learners. In other words, bringing methods to bear in the classroom which are inclusive.

This chapter will focus on three aspects of literacy and underachievement. The first is how to enable pupils to become fluent writers. The second is how to help them become good spellers and the third is how to enable them to communicate their ideas in a fluent and coherent 'cool' form, despite the linguistic and cognitive disadvantages created by culture and social background as described by Freeman in Chapter 2.

In relation to intervention an emphasis will be placed on early identification of difficulties and abilities in reception classes as well as at the later stages. Developmental, corrective and remedial approaches to intervention will be described.

Handwriting

Lee-Corbin and Denicolo (2000) compared achieving and underachieving able children and found that family stability, social class and handwriting competence were closely associated with achievement. Their underachieving children did not seem to have a lower self-concept or an external locus of control. There was a trend for boys to be more likely to underachieve than girls. As in many other studies, marital breakdown and lack of family stability were significantly associated with underachievement.

In all the three schools studied, fluent handwriting was significantly associated with achievement, which confirmed earlier studies by Wedell

(1973), Whitmore (1982) and Montgomery (1990, 1997a, 1998). They make the point that although family stability and social class cannot be influenced by the teacher, handwriting can be.

It was in fact Jane Taylor, then of the National Association for Gifted Children (NAGC), who in the early 1980s first drew the issue of the scrawly handwriting of highly able children to my attention. She wanted some help with a survey into the subject and has since gone on to pursue the topic in depth as one of the members of the Handwriting Interest Group (Alston and Taylor, 1987). When my in-service development LDRP work began with Cowdery, Morse and Prince-Bruce in 1983 to help them write their Teaching Through Spelling Programme (TRTS 1983–87), I was in a position to study able dyslexics' work at close hand for more than five years. Morse was the group's handwriting expert, but members of the group had all been trained in Palmer cursive by Hickey (see Augur and Briggs, 1991). Hickey had based her programme on that of Gillingham et al. (1940, 1956). They had demonstrated over many years that the remedial dyslexia programme must train the dyslexic in cursive, or fully joined writing, with each letter starting on the line. However, our pupils were going back to classrooms where joined writing was banned until they were eight years old or could write neatly! Thus it was that we set out in the LDRP to change this attitude through conferences and in-service development work. By 1990 more than half of the Kingston Local Education Authority infant schools taught cursive from the outset and recent SATs results show that in schools where this has been maintained, by Key Stage One most pupils have reached level three (Jones, personal communication 1998).

Portsmouth primary schools operate a similar strategy, having been introduced to TRTS and 'Kingston cursive' through the development of STRANDS, a worksheet version of TRTS produced by the local education authority team. Other clusters across the country also operate a cursive régime. However, not all schools do, and it is time to say that all schools must do so if they are to cease disadvantaging their pupils.

The main concern that teachers express about introducing infant cursive is the use of the lead-in stroke to letters. However, only recently, when one headteacher in the Portsmouth group reported the problem and decided to discontinue using the lead-in stroke to all letters, three other headteachers reported no problems with this. Difficulties are often more in the teachers' minds and perceptions, and in their methods of teaching, than in the actuality.

In addition, all junior and secondary schools need to implement a programme of changing to cursive for all current pupils to get them over their learning disadvantages. Pupils with coordination difficulties or with dyslexia will need remedial writing training.

It has been a significant finding that schools which have adopted cursive in the early years have not always seen this carry over into spelling. This is often because the two are kept separate and handwriting is used only in copy exercises and not in developmental spelling activities as well. It was this finding when engaging in appraisal work with one particular infant school that caused me to write the handbook *Developmental Spelling* (Montgomery, 1997b) to try to help them. The result was that the spelling SATs improved by more than 40% and the reading SATs by 10%. This is not an uncommon finding and was frequently quoted and evidenced by Cowdery et al. in our discussions.

However, the reverse does not necessarily follow, as the NLS has demonstrated. Reading teaching does not transfer to and enhance spelling. Part of the problem is that there has been too much emphasis over many years in the UK on reading as the dominant basic skill and a neglect of spelling and handwriting. Spelling and handwriting also need specific methods which are not covered in reading.

Although reading is an essential skill, the amount of time and effort pupils are still expected to put into writing means that the balance and direction of our teaching in schools needs readjusting and teachers need retraining to do it. Not only this but researchers and trainers also need to redirect their efforts. It is not satisfactory that literacy reports discuss only reading; and that the Department for Education and Employment (1997) in *Excellence in Schools* can write 'dyslexia, or reading difficulties' (p. 14) when dyslexia is both a reading and a spelling problem, with spelling more severely affected. Frequently assessments for statementing only include reading test scores, and researchers formulate and interpret their work on literacy and dyslexia in terms of reading difficulties even though they now look at the phonological subskills of it. Dyslexia may or may not be associated with handwriting difficulties or a range of other difficulties which stem from the phonological problems, such as digit span (short-term verbal memory problems), verbal sequencing, reciting tables and so on. In the sample of 300 dyslexics already cited, 30% had a dysgraphic difficulty associated with coordination problems.

However, there is a significant minority of pupils who will have handwriting coordination difficulties across the ability range without any dyslexic-type difficulties. Estimates vary from Sassoon's (1987) report of 40% of boys and 25% of girls at age 15 stating that they found writing painful and avoided it whenever possible, to 10% in other studies where the fine motor control itself was examined (Gubbay, 1975; Laszlo, 1987). Many of these difficulties would seem to be more a result of lack of fluency, form and speed than any disability per se.

Alston (1993) found that 21% of 9 year olds in some Cheshire schools were ill equipped for the writing demands of secondary schools, and this does not seem to be uncommon in the 1200 lessons observed and appraised by Montgomery (1999). There is no need for writing to be painful. A significant proportion of such difficulties is brought about by bad posture, incorrect writing positions, inappropriate furniture and wrong positioning of the paper (Sassoon, 1987). These can easily be dealt with by a more careful consideration of needs and a more flexible approach to provision.

Difficulties will indeed become handicapping if a print script is insisted on until the writing is neater (Early, 1976). For those with handwriting coordination difficulties such a time of neatness will never come unless they are taught cursive. Even so, there will be the rare occasion when a pupil with spidery, shaky writing cannot improve whatever style is used because the underlying difficulty is not amenable to training. This may be the case in motor impairment when the effort needed to write is excessive, and then the pupil should be given a laptop and there must be a classroom computer on which the work can be downloaded. In some such cases it may be sensible to introduce only some limited handwriting skills as the pupil gets older for signing cheques and form-filling.

Some pupils may have mild handwriting coordination difficulties alone and cannot write neatly. The writing will be scribbly with uneven pressure and poorly formed. This will attract substantial criticism from almost all teachers, who tend to regard poor writing as lack of serious effort. In the more severe cases the pupil has such difficulty and pain with writing that very little can be produced. Spelling thus gains little practice and they become pupils with spelling and handwriting difficulties. According to Alston (1993), 40–60% of secondary school pupils in her sample complained of such pain and difficulty.

Handwriting coordination difficulties belong to a wide group of problems referred to as Developmental Coordination Difficulties (DCD) and developmental dyspraxia. In dyspraxia the pupil may have a specific problem such as dressing difficulties or handwriting problems, or a whole range of such difficulties including an inability to plan complex motor behaviours, an ideational planning problem. This is sometimes detectable in an early inability to assemble jigsaws as easily as peers. DCD tends to confine itself to difficulties with gross motor control, such as in locomotion, and/or fine motor control, such as required by buttoning, sewing, cutting, tying and handwriting without the more complex ideational difficulties. In this chapter the significant difficulty, handwriting, from whatever source will be addressed and will be called 'developmental dysgraphia' or 'dysgraphia' for short. Spelling difficulties will be dealt with in a separate section as dysorthographia.

School-age pupils with DCD studied by Schoemaker and Kalverboer (1994) compared with controls were more anxious, lacking in self-esteem, more introverted and judged themselves to be less able both physically and socially, even children as young as six years. The researchers put this down to the importance placed on proficiency in physical activities by the child and the peer group.

Pupils who cannot write neatly however hard they try are castigated by teachers at all levels to try harder, to write neatly, to do it again – and even harsher statements are made. This constant barrage diminishes these pupils' self-esteem and gradually causes them to seek to avoid writing whenever possible and also to become upset because the content is often not taken into account, especially by subject teachers. It is most disheart-ening for them and it is little wonder that many become angry and refuse to write and that others engage in all sorts of tactics including misbehav-iour to avoid being shown up.

Speech delay was a most frequently appearing concern in DCD studies, with more than 50% of children with DCD requiring speech therapy. Half of the groups were doing well in maths at school but their problems in spelling and handwriting were hampering progress in other subjects. In addition to the DCD there was an association with poor social skills, emotional problems and a predisposition to hyperactivity.

Roaf (1998) found that 25% of pupils entering her secondary school were unable to write faster than 15 words a minute. These were the pupils who were struggling in all lessons where a lot of writing was required. The survey suggested a close link between self-concept and handwriting presentation. Most of the slow writers showed difficulties with motor coordination, spelling and letter formation. A speed of 20 words a minute in year 7 could be regarded as a successful rate. In year 10+ a speed of 12 words per minute should trigger 25 per cent extra time in GCSEs (Allcock, 2000).

1. Teaching handwriting

Teaching cursive handwriting to all pupils can have widespread positive effects because it increases fluency and speeds up writing, which enables more thoughts to be written down. Fluency reduces the physical and mental effort needed to be put into writing. As writing also involves spelling, this too becomes more fluently recorded and automatic (Montgomery, 1997a). It is therefore important that spelling teaching is linked with handwriting teaching, and that there are developmental, corrective and remedial strategies available for this as appropriate.

Lined paper should be given. Lines improve the look of the writing and help the pupils locate the position on the paper where they should begin the letters. It does not harm their creativity or style (Burnhill et al., 1975).

Thomas (1998) described a policy adopted in her Kent infant school that the creative aspect of expressing children's thoughts was, in the first instance, developed only orally. Teachers spent a longer time than before on developing an automatic joined hand. As a result they have seen a new quality in the creative written work. The teachers did not act as scribes and the pupils did not engage in copy writing. She compared the usual system in the UK with that which operates in France, where cursive writing is a lengthy process, has high priority in schools and teacher training, begins on entry to school and takes precedence over reading. She suggested there is much to be learnt from the French experience.

Developmental approaches to handwriting

An ovoid, slightly sloping style is more natural to form, and more fluent than an upright round style.

Guidelines for introducing cursive writing teaching in the early years (and in remedial settings)

- Teach the basic letter shapes as a single fluid motor movement, *not* in copy writing or tracing.
- Teach the letters singly but encourage joining immediately in blends and syllable units, not meaningless patterns.
- Teach the letters for writing in USE order with sounds and names, not in alphabetical or shape families as for reading. For example, start with i t p n s – the most frequent and useful writing letters. (It is perfectly reasonable to teach a different order for reading as it is a recognition skill, and much easier to learn.)
- Use lined paper from the beginning and until pupils can write neatly and fluently without lines, and then always offer the choice of lines.

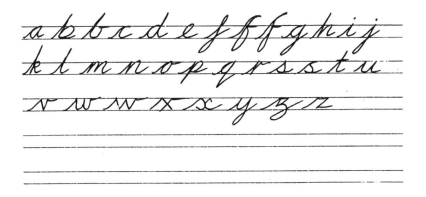

Figure 10.1: Handwriting teaching – ovoid cursive style: example of the Learning Difficulties Research Project (LDRP) style (I)

- Sometimes use double lines as above to help develop stability in body size of letters and the appropriate length of ascenders.
- Start each letter on the line with a lead-in stroke.
- Teach joining as soon as two letters with their sounds and names are known, and use these to generate spellings: i t it ti tit and so on.
- Teach base words, syllables and affixes as one writing unit wherever possible, a linguistic and logical approach.
- The right-handed pupil should hold the paper down with the left hand. The paper should not be vertical but should be tilted at an angle of about 25–30° to the right (between 4 and 5 o'clock).

Teaching left-handers

The left-handed pupil should hold the pencil or pen slightly further from the point than the right-hander so that the writing is not obscured.

The paper should be held down by the right hand and should be tilted much more than for the right-hander. A tilt of about 40° is common. Some pupils need a tilt of 90° so that their writing flows downwards. Over time each pupil will gradually find the most comfortable and legible-inducing position for themselves. They should be encouraged to be free to experiment and to take an intelligent interest in the skill.

Seating arrangements for left-handers are crucial. In pairs seating, the left-hander needs to sit on the left-hand side of the pair to allow both pupils room to wield their pens without interference. This is more problematic where there is seating round a table: then, chairs need to be given more space to the left of the left-hander to allow for freedom of movement.

Corrective cursive training

Pupils can be encouraged to collect samples of elderly relatives' writing (the *Lord's Prayer* is quite useful for this, or a nursery rhyme) to analyse as part of early 20th-century projects for style and form, and even spelling. No pupil should be introduced to a series of lessons on cursive without detailed preparation. This should first include analysing their own handwriting for errors and problems with the aid of checklists. When this is complete they will need examples of the use of cursive and a rationale for it, for often they have developed a semi print rounded script which teachers like and find highly legible, and so there may be anxiety about making changes. Concern is bound to arise because for about a month or so they will feel that their writing has deteriorated and that they are slower than they were. However, a gradual approach to this will overcome a lot of problems. For example, all small connecting words can be rewritten straight off as a single unit (the, if, we, and, why, off) and all words' begin-ning letters must start on the line. Never spend too long on strings of single letters perfectly formed. The pupil needs to get the feel of the letter in movement in the air, then with eyes shut, next on paper and then start to use it in writing words.

If this preparation is not an appeal to the cognitive then older pupils in particular will feel insulted at having to go back to learning to write all over again. I clearly remember our feelings and conversations when the Latin master tried to do just this.

Reasons to tell pupils for switching to cursive handwriting

- Aids left-to-right movement through words across the page.
- Stops reversals and inversions of letters.
- Induces greater fluency in writing which enables greater speed to be developed without loss of legibility.
- More can be written in the time available.
- Speed and fluency can make a difference of a grade at GCSE, A level or in degree programmes.
- The motor programmes for spelling whole words, their bases and affixes are stored and so improve spelling accuracy.
- Space between letters and between words is orderly and automatic.
- A more efficient fluent and personal style can be developed.
- Pupils with handwriting coordination difficulties experience less pain and difficulty.
- Legibility of writing is improved.
- It reinforces multisensory learning, linking spelling, writing and speaking.

In addition, if taught from the outset:

- It eliminates the need to relearn a whole new set of motor programmes after the infant stage. This relearning can be a double handicap for those with dusgraphia.

Identification and analysis of letter formation errors

A list of the general types of errors made may be found in Figure 10.2 (Montgomery, 1990, after an idea by Waller, 1973). They usually derive from inadequate teaching and learning.

The pupils, with help, should make an analysis of errors in a sample of their own handwriting. The more opportunity the pupils have to discuss the errors they find, the more likely it is that they will have the interest and motivation to try to improve their writing. The key points to address in

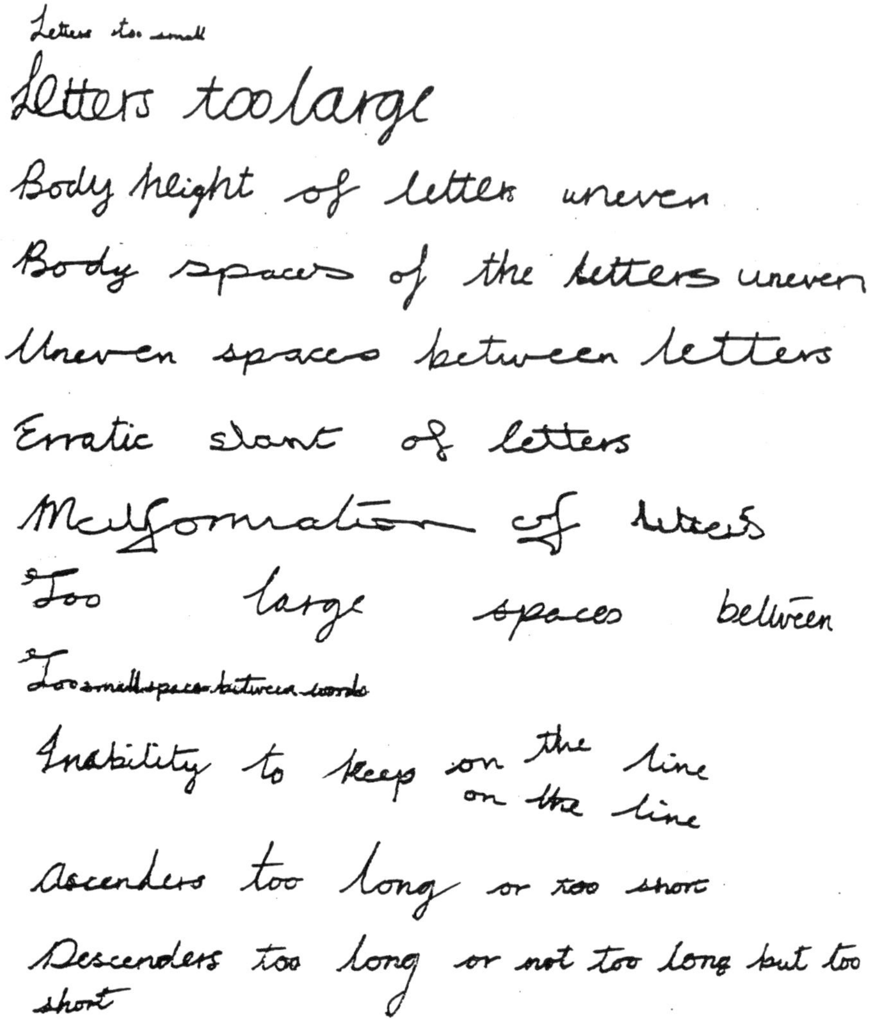

Letters too small

Letters too large

Body height of letters uneven

Body spaces of the letters uneven

Uneven spaces between letters

Erratic slant of letters

Malformation of letters

Too   large   spaces   between

Too small spaces between words

Inability to keep on the line

Ascenders too long or too short

Descenders too long or not too long but too short

Figure 10.2: Handwriting teaching letter formation errors

correcting handwriting errors as cursive is introduced are body size and then slant.

Begin any intervention with practice, using double lines to get the body size of the letters all the same. Next, address the slant of letters to get them all sloping the same way, whether forwards or backwards. Stress that all letters should have a lead-in stroke and that this should begin on the line for every letter made separately. All words should be practised with a lead-in stroke to help override previously learned motor programmes. Copy writing and writing verse from memory is best at this stage, for thinking about what to write and how to spell it add too much cognitive demand when changing or learning a skill.

Changing from print to cursive should not include half-measures in which arbitrary groups of letters are connected because they are easy to join and are in small groups. Nor should all the letters of the alphabet be taught separately for later joining. Instead children should practise writing whole small words, base words, prefixes and suffixes – that is, meaningful units. Some words are particularly pleasant to practise, such as little, butter, apple and so on.

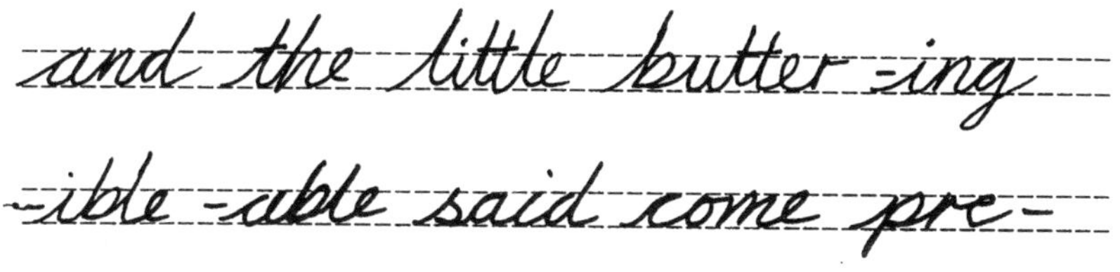

Figure 10.3: Some example words and syllables

Identifying handwriting coordination difficulties

Checklist of motor coordination problems

- Writing pulling in from the margin towards the mid-line.
- 'Rivers' of spaces running down through the writing.
- What seem to be capital letters spotted about, but which are really large forms of the lower case out of control, especially of s, w, k and t in the middle as well as at the beginning of words.
- Writing that looks scribbly or spiky.
- Shaky and wobbly strokes on close examination of letters.
- Writing that varies in 'colour' so that it is sometimes dark and in other places faint, indicating variation in pressure.
- Writing that produces ridges on the reverse of the paper and even holes in it due to pressure exerted.
- Inability to maintain the writing on the line.
- Difficulties in copying fluent letter shapes in one fluid movement

An example of motor coordination is shown in Figure 10.4.

'My Christmas Party'

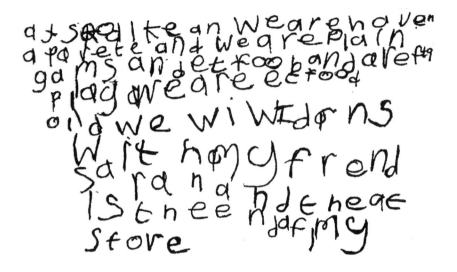

Figure 10.4: An example of coordination difficulties in handwriting: Sarah aged 6 years

Teaching remedial and developmental cursive

Whatever stage and level of handwriting has been reached by a pupil, if it is made in a print script then an attempt needs to be made immediately to switch to an ovoid cursive to increase fluency and speed. Not all pupils will want to transfer to cursive and may have parents who refuse to let them, even when provided with relevant evidence. Most, however, will be willing to try, although for a while their writing may not look so neat to them or might feel less under their control.

Beginning writers should be taught to use a joined hand from the outset with lead-in strokes. Dyslexics and pupils with handwriting difficulties must be taught a joined hand to reinforce the spellings they are learning and the word-attack skills for reading, as well as to overcome their dysfluent perceptuomotor problems in handwriting. The following multisensory training technique is recommended (Cowdery et al., 1984; Hickey, in Augur and Briggs, 1991).

As well as teaching a full-flowing ovoid-style cursive, a multisensory training technique as shown below should be used, as detailed by Morse in Cowdery et al. (1984):

- Show the cursive form of lower-case letter i on the board.
- Explain how it is made by talking them through the letter, for example 'Start on the line and flow up then back down and round a little. Now

add the dot over the top.' Repeat this several times and ask them to join in the talk-through.

- Give them the sound of the letter unless one of the children knows it (i). Talk through the letter once more and get them to do so too and say its sound as well.
- Now demonstrate the formation of the letter i in the air with your back to the children. Repeat with left hand for left-handers.
- Each time the letter is written its sound should be spoken, that is the short vowel sound (i). Introduce the idea of a key word to remember the sound, for example imp, ink
- Ask pupils to imitate the movement in the air altogether once and then trace it with forefinger on the table, saying the sound at the same time. Repeat the sequence a few times with the class and table groups so that every pupil can be observed.
- Individuals can be asked to come and show the rest of the class how to trace it in the air.
- The teacher then writes the cursive i on the board and pupils can volunteer to come and write i next to the model. (The model is always covered up, and then uncovered for matching.) Small pupil-sized blackboards can be very helpful now for practice.
- When pupils have the feel for the letter they can be encouraged to try it on paper.
- When they have the correct form they can then try a joined group of i letters, murmuring the sound as they write it (a phonological strategy).

(a) 'Please don't let the children cross the road' (Alison aged 5.1y)

Figure 10.5(a): An example of a beginning writer with coordination difficulties

Figure 10.5(b): An example of a beginning writer with coordination difficulties

Only when a pupil has developed a fluent style should any calligraphic variation or art form such as italic be introduced. For pupils with handwriting problems such as graphomotor dyspraxia or developmental dysgraphia, calligraphy may not be a suitable study in school. The following are case profile notes given by a parent of David (A Parent [pseudonym], 1995).

Before David started school at 5 he had always been a happy, confident and lively little boy. At the end of Year 2 his report described him as:

> well motivated, enthusiastic, concentrates well, has good vocabulary, speaks up for himself, gives opinions and reads very well. The quality of content in written work is good, very thorough and very imaginative, but unfortunately, his pencil control lets him down. (1995: 29)

Here we have it – bright but with a distinct fine coordination problem. By now he should have been on a special developmental and full assessment programme to see whether the problem was amenable to cursive training and whether there were wider dyspraxic difficulties. If there were severe difficulties he should have been switched to a laptop and given keyboard training in Year 1. What actually followed is very common.

In Year 3 he was still having difficulties with sporting activities (indications of the gross motor as well as the fine motor problems) but did learn to swim a bit. He failed to stand up in ice-skating and fell behind in judo; he persevered but eventually dropped all but swimming which was compulsory. His younger brother started school and could do all these activities. He was assessed at the parents' request and it was concluded that his coordination was good and nothing needed to be done except that he should be given advice on letter and number formation.

In Year 4 he had 15 minutes of individual help (unspecified) with his writing. Although his letter formation did improve, it did not transfer to work in the classroom. This is characteristic of training in neat print script, letter by letter. He was still experiencing difficulty in organizing himself and his work, and was forever misplacing it and his possessions. This is typical of Gubbay's (1975) 'clumsy child' syndrome. His teacher was very under-standing of the problem and David in this year was generally more settled.

Year 5 was a bad year. He went home complaining of bullying and name calling. The tone of this was obviously set by the new teacher.

'David became very anxious, frightened, easily upset and each evening had to be comforted and consoled and would not go to sleep without someone sitting with him'. (p. 30)

In Year 6 he would not report incidents any more as nothing was ever done and it only made things worse. He was becoming completely 'switched off' with regard to school. The parents got in touch with the Dyspraxia Trust which advised that David should be statemented and have special support. He was assessed as dyspraxic and with an IQ on WISC-III UK as in the top 2% of the ability range. David was greatly helped by this assessment and learning he was not stupid, but the school said it was unable to dedicate a laptop to his sole use.

The account ends with the parents sending him to a different school in Year 7, away from those who bullied him. He uses a notepad computer in class, has learning support in PE and is withdrawn to the special needs class during English to try to alleviate his anxiety. This is just one of many tragic careers in schools because of a failure to write neatly and compete in sports. It is a bullied life experience unwittingly conducted and modelled by many teachers. Why?

The essential factor in changing handwriting is to involve the pupil in the evaluation and the redevelopment strategies, as motivation to want to change is a key factor and some may be frightened to change at first, given the difficulties and distress they may already have experienced.

It is especially important to teach handwriting and spelling together so that one skill can act to enhance the development of the other and so give the practice activities in handwriting added value.

Before training

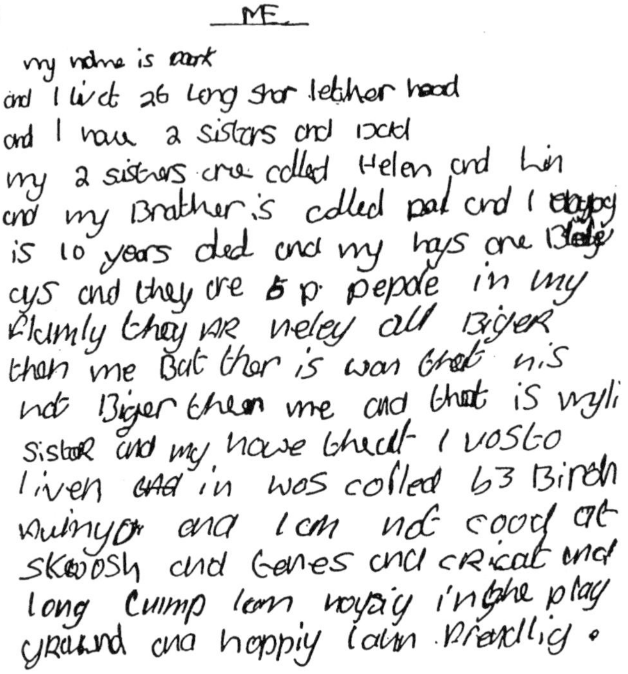

ME

my name is mark
and I live 26 Long star letther head
and I have 2 sisters and Dad
my 2 sisters are called Helen and Lin
and my Brother is called pal and I babey
is 10 years ded and my has one Babe
cys and they are 5 p. pepde in my
Famly they AR neley all Biger
than me But ther is wan that his
not Biger then me and that is myli
Sister and my have thecdt I vosto
liven and in wos colled 63 Birch
wuinyor and I am not cood at
skwoosh and Genes and cricat and
long cuimp iam royaiy i'nthe play
gRawnd ano hoppiy iam Praxllig.

After 5 mins training per day for a fortnight

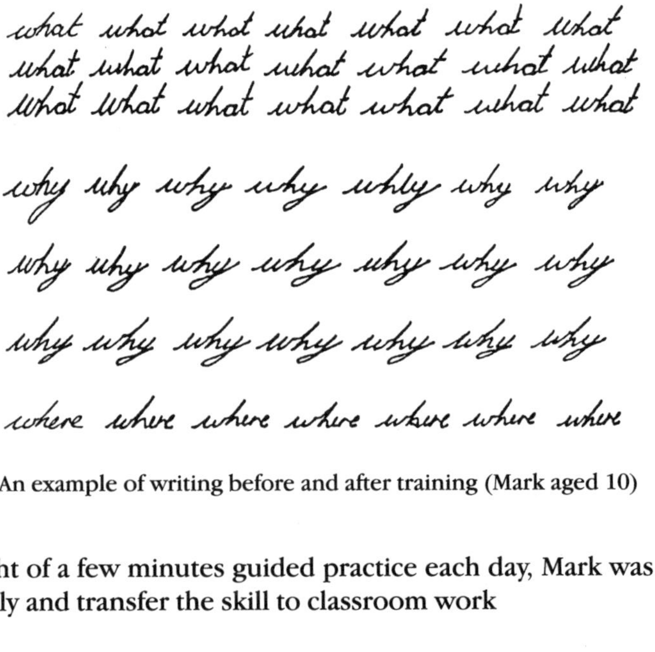

what what what what what what what
what what what what what what what
what what what what what what what

why why why why whly why why

why why why why why why why

why why why why why why why

where where where where where where where

Figure 10.6: An example of writing before and after training (Mark aged 10)

In a fortnight of a few minutes guided practice each day, Mark was able to write fluently and transfer the skill to classroom work

The next section outlines suitable approaches to teaching spelling for all pupils, but which for the highly able are essential and a great relief.

2. Teaching spelling

Recent surveys by HMI (1996, 1997) have shown that more than one-third of pupils age 11 years are unable to read and write adequately for their studies in secondary schools. Even the NLS has failed to improve spelling, which is not surprising since it is focused on reading. In teaching some phonics in a course of reading plus a few spelling rules such as 'magic e', teachers often think they are teaching spelling but this is only a minute part of what they might be doing (Montgomery, 1997b). There is perhaps still a fear of what used to be called the 'spelling grind'. Pupils used to sit in rows chanting spellings, learning sections of the Bible and whole books of poems by rote (Barnard, 1961; Chalmers, 1977). The reaction was to drive teachers towards 'meaning emphasis' methods, particularly the Look and Say approach to teaching reading, and then various whole books and apprenticeship methods during which spelling was mainly 'caught' during reading (Peters, 1967, 1985) and reinforced by copy writing. In addition, a generation of teachers has grown up in a system where the linguistic aspects of the language were not divulged. Although mixed methods are now being fostered and phonics is being extended into linguistics, this is not systematic enough nor supported by accurate materials in many instances.

In December 1999, the Secretary of State for Education David Blunkett announced that spelling tests would be introduced in a national system of testing for pupils at 7 and 11 years. We can predict once again that many teachers will give lists of spellings to rote learn and that the good spellers will do well and the poor spellers will not. Poor spellers will be further disadvantaged and will experience that learned helplessness and fear which can generalize to all school work. If we could this time concentrate on learning processes and not just outcomes, we might actually help children rather than punish them.

Spelling is a recall skill in which the correct letters have to be given orally or in writing in a precise order. In our writing system 26 alphabet letters represent about 44 speech noises in which all the vowels have two sounds – short, and long when the vowel 'says' its own name. There are also consonant digraphs where two letters make one sound, for example ch, sh, th, th (voiced), ph and wh, and this is different from each of the constituent sounds. The double vowel oo has a short and long sound of its own and acts as an extra vowel, and y may be a vowel or a consonant. There are four diphthongs in which two letters in one syllable are blended to make a completely new sound reminiscent of two vowels in succession, for example oi, oy, ou and ow.

Most words used by beginning spellers can be represented by 80 phonograms, according to Spalding and Spalding (1969) in their *The Writing Road to Reading* scheme. Different phonograms may represent the same sound, for example i, ie and igh may all represent the long vowel sound of letter i or capital I.

According to Hanna et al. (1966), at least 85% of the English language is regular in that the spellings follow an ordered pattern of sounds and linguistic rules. A computer given the basic sounds of the alphabet can produce a correct spelling only once in five words, but about 15 key words can unlock linguistics and give the correct spelling of most of the words that pupils need to use in extended writing in schools, especially if 'engage brain' strategies are used to help overcome learned helplessness and to motivate pupils.

A regular word is one in which the alphabet symbols correspond exactly to the sound represented – a system of basic phonics, for example pin, bag, stop, trust. When beginning spellers or those with spelling difficulties have cracked this alphabetic code, a system of 'skeletal phonics' can be seen, for example 'mi mum got me a cmputa fr mi bthde'. Typically, medial vowels are omitted or wrong vowels are inserted even in relatively regular words. Irregular words such as come, said and women may be represented as they sound, for example cum, sed and wimmen or wimen. At an even earlier stage single letters may be used by five year olds to represent a cluster of letters or several similar sounds.

Adults looking at children's spellings often forget that it takes time to learn and that the wider the vocabulary used the more potential there is for misspellings. Even when pupils seem to have learned to spell well, whenever a new vocabulary is introduced mistakes will be made. Some creative misspellings of a five year old and a six year old are as follows:

> *William, 5 yr 2 mos*: 'teh tre fel on to f ten ottn telfn pol riu' (the tree fell on top of the other telephone pole wire).
> *Ryan, Year 1 pupil*: 'I wen to see Tottenham and noting Fors' (I went to see Tottenham and Nottingham Forest).

It is easy to see which team was supported.

As well as the lexicon of correct spellings which most people carry in their heads, a number of errors will also be securely stored. Some common ones are: seperate, accomodate, dessicate, potatoe and so on. Errors once ensconced are particularly difficult to eradicate, and no amount of writing them out neatly five times will correct them (otherwise they would not still be there).

Pupils vary in their ability to develop good spelling without help. There are some who are generally poor at spelling and some who, for a variety of reasons, may have severe, persistent and specific difficulties. Poor spellers do not seem to have specific difficulties, but are generally slow to develop literacy skills, and because of this may miss out on many key teaching inputs for they may not be ready for them. Others have had unsatisfactory opportunities for learning and carry forward with them a range of basic errors which they are unable to correct alone and which handicap their progress later. Handwriting difficulties may further delay spelling development. For example, Ryan in Year 1 also had a handwriting coordination problem which was hampering potentially good spelling.

Most pupils in mainstream need only a corrective and developmental spelling programme whereas beginners need a developmental programme per se. The next section therefore begins with corrective techniques and is then followed by lessons in developmental and then remedial spelling.

Corrective spelling strategies

There are a number of words in common use that most people will spell wrongly. Sometimes they know they are prone to misspelling them but forget the correct spelling each time. The area of error is usually only over one letter. As the teacher moves around the class, the more common errors can be collected and individual errors can be recorded in the margins of the book to be saved for intervention. Sometimes a whole class session can be devoted to a new or problematic spelling. A few minutes every day can help spelling development significantly using the cognitive process strategies outlined below (Montgomery, 1997a).

Pupils can be asked to give some words with which they have difficulties to see whether they can learn to use the corrective strategies. Younger pupils tend to make lower-order errors, such as articulatory, phonic and syllabic errors, so that the strategies can straightforwardly be directed to these. If they make higher-order errors then they will need to use the full protocol, which includes the dictionary work.

Spelling errors tend to be made early on in spelling development, and once stored in the brain they cannot be unlearned although they can be overridden. What is seen is misspellings cropping up under duress in tests or examinations, appearing in different error forms in general writing and appearing in the same piece of work with the correct spelling so that it looks as though the pupil has just been careless.

The pupil may be fully aware that certain words are problems and may have tried to correct them, but now is totally confused as to whether there should be an e or an a in the middle of separate, or two ms or one in accommodate and so on. They often cope by alternating between the two or avoiding problem words and using a much simpler vocabulary. This is noticeable and also takes extra time.

Corrective spelling

Twelve cognitive process strategies for correcting misspellings

The cognitive process approach focuses all the attention on the area of error to identify and correct it. This attention gives it a higher profile in the memory and rings warning bells as the spelling approaches so that the strategies can then be applied. After a while the pupil experiences heightened awareness and writes through the word, giving the correct spelling. Eventually, the correct motor programme is elicited on every occasion. Thus it is essential that all corrections are written in full cursive to establish the automatic motor programme.

- Articulation – clear, correct speech, 'chimney' not 'chimley'.
- Overarticulation – parli(a)ment, gover(n)ment.
- Cue articulation – say it incorrectly, Wed - nes - day.
- Syllabification – break it down into syllables, mis - de - mean - our.
- Phonics – try to get a comprehensible skeleton of the word's sound.
- Origin – the word's root in another language may give clues.
- Rule – the l - f - s rule and 'i before e except after c' can help.
- Linguistics – syllable structure and affixing rules govern most words.
- Family – bomb, bombing, bombardier, bombardment give clues.
- Meaning – to pare or part helps spell 'separate' correctly.
- Analogy – 'it is like braggart' helps spell 'braggadocio'.
- Funnies – 'cess pit' will help me to remember how to spell necessary.

Using the full Cognitive Process Protocol to correct misspellings.

- The pupil proof-reads to try to identify misspellings.
- Teacher also proof-reads for errors.
- A composite list of all misspellings is made by the teacher.
- Pupil selects with teacher two spellings to work on.
- Pupil looks up the words in the dictionary.
- Pupil puts a ring round the area of error – the wrong letter or omission.
- The words are studied in the dictionary for clues to meaning and origin.
- Teacher discusses with the pupil two cognitive strategies from the list of 12 for dealing with one of the errors.
- Pupil applies the strategies and checks to see if they have been successful using SOS (see following section).

- Pupil now addresses the other word, identifying two strategies which can be applied.
- The pupil now reports to the teacher on progress.
- A day or two later the teacher asks the pupil to spell orally both of the words as a check that they are still remembered.
- When these words have been learnt it is then possible to tackle two more. After a while the pupils will be able to manage this process themselves.

Some examples of the use of the protocol for correcting higher-order errors

Typical problem words as spellers become more advanced are those associated with the 'schwa' (uh) sound in syllables and with affixing and errors at syllable boundaries: separate – usually misspelled seperate and seperat; accommodate – usually misspelled accomodate, sometimes acommodate; opportunity – usually misspelled oppertunity or even opurtunity.

- First, look up the spelling in the dictionary.
- Next, put a ring around the region of error, for example the second e in separate, the omitted m in accommodate and the second vowel in opportunity.
- The meaning of separate is to divide or part; the prefix is se (aside) and parare is from the Latin meaning to put. Learning to apply the meaning 'to pare or to part' to the word's spelling usually sorts out the problem.
- The origin of opportunity is from ob (before) and portus (a harbour) which can be linked to port to make 'opportunity', which has the meaning of a timely event like coming upon a harbour or port in a storm. Ob is assimilated to op before portus.
- After the short vowel sound in com the consonant 'm' is doubled. Other examples are in ad - gression, aggression, ad - cumulate. It is therefore important that the common prefixes and their meanings are learnt.

When most errors are to do with basewords and the addition of prefixes and suffixes, these are the errors of more mature writers and make up 75% of all misspellings of normal adults.

Developmental spelling strategies

Early identification of potential difficulties

In the first month in school, screen all the pupils in the class as follows:

- Find out which letter names and sounds they know.
- Take a sample of their writing and spelling, for example ask them to write their names on a piece of paper; ask them to copy their names and a short sentence ('My name is X'); ask them to write a message or a story unaided. This should follow some discussion of, say, a storm and what they saw. It is essential not to give any help with writing or spelling and to collect with pleasure all their scribbles. Then undertake an error analysis as follows.

Developmental error analyses

After marking the writing for content, note each spelling error or photocopy the page and underline every spelling error so that a general plan of intervention and development can be drawn up. Select one simple misspelling on each pupil's paper to try an intervention on, so that responsiveness to teaching and readiness for learning can be assessed. Dictation exercises can be used as the pupil's writing develops.

Interventions

- Both William and Ryan (p. 170) are promising spellers. Continue introducing sounds for spelling and teach 'the' and 'and' as a writing unit.
- Teach William to spell 'tree' and Ryan to spell 'went' and 'forest' as these are already nearly correct. Get them to articulate clearly for spelling and teach William the initial blend 'tr' and Ryan the end blends '-nt' and '-st'.
- Get them to try to generate some more words with the blends.
- Use a writing strategy with the spelling so that they learn to write the words more fluently. Use the developmental and remedial cursive strategy described above.
- Sit with them and ask them to read their sentences articulating clearly for spelling to see if they can see how to improve some other spellings.
- Explain that this is what real writers do – they edit and redraft what they have written, often many times so that they get it right. Illustrate with copies of famous writers' pages on display boards.
- Teach syllabification for spelling to begin to correct 'telephone' and 'Nottingham'. Link this for Ryan with Tottenham.
- Ask them to produce an edited and final version of their pieces of writing from memory unless they are already tired. Put both pieces of work in their assessment file for reference.

Identification of spelling errors with older pupils

Older pupils can be asked to:

- Write their names and addresses.
- Write a short story in their own words without help or bring a piece of narrative writing from a subject area.
- Write from dictation – Peters and Smith (1993) provide a set of these for different year groups; or use an extract from a current story/textbook.
- Do a spelling test such as the Schonell Spelling Test (A or B) (Schonell and Schonell, 1946) or that of Daniels and Diack (1958). The spelling scores are not as important as the collection of errors and their analysis.

The spelling test errors and all the errors on the other tasks should be subject to an analysis for patterns of errors and omissions so that an appropriate corrective or developmental programme can be drawn up. For example, most schemes deal with phonics but provide many worksheets which can be completed without actually using phonics, leaving out the multisensory and articulatory (Montgomery, 1997a) nature of the training needed, particularly with dyslexics. So the tests can identify which phonics need reteaching; frequently these are end blends, particularly -lt, -nt and -nd.

What most general schemes omit is the graded introduction of basic linguistics for spelling. Rules are frequently introduced but not in the order that pupils best profit from knowing them. The order in TRTS which was developed over many years of experience by Cowdery et al. (1983–87) is one of the best examples, and the *Developmental Spelling* handbook is based on it (Montgomery, 1997b).

SOS is a rote learning remedial strategy first published by Gillingham et al. (1940). Because it is rote learning it must be used sparingly otherwise it annihilates a pupil's powers to generalize and use analogies, making them become dependent rather than independent spellers. Look – cover – write – check (Peters, 1967) is not the same strategy, as it omits the spelling element.

The SOS protocol is as follows:

- Look up the word in the dictionary with help if necessary.
- Write down its spelling from the dictionary, **naming** the letters.
- Check that the spelling is correct. Here the teacher should also check so that the word is correct from the outset.
- Cover up the spelling and then the pupil should write it from memory, saying the name of each letter as he or she does so.
- Now the pupil checks against the original spelling.
- They should repeat this SOS procedure three times.
- The criterion is three correct spellings in a row.

- Next day it should be checked to see if it has been retained.
- If it has not, identify the area of error and this time use lower-case wooden or plastic letters to build the word correctly three times, saying the names of each in the process.
- Repeat the SOS procedure and check again.

Developmental and corrective spelling approaches have been discussed and exemplified. What is clear is that any method which systematizes and presents an orderly approach to the teaching of spelling during the course of reading and writing development will prove helpful to most spellers. Over-reliance on worksheets as a substitute for direct teaching will be unlikely to lead to good spelling development, particularly in children with difficulties. The techniques need to help children develop strategies and generalizations to new vocabulary. Thus rote learning strategies give poorer results and sometimes no return.

Some guidelines for remedial spelling

For more effective learning the dyslexics must be taught in matched pairs. Individual tuition (one-to-one) creates too much pressure and prevents consolidation by the learner. They need at least two such sessions of 50–60 minutes a week (Ridehalgh, 1999).

They need to have the stage system of the Code of Practice short-circuited, for the earlier the proper remediation takes place the better the rates of recovery. Remediation should begin in the reception class directed to spelling and handwriting.

Phonics and multisensory training for dyslexics are necessary but not sufficient. Dyslexics need a full APSL (Alphabetic-Phonic-Syllabic-Linguistic) programme to bring them up to grade level. We should be expecting a rate of progress each year not of six or seven months but of at least two years. This can occur when programmes such as Alpha to Omega and Hickey (including the Dyslexia Institute Language Programme (DILP) and TRTS) are used. When teachers 'do not bother with the spelling pack' (M. Prince-Bruce, personal communication, 1995; Ridehalgh, 1999) or use a 'pick and mix approach', reading may progress but spelling does not (LDRP, 1999).

Whole-school strategies

Every teacher must make a positive contribution to dyslexics' and underachievers' learning in the literacy area. However, they need a whole-school policy and in-service training to support them. For example:

a. With 15 key words in any National Curriculum topic linguistics can be taught.
b. With 12 cognitive strategies every teacher can reinforce the school's policy on spelling and give some 'brain engage' stimulation to the more able who avoid rote learning.
c. With a cursive handwriting policy schools can ensure that every pupil in secondary school can write at the speed of 25 words a minute (unless they have a severe motor disorder).
d. All teachers and pupils can undertake an error analysis of pupils' spelling and handwriting errors.

15 keywords to competence

This strategy can be used for a visit to Maldon's barges in Essex as a local studies or settlement topic, for example. Any subject teacher can produce such a list for a year group to teach or reinforce the strategies. Pupils should master one 'key' before proceeding to the next or to exceptions.

1. *Hull* (cvc, cvcc, ccvc, ccvcc) cot, block, deck, winch, list, wind, wet, cvc. The short vowel sound and L-F-S RULE – must double l-f-s after short vowel.
2. *Rudder* (cvc/cvc) after short vowel sound must double consonant and (cvc + c + suffixing DOUBLING rule) running, setting.
3. *Rope* (cvce) lines, mate, wire, life, made. Long vowel sound + suffixing DROP RULE, roping, lining.
4. *Sail* (cvvc, cvvcc, ccvvc, ccvvcc) rain, pail, bail, paint, faint, maid, paid (said), cleats, cheats, meets/meats, wheat, load (TWO VOWELS RULE; and ADD suffix RULE). When two vowels go walking the first one does the talking (usually).
5. *Cook* (cvvc) book, look, took, rook, nook, shook, hook, good (blood!) and ADD RULE (oo extra vowel, short).
6. *Noon* (cvvc) fool, cool, room, school, soon, stool (oo extra vowel, long).
7. *Barge* (vr) (ge, e softens g) ar and air words large, art. Fair, air, stair.
8. *Wheel* (wh ? words) wh digraph and question words (only six consonant digraphs – th, th, wh, ph, ch, sh).
9. *Cabin* (cvc in/ic/id) robin, rabid, titanic, manic (mania). We perhaps say them differently, or their origin is different. Open first syllables: ba-con, o-pen, spo-ken, to-ken.
10. *Mast* (cvcc/cv st) master, last, fast, past - dialect change.
11. *Water* (wa - or) wa - words, war, walk, ward.

12. *Work* (wo - ir) wo - words, world, worst, word.
13. *Round* (ou - diphthong) 'ah-oo' ground, found, sound, confound (and consonant prefixes).
14. *Sign* (cv gn) silent letters, family words, signal, signing: -igh, ight: kn - knife, knight, knave.
15. *Pay* (cv y) + CHANGE RULE paid, said, repaid (vowel prefix).

3. Inclusive teaching and learning

In the previous chapter a framework for teaching to promote effective learning was outlined based on studies found to promote the learning of all pupils but which is essential for the more able and the able under-achiever. In this final section of the chapter some of the recommended techniques will be explored in more detail to show how, for example, Holland's underachieving boys might be helped to overcome their stereotypes without handicapping the girls. In other words, methods will be brought to bear in the classroom which are inclusive and focus first on oracy and learner participation.

Learning new material is dependent on a pupil's existing knowledge (Ausubel, 1968; Gagné, 1973). This knowledge extends far beyond that which was taught in the previous lesson to the pupils' life experiences up to that point. It is impossible to categorize this prior experience. It will be different for each individual, and the same experiences will be drawn upon differently by them. What is important is that they should have time to go through the process of reconstruction to incorporate the new into the old and to reframe the whole. Answering teacher questions and filling in worksheets does not serve the purpose and can literally prevent thinking. Pupils need time to reason and reflect, and motivation to do so – particularly if they have been trained out of it by the earlier schooling process. These opportunities arise particularly during collaborative work, in explaining and 'teaching' someone else to understand your point. Nisbet (1993) identified five methods which promote self-regulation and which help pupils reflect on their own learning. This is an adapted and extended list:

- *Cognitive apprenticeship*, in which the teacher models methods and demonstrates processes that experts use with complex tasks.
- *Talking aloud* – the teacher talks aloud while working through a problem.
- In *reciprocal learning* the pupil can take over the teacher talk as and when ready, which enables the pupil to use the teacher's repertoire of skills and knowledge where necessary and where the underachieving pupil has gaps.

- *Discussions* in which the processes of argument are also analysed. Sometimes discussion is wrongly taken to mean a question and answer session in which the pupil tries to find the answers in the teacher's head at the start of a topic – finding out what we know.
- *Cooperative learning* – ideal for developing higher-order thinking in that pupils discuss, share, question, teach, tutor one another.
- *Socratic questioning*, which helps pupils explain what they know and think.
- *Mentoring*, where possible mentors are introduced who may be experts or older pupils who promote the interests and views of the pupil and may act as personal tutors.

In a summary of current international research for OFSTED, Freeman (1998) lists conclusions about teaching the very able as follows:

Improving task demand by:
– presenting information in a conceptual framework, not in isolation
– taking a problem-posing as well as problem-solving approach
– teaching for clear 'scientific' thinking skills to a greater depth
– emphasizing abstract as well as basic concepts
– materials should demand complex responses and avoid repetition
Using language:
– the intellectual demands of a lesson can be recognized by the level, speed and quality of the verbal interactions that go on in it
– the talented should use the appropriate technical language rather than a simplified version
– encourage play with words, especially proverbs and idioms
– encourage questioning as a part of everyday learning to stimulate thinking and creative problem-solving
Communication:
– enable pupils to explain out loud, comparing old and new learning and ideas with ability peers
– teach research skills so that pupils can expand own materials for themselves
Encourage excellence (Freeman, 1998: 52).

These techniques and those described in Chapter 9 do not necessarily require whole lessons to be given over to them; sometimes an introductory 20 minutes can get the students off on the right foot for a whole series, and on other occasions what they would traditionally be doing is modified.

There is, of course, the major problem of teacher time and how it can be distributed. If every pupil is required to give extended answers to questions then the day would not be long enough. What needs to be developed is a strategy to promote legitimate talk in classrooms and this means that multiple audiences need to be engineered. Able under-achievers particularly need the stimulation of oral work, because their writing skills will take longer to develop. The challenge of real audiences may be the only way to promote written work in some highly able learners who see little point in writing things down for the teacher to read, as the teacher already knows the stuff.

Some examples follow to show how increased talk, or oracy, can be organized in classrooms based on the teaching model already described – that the two primary objectives in education should be to enable the pupils to think efficiently and then to communicate those thoughts succinctly in the context of any subject area (Montgomery, 1981).

Real problem-solving in history

In this example, real problem-solving, creativity, a simulation game, an audience, argument, evaluation and collaborative learning are all involved. As the series of lessons proceeds then study and research skills would be required.

The class is shown an outline map with six potential sites – a plateau, hills, an island in a lake, a village, land surrounded by marsh, and land on a peninsula between rivers – and each group is assigned a site at random. The groups are then given the task of preparing a marketing brief to sell their site to the potential Lord and Lady owners who wish to build a castle. The map also shows quarries, marsh, woodland, tracks and so on. The year is 1250.

No other help is given but the mixed-ability groups are given 10–15 minutes to discuss the problem and then give a presentation to the buyers – the teacher and the rest of the class. Starting a series of lessons on medieval castles, why and where they were built, and the needs of the people of the time, can prove to be a lot of fun. Pupils as young as six years old will all know something about castles from TV and films and can contribute to a group's deliberation. They all get an opportunity to talk, question and explain or merely listen. They can all help in the presenta-tion, although one of them will emerge as the lead presenter. After hearing each group's presentation the teacher can then begin to draw out and systematize the key points with the whole class. By a process of compare and contrast they can be led to classify the advantages and disadvantages of each site and maybe even tabulate them, probing deeper into the issues. At the next stage they can be introduced to pictures and videos of signifi-cant castles in the history of different or particular countries and identify their main attributes. This can lead on to the stories of those castles and peoples. From this a variety of forms of writing can be derived – descriptive, narrative, personal and imaginative. Castle development through history can be examined, model making with a limited range of materials can be undertaken for design and technology, or model building on screen can be accomplished with suitable Information and Communication Technology (ICT) databases. Castles can be illustrated in art using a variety of techniques, and pictures of castles in art collections and on stamps can be collected and studied.

The teacher who first designed the activity on which this simulation and role-play were built actually wrote detailed information on the worksheet such as the following:

- Eldon Hills: Good view of countryside. Plenty of stone. Good for water but short of timber for firewood. Good foundations, easy to build. Good for defence.
- Lake Island: Excellent for defence on island. Fish in lake good for food. Close to quarry and near village, but hard to build on soft swampy ground.
- Eagle Rock: Excellent for defence. Plenty of stone and timber. Water would have to be stored.
- Village site: Close to workmen. Plenty of wood and food from farming. Poor defence and so on.

In doing this the teacher has taken all the cognitive challenge out of the task, even though it was first designed for the highly able. The children have been told what to think rather than first recalling, organizing and thinking about what they already know. There is a wide range of such Real Problem-Solving (RPS) and games activities which can be designed to introduce all subjects in the curriculum. The response of the underachieving pupils was typically 'this is much better than the usual boring stuff we get'.

If we look at the method of experiential learning, a sequence of lessons might begin in some countries with a visit to a nearby castle. An example of experiential learning which is specific to my local area is that a semester of work can be based around a five-day sailing trip for groups of 12 students aged 9 years and upwards (as well as company executives) on an historic 19th-century Thames sailing barge. These have the traditional red ochre sails, hammocks, sea chests and no television. Anchors have to be weighed by the student crew and sails hauled aloft by hand and winch. They learn to sail the ship and the ship's tender, to fish and to work as teams on all the boat's chores such as provisioning, cooking and cleaning. History, geography, language and literacy, music, physical education, design and technology, art and religion can all be pursued under this umbrella project and in a period context. They live in 19th-century time and learn new skills such as ropework and a whole new vocabulary and the meaning of many common sayings such as 'top quality', 'sea legs', 'make way' and so on.

A different starting point for problem-solving and medieval castle building, or part of the project after the initial work above, might be the following:

Problem: 'It is 1280. You are King Edward I's master mason. You have been told to design and organize the building of a new castle at David in North Wales.'

Information given to pairs of pupils:

- Labour force details and costs
- Materials and equipment costs
- Purposes of the build – defence
- Site of gatehouse
- Bursary for reconnaissance visit
- Budget for the whole project

  Additional costs to be built in:

- Round versus square towers
- Price per crenellation
- Windows and doors versus slits
- Overhang
- Accommodation, storage and armoury.

After work on this they could price a particular castle build as a maths project or extension work. This can be linked to real-world careers in quantity surveying and architecture. Some students might decide to model the build on the computer.

A case example in modern foreign language teaching (Burton and Anthony, 1997)

According to Burton and Anthony (1997), research on learning and teaching has been separated by a failure to explicate the relevance of one to another. This has resulted in an absence of pedagogical rationale grounded in a theoretical understanding of learning needs. They suggested that the consequence was an imbalance in the emphasis placed on the activity of teaching rather than the facilitation of learning.

In a series of French lessons they explored the challenge of meeting the intellectual needs of all pupils within a mixed-ability class using carefully structured open-ended tasks.

The French class consisted of 25, mainly Muslim girls, in a 13–18 inner-city comprehensive. They were set the task of creating a scene in a florist's shop using the transactional language learned in the study unit. A basic set of phrases was given them and they were told they could either work on their own or in groups and could use the teachers as a resource alongside books and displays. The aim was to provide a framework for successful performance among pupils of a wide range of ability. The performances were recorded on videotape. Having taught the necessary procedural knowledge to complete the task the researchers hypothesized that the follow-up use of an open-ended task would provide opportunities to extend and communicate meaning beyond the prescribed text.

Their rationale for the strategy was provided by reference to cognitive and social psychology. Of particular relevance was the phenomenological perspective – for example, the notion of associative schemata and the diversity of learning styles in relation to concept development.

They described their findings as convincing, despite some evidence of task resistance due to the novelty of it. All pupils in the class achieved success and were able to alter or add to the given structure of the transaction in some way. The greatest extension of ideas and language occurred among the pupils of high ability who went far beyond the basic task. They added meanings from their significant personal experiences and from previous learning.

The researchers concluded that the open-ended task clearly acted as a catalyst for the meaningful construction and communication of both declarative and procedural knowledge. They suggested that the 'freedom to learn' which Carl Rogers (1985) had advocated was facilitated by this collaborative strategy because it fostered the complex interplay between a learner's inner resources and external influences, which constitutes the dynamic of individual development. They concluded that the strategy crossed subject boundaries and had clear applications to work with high attainers as well.

Cognitive Study Skills

An example of cognitive study skills follows. The task is 'concept completion' in which pairs of pupils try to reconstruct the original author's meaning. It is not the same as a 'cloze procedure' exercise where words are deleted in random cycles, for example every seventh word.

Under Ground by James Reeves
In the deep kingdom under ground
There is no light and little ——

Down below the earth's green ——
The rabbit and the mole explore.

The quarrying ants run to and fro
To make their populous empires——

Do they, as I pass ——

Only part of the verse is repeated here to illustrate the method. On the basis of it pupils can then be questioned about how they came to the conclusion that it rhymed: there are at least four possibilities to explore here and they learn more about the meaning of the poem and remember it better than if they merely read it through and are asked comprehension questions.

In *Ultima Ratio Regum* by Stephen Spender we have an even more difficult example for older students. Again, only the first part of the poem is given:

The guns spell money's ultimate reason
In letters of _____ on the Spring hillside.
But the boy lying _____ under the olive trees
Was too young and too _____
To have been notable to their important eye.
He was a better target for a _____ .

The deletion of concepts is frequently applied to prose and as tests in science, for example, but less frequently to poems. It can be a powerful technique for learning.

Another key technique in study skills approaches (Montgomery, 1999) can be to get the pupils to identify the main and subordinate points in a chapter, article or poem. It means that they have to apply a range of reading strategies to the text, not just a straightforward receptive reading run as with a novel or newspaper. Once the points are identified they can be converted to a flow chart, if desired. Another strategy is to identify the type of text structure and not just its contents. This is an area in which underachieving and disadvantaged pupils fall short, as shown in Chapter 2. If we can actually teach them these text 'scaffolds' they can learn to recognize and use them in their own writing. A similar strategy was used with teachers on in-service courses who had problems in writing essays. After only a few short lessons on education essay structure they were all enabled to pass. Pupils equally respond well to this and the text on the Pueblos (see below) is regularly used as a training exercise (Montgomery, 1996, 1998).

Narrative text schema or scaffolds

- Explain – a process or how it works.
- Describe – the way things are.
- Instruct – how to make or do.
- Recount – retell events.
- Persuade – argue a point of view.
- Discuss – present an argument or case, essay.

An environmental studies example

A training example of reading for the main point and then schema training can be undertaken on the following piece of text:

> With a food surplus, the Pueblos were able to turn their attention to other activities besides locating or growing food. In one particular area – pottery making – the Pueblos developed a high degree of artistry. Potters became artists and developed individualised techniques, painting fine-lined geometric designs as well as reproductions or life forms on their vessels. Paints were improved and pottery has been found that contains three or four different colours. (Royce-Adams, 1977, taken from *Columbus to Aquarius*, Dryden Press, 1975: 145)

Pupils are asked to identify the main point of this extract. Although this was originally designed by Royce-Adams as a paper and pencil activity for individuals, it has a much more powerful use as a teaching and learning strategy if the pupils in pairs read the passage and discuss with each other the answer they are going to offer and its justification before sharing this with the rest of the class in a whole-class interactive teaching session. Their different responses can then be presented and argued through. After this they can do similar activities on other material in the subject area in which they might learn that most simple texts contain the main point in the first sentence – useful knowledge for scanning activities.

They can also be introduced to paragraph writing patterns as below: Which of the following writing patterns is exemplified in the Pueblo passage?

a. illustration – example
b. definition
c. comparison – contrast
d. sequence of events
e. cause and effect
f. description
g. a mixture – state which.

Highly able pupils might be asked to try to write the same paragraph in all six forms. Underachieving able pupils need to be put into pairs (mixed or matched) to discuss how to draft two of the paragraphs.

Scaffolding imaginative writing

It is usual to begin teaching about the structure of open-ended writing or so-called 'creative' writing by discussing with pupils that stories must have a beginning, a middle and an end. They need then to analyse some stories, perhaps for younger children, to study this and the main points can be written in the scaffold boxes. At various stages teachers may be heard to urge pupils to use more describing words and then teach sessions on adjectives, but this can give a poorer return than if the first lines/paragraphs of half a dozen books are studied to see what effects are created by the words, for example mood, historical setting, suspense and so on. Similar strategies can follow with other aspects of real stories, and more complex story scaffolds such as the following can be developed (see Figure 10.7 p 187).

Causal reasoning in English

When studying text, various methods of getting at the deeper structure can be used which both promote higher-order thinking and give practice in doing so.

Thinking carefully about causes. Question: Who, if anyone, was responsible for the death of Romeo and Juliet?

a. Feuding parents?
b. The Prince?
c. Friar Lawrence?
d. The lovers?

In pairs discuss and draft an argument which holds each one in turn responsible for the deaths.

Select your 'best' argument and draw the causal chain you describe. Further questions to promote class discussion. Brainstorming might be used as a starting point.

Q. On what basis do we hold people responsible for their actions and the things that happen?
Q. Are there analogies between the play and real life today?
Q. Are there any similar issues in our own experiences?

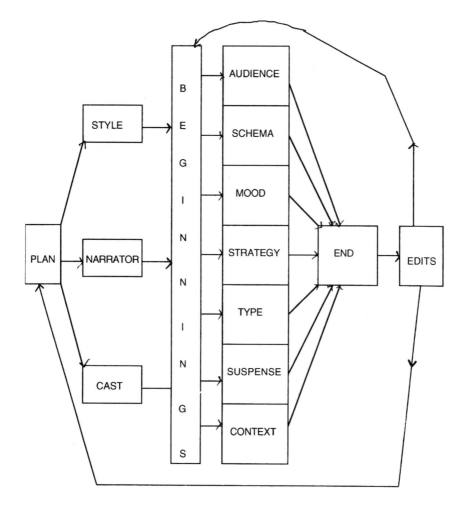

Figure 10.7: A 'scaffold' for story writing

Different 'voices'

Eyre (1997: 60–1) gives an example of an able pupil who writes about the reivers, robber gangs of the 16th century, in different voices: the diary of

Petra Carrson on 14 March 1595; a school history book; a letter from Anne who escaped to Carlisle; and a report from the newspaper of the day on the troubles. It can easily be seen how this idea can be developed further as pairs work and can also be recorded in different styles using a study of handwriting of the day and printing techniques. Alternatively, the whole project can be drafted in pairs work on the computer using different formats.

The village of Eddington enrichment pack is a useful resource for this type of historical approach (Maidenhead Group of Teachers, Adams et al., 1987).

Newspaper topics (Montgomery, 1991) can also provide great incentives to write and modern-day events lend themselves to the different voices approach.

Cognitive acceleration through science (CASE: Adey, 1991)

Adey with his colleague Shayer have been working on this project for more than two decades. They found that only about 30% of 16 year olds were capable of demonstrating formal operational thinking. The project aimed to make more children able to think in this way. In order to do this they emphasized the importance of metacognition in learning. They designed a series of 30 science activities which would develop metacognitive activities and a training course of one-day workshops with follow-up visits to the schools in the project for teachers. The CASE lessons occupied one science period every two weeks over a period of two years.

The critical features of the programme were to ask pupils to reflect on the difficulties and successes they had with problems, to discuss with each other how they had solved or failed to solve them, and to accrue understanding of the vocabulary of reasoning, so that they could more easily transfer the reasoning patterns from one context to another. The language of reasoning mediates meta-learning.

For example, in a classification activity they were asked to reflect on their thinking processes after they had sorted animals into groups according to their own criteria, arranged foodstuffs on a shelf, sorted chemicals in two ways by colour and solubility, and so on.

They were asked what was the easiest and the most difficult and why, as well as their feelings about the tasks. They compared their answers with those of other groups. A classroom atmosphere was encouraged which facilitated pupil talk about how they had solved problems and they became familiar with the terminology of problem-solving and reasoning. Their pupils in nine classes in Years 7 and 8 of secondary schools showed significant gains in comparison with control subjects, not immediately, but two years later in GCSE science, maths and English. The research work continues and has now been applied by others to maths and geography (CAME and CAGE). Its processes fit the cognitive learning spiral (Chapter 9).

Problem-solving in mathematics

Mathematical problem-solving can be deceptive in that it does not engage the pupils in real problem-solving where cognitive skills are required. Labelling a task as problem-solving because it is a presented in word form is a lower-level task. A typical example is that pupils are given a budget of, for example, £10.00, and asked to design a party menu for five friends. They are given a list of prices of typical items. The only problem is the conversion of the words to numbers and portions and then the use of number skills based on five to use up the money. It is better if they work in pairs so at least the think – pair – share strategy can be used to promote thinking and communication. RPS is more open and would begin thus – You have been given £10.00 and you decide to have a party for some friends. How would you plan it and spend your money?

Eyre (1997) gives the example of two good mathematicians in Year 2 being given a car-parking problem. The school was to have a celebration to open a new set of classrooms and a lot of visitors were expected. They were set the problem of finding out the most effective use possible of the playground for car parking. There are many similar such problems that can be found not just for the most able. Many children can do these problem-based tasks once they have some experience of the approach and learn how to question themselves and each other, and reflect on what they are learning and how they are learning. This is the power of the second cycle of talk, the reflective talk, which is illustrated by the cognitive learning spiral. It is this second cycle of reflective talk which is too often missing from most classrooms and from which all pupils would benefit. Watson (1996), for example, uses such reflective talk in lessons with pupils with moderate learning difficulties and finds that their standards of attainment improve.

Summary and conclusions

The purpose of this chapter has been to draw together the three main strands in underachievement which run through this book: how to teach to the needs of able underachieving pupils, how to include them in mainstream education, and how to motivate them to learn.

The approach adopted has been that it is the school and the educative environment and techniques which are basically at fault and where the main effort for change can be made. Whatever disadvantages pupils bring with them, the school and teachers can make a powerful difference.

First and foremost, the school needs to provide a positive and supportive ethos without losing opportunities for cognitive challenge. Second, the work in all areas must provide cognitive stimulation and motivation to learn based on effective learning principles. Third, identification of pupils' abilities and talents is essential in order to recognize, celebrate and affirm them, and also so that any difficulties they bring to the learning situation can be analysed with their help and appropriate support be given, especially in the areas of spelling and handwriting.

A cognitive approach in all of this – *Thinking Classrooms* (McGuinness, 1999) or whatever we call the approaches – must engage the brain of the learners so that they become active participants in their own learning development. This will help to overcome or avoid 'learned helplessness' in all areas of life and work and will enable them to become lifelong learners. Too often schooling 'switches' learners off, especially where it is pervasively didactic and ignores needs; it then promotes disaffection and disadvantage and puts these pupils on pathways to disruption and exclusion or into retreat.

Although schools are improving their results in the league tables year on year, the numbers of the disaffected and excluded grow. UK education is thus not inclusive yet. To be inclusive there needs to be a form of differentiation described as 'developmental differentiation', because most classes in most schools and subject areas are going to remain mixed ability whatever special treatment is given to a few. Making the ordinary special can be achieved by the methods described. The methods are based in theory but also are grounded in research in classrooms which have analysed with pupils and teachers what was needed and what can work.

Current text-based didactic methods are not catering either for the education of the emotions and the development of empathy or the development of intellect. Such things as emotional intelligence do not come as a curriculum package which can be told to pupils and reinforced in worksheets. It arises out of the everyday interactions between people. Empathy and understanding grow out of stable and supportive interactions.

Teachers can have time in the methods described to model such behaviour and help children who do not otherwise have these experiences. One significant adult can make a difference. All children need such mentors but especially the underachieving and disaffected.

CHAPTER 11

Shaping my life – evolving strategies of highly able women: biographical studies

JANICE A. LEROUX

Introduction

Women have always lived, listened, read and built analogies with a double perspective. In order to maintain a comfort level in the established order, females have to shift their perspective, their own point of view, to reflect the realities of a male world. Perhaps they have never reflected on these motives, these actions. It is not until someone or some incident causes them to reflect on personal responses that they are forced to confront the particular strategies and the unique choices made each day. Is there a value in having a wide selection of various strategies to choose from, depending on the situation and its intensity?

If the coping leads to a sense of control over the situation, an adjustment that reduces anxiety, then we consider the choice to be efficacious and effective (Billings and Moos, 1981; Kessler et al., 1985; Wetherington and Kessler, 1991; Bandura, 1995). If we are passive and try to deny the stress, can there be value in this response? Is it situationally useful depending on the depth and severity of the pain?

Not much research has been done on the special abilities of high-ability women who have made contributions to society. This chapter will explore the versatile coping strategies of Canadian women in order to see how their lives can guide others towards greater knowledge of personal motivations, sense of identity and responses to daily situations. Their examples can also provide ideas for shaping teaching strategies for those working with young girls.

A narrative

Angela, at 48 years, is proud of her position as vice-president of an international company whose business continues to expand. She recalls the words of her father who spoke of paddling her own canoe or else being left to drift in the waters of business life. In the past, when dealing with male competitors, she chuckles at how she would wink at one across the negotiating table to disarm him, or smile at a contentious competitor who asked her to get him a coffee during a meeting. She told him this would happen after he got her a cup.

Angela would read four or five papers early in the day to be prepared for discussions at meetings. She had always been a voracious reader. The sports pages were particular favourites because she had learned that talk of sports was a common ploy to keep her out of conversation in many all-male environments. She enjoyed the looks on male faces when she extolled the virtues of a popular hockey player or local baseball team.

In the midst of every busy day, she always made time to phone her daughters to check on their school work, music lessons or sports practice. As a single mother, she felt a keen responsibility to try to attend important events with the girls as often as possible. Recalling the trauma of her own rape at the age of 10 by a trusted family friend, she is intensely protective of her daughters, and even if out of the country on business she phones them daily to let them know she loves and cares for them.

Angela credits her patient parents with helping her deal with the investigation and trial of her abuser, but his subsequent suicide left her with mixed feelings of guilt and responsibility for many years. It was only during university and with the support of a trusted tutor that she began to believe in the talents she remembers won her awards in grade school. Her drive to succeed in business, particularly in a non-traditional field for women, helped her to rebuild her confidence, but also caused dissension with a young husband. When he told her that she should not think she was smarter than other people, and that she should stay at home more to care for him and the girls, she decided to stand her ground. The resulting divorce caused her pain, but with the help of female friends she realized that the marriage had been more beneficial to her ex-husband than it was for her and her dreams.

Angela is now aware of the power of her own independence and, although often alone, she rarely feels lonely because she knows she has friends she can talk with, a job that gives her many satisfactions, and the knowledge that her daughters have a role model who trusts her own choice. She is committed to creating new business opportunities in her career because she thrives on challenge and believes she has a responsibility to help to improve the lives of the people who work for her and with her.

In looking at this synthesis of a woman who is energetic and enthusiastic about life, we wonder what are the underlying constructs of her success? Can such a woman's life provide a mirror for other girls and young women as they try to believe that they have what it takes to succeed?

Coping mechanisms

Often in trying to understand our abilities, we come up against a male model of behaviour; an established expectation that the male patterns are the valued ways of knowing and acting. Females come to believe that their achievements are unimportant, and that their ideas are commonplace when compared with the socially defined expectations based on men's achievements (Belenky et al., 1986; Miller, 1986). It is only with the development of versatile coping strategies that women come to realize that what they do is important and has value in the relational world. Through this knowledge we come to understand that we can be both instrumental and expressive in our behaviours, becoming androgynous women as appropriate to our contexts.

If we value our self and act in ways which demonstrate this, then self-reliance and ultimately self-agency result (Jarvis, 1992; Landrum, 1994; Bandura, 1995). Self-agency refers to the reciprocal interplay between motivational incentives and achievement mastery. It is the action which results from self-efficacy beliefs, which, in turn, fuels further cognitive control and affective regulation of additional and goal-orientated success (Bandura, 1995).

Efficacy beliefs influence academic achievement and career achievement behaviours, 'one's capabilities to organise and execute the causes of action required to produce given attainment' (Bandura, 1997: 3). Self-assessment of control seems to facilitate the construction of greater metacognitive knowledge, and this in turn impacts on motivation and further success.

Through self-regulatory and reflective capabilities, a resilience is developed which provides great strength for handling times of stress. Resilience is the willingness to act in the face of politically dangerous reality, to successfully master change (Flach, 1988). For a woman perhaps, this might be the courage to be 'not nice', to risk disillusioning others for the sake of discovering truthful connections (Gilligan, 1994). To achieve this belief that we can control and transform our own environments requires the courage to confront potential disconnections and maintain an adaptive functioning in spite of serious risks. Resilience allows one to cope and succeed and is important in providing protective factors useful in overcoming adversity (Pearlin and Schooler, 1978; Zarit et al., 1986).

There is also a great deal of literature on the benefits of versatile coping responses to practical problems (Billings and Moos, 1981; McCrae, 1984;

Folkman et al., 1986). Wetherington and Kessler (1991) suggest that active behavioural and versatile coping (a combination of multiple coping strategies) are efficacious strategies that show good emotional adjustment. It seems that in acute crisis situations at least, action is preferable to passivity and versatility is the hallmark of an emotionally healthy person.

Another element of healthy coping is the belief that one's fate is in the hands of a higher power. Religion can help effect positive reappraisal of difficult situations, particularly those involving death and high degree loss (Wetherington and Kessler, 1991). Whether one belongs to an official religion or deeply believes in the importance of an 'awe-filled' sense of connection to the world, a sense of spirituality contributes to good emotional adjustment to practical and interpersonal events.

It is this belief in the importance of connectedness that shapes women's sense of identity and transformation (Miller, 1986). For women, identity and intimacy are intricately conjoined (Gilligan, 1994). Women, through their preference for connections, come to see self as a caring and responsible entity (Gilligan, 1982). Whether interacting with friends, accepting social responsibility, learning through relationships, collaborating with colleagues, or supporting through an ethic of caring, females build self-knowledge and self-efficacy through multiple connections in their daily lives (Simon, 1987; Gilligan et al., 1990; Skoe and Marcia, 1993). Even when cognitive self-efficacy is not enough, women will turn to social efficacy to help them reduce stress and enhance personal efficacy through their social support systems (Bandura, 1995).

Along with connectedness, the literature points to the importance of personal autonomy in the development of human success. As an individual culls her past experiences, she comes to know that she can create ideas, make new knowledge and trust her own decision-making (Belenky et al., 1986; Miller, 1986; Gilligan, 1991; Silverman, 1991; Jarvis, 1992). With this grows autonomy – the ability to trust experimentation, to loosen constraints and to choose to create totally new situations for ourselves (Jarvis, 1992). Autonomy is the willingness to trust one's inner voice and act on it (Goldberger, 1996). For women the importance of the particular and the personal is at the heart of feminist epistemology.

Women become acutely aware of their femaleness when they encounter autonomous self in relation to others. Personal ability is seen as complementary, not competitive, and sharing of strengths is the accepted norm. For women the need to connect, withdraw and connect again is clearly the path of development, and being female allows one to find authentic self in connected ways that differ from those of men (Gilligan, 1982; Heilbrun, 1987; Miller, 1994; Leroux and Butler-Por, 1996).

It seems from the literature that there are major constructs which exemplify how women confront stress and change in their lives. Are career women actively choosing such strategies? In a study of 40 eminent Canadian women, the constructs identified above were supported and led to a Spiral Model of Female Achievement.

The biographical study

Interviews which lasted from two to three-and-a-half hours were held across Canada with 40 eminent women aged 28 to 79 who have demonstrated leadership success in careers such as law, business, engineering, the arts, politics, sports and academics. Demographic data on family constellations, marital status, parental background, careers and so on were discussed and then open-ended questions based on constructs from the review of literature ensued. Interviews were tape-recorded and personal observations were noted after the interview was concluded.

Frequency counts were used with the demographic data, and a series of reductions elicited the similarities and differences that emerged (Miles and Huberman, 1984; Strauss and Corbin, 1990). Triangulation of the emerging commonalities was achieved through independent readings by two graduate assistants, and through discussion and comparison with demographic data (Lincoln and Guba, 1985). Emerging patterns in the women's lives were compared with the literature on females, with a particular view to achievement, relationships and constructs of self-agency.

Versatile coping responses were used by most of the women, with social supports, active cognitive and active behavioural responses as the most prevalent adjustments. From reflections on their experiences a series of six constructs emerged to form a spiral model of achievement representative of women's ways of knowing and doing.

A spiral model of female achievement

From the women's stories there were many commonalities. Most of the women described using a variety of strategies when they worked through challenging incidents in their lives. They would appraise the situation, 'integrate all that I have attempted before', said one businesswoman, actively trying to change the environment, or 'become very efficient' in working out solutions. If the stress caused deep grief, they would spend time 'soul searching', seeking spiritual consolation or talking with dear friends. Sometimes reading, riding a bike or meditating while running were useful coping efforts the women chose to help them adjust to the demands of their lives.

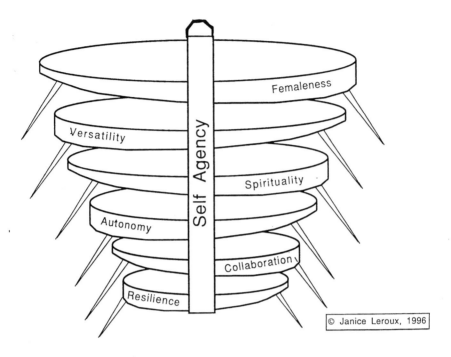

Figure 11.1: Chandelier model of female achievement

This combination of various cognitive, active reappraisal, active social and to a lesser degree spiritual coping strategies points to a versatility common in the eminent women (see Figure 11.1).

As the women learned to recognize their inner strengths, they spoke of daring to act in ways which often seemed to be contrary to socially defined expectations. These women recognized their own motivations to achieve, and were willing to use their energy and enthusiasm to both protect their personal dreams and to move their goals ahead with whatever means were at their disposal. Even in the face of harassment, they become successful copers and doers. As one academic said: 'I have less grief and less pain if I take action on an issue. I break it up into component parts: that's helpful.'

Some recognized that even as young girls they had always 'been a fighter', or 'been a mouthy girl who was not always nice to others'. They liked to use challenges or even indifference as motivators to further achievement. An artist recalled: 'My brother used to tell me how useless I was and that was an inspiration: 'Oh, you think I'm stupid. Well, I'll show you!' Another artist said: 'As a woman conductor (and composer) I know I have to work ten times harder and a hundred times smoother than a man. So that's been an influence on my career.' For these women, perceived beliefs of ability, self-efficacy and control led them to work hard at overcoming obstacles through a resilience that imbues all their accomplishments. They have learned that being resilient is a powerful tool for building success (Flach, 1988).

Another attribute combines the constructs of connectedness and interaction. Collaboration, the 'co-labour' of women's interactions, may be described as participation that interacts and empowers all in a concerted effort. These women see collaboration as an integral part of life, sharing ideas, sharing responsibilities and sharing power. For them, talking things out, whether at home or on the job, and finding support in others were an understood part of problem-solving.

Strength is discovered through a multiplicity of forms of collegiality and friendship. As an engineer stated, 'When an aggressive colleague plays a dirty, silly game I get very angry and know that I need to decompress and deal with it right away. That's when I talk to someone I can trust – a friend, a colleague, my husband, whoever is the best person to listen to that particular problem.'

Many women spoke of the mentors who 'guided me right from the beginning', or who were 'a network of intellectual mentors' who encouraged confidence and tenacity. Working in harmony with others grew from this base of connectedness.

While valuing collaboration, these women also recognized the need for autonomy in their lives. They see autonomy as an ability to direct their own lives to the fullest development of self while at the same time encompassing knowledge of their own power, to trust their own judgement and to foster mutual psychological development with others. Generally they see themselves as independent people who must make decisions and 'bear the consequences' themselves. They have learned to define their own reality through self-regulated behaviours.

Another emerging construct may be called 'spirituality'. Many of the women spoke of an ethic which guides their lives – the spiritual aspects which create linkages to all life. Using different words, these women perceived spirituality as a living factor, an 'inner peace' that provides a necessary basis for the values that informed their decisions. As one athlete said, 'I only do those things that fit with what I believe, that soul place for me'.

They draw on every relationship, every piece of background, the wellsprings of who they are, from family history to marriage or children, to maintain a sense of balance. The interconnectedness of human will, spirit and community are all part of these women's personal motives and they perceive an obligation to act from this base of beliefs.

A total sense of femaleness emerged from the words of all the women. As one academic said, 'In a sense, being a woman is my work.' Being female gives them a sense of freedom, comfort and a sense of caring that liberates their lives. They have learned to believe that they can be anything that they want to be, have a career, or choose motherhood or often try to combine these roles.

Sometimes a woman might be a public role model, at other times she is a quiet strategist working hard behind the scenes to support a valued outcome and a loved family. Their sensitivity to themselves, to others and to the world flowed from a belief in the value of connectedness and caring that was essential to their femaleness.

Women in this study did not always choose their career path by deliberate design; nor did they choose their professional way in the world by accident. Their paths, however, evolved from a self-agency based on their wide range of experiences, backgrounds, training, talents and abilities. The means they use to achieve may vary, but the relentless motivation to make a difference, to contribute to a better social order, shines as the inner light of a chandelier for all to see. Supporting the light is a core of personal efficacy that stems from belief and action.

With personal strength as the energy core of light inside, the chandelier model, with crystal prisms outside, represents a paradigm for the evolution of female experience and success. As self-efficacy develops, they learn to recognize realities and 'still follow their bliss'.

Research applications

The lives of women who have succeeded in a variety of careers hold much information for younger women, their educators and parents. How can the spiral model of achievement help girls develop a base for modelling behaviours? Success is rarely attained at a young age. But what educational strategies can help females to accept and value the complex strengths inside?

Home and school

Parents and teachers must encourage discussion and exploration of the constructs in the model and create opportunities for females to risk acting in ways that contradict cultural stereotypes. One way, for example, is to talk with them about social expectations around the beauty myth. In the safety of home or with a sensitive teacher, girls can learn to debunk the media visions of beauty. They can compare the fantasy of advertising with the reality of female body images. They can question the portrayal of women in music videos, learning to poke fun at the subservience of female characters.

In both informal and formal group sessions, girls as young as six years of age can learn to make choices about their appearance, their individuality, their speech and their non-typical behaviours. Listening to older females (teenage girls can also share experiences with the young), they come to see the wider range of possibilities that are available to females who value their independence and trust their beliefs. For example, rejecting the thin body image promoted by media is hard for young adolescents who want to be 'beautiful'. Sociodrama and reverse role-play can help females see the various pros and cons of healthy life choices.

Schools

Single-gender classes or seminars can provide a range of confidence-building opportunities in an atmosphere of trust. For example, cluster groupings of females in science or mathematics can allow girls the luxury of deeper sharing of learning without interference. Reading about the lives of successful women, creating and operating all-female business experiences, and shadowing women in a variety of careers can all help young girls acquire knowledge about their own abilities.

Role playing potential stress situations, or problem-solving about the costs of various career possibilities, can help young women recognize the merits of collaboration as well as autonomy in their lives. Knowing that she carries within her the strengths of her cognitive self as well as her emotional self, the young girl can practise ways to manage the cultural and relational stressors that will invariably be part of her future.

In heterogeneous classrooms, reverse role-play with males can help all better understand and be sensitive to some of the uncompromising stereotypes about females in our society. All young people want acceptance, and recognition for real abilities and strongly held values. But at the same time, girls have to feel that it is safe to be unpopular. Male students, through role-reversal exercises, can experience how females feel about teasing about being smart in maths. Girls can show boys the benefits of learning from stories and being emotionally connected to others and the world.

All students need recognition for achievements based on real, not ritual abilities. (Being praised for being 'highly able' or neat is no substitute for hearing praise for a great new idea, or an original short story. Gifted children know the difference.) Knowing that her ideas are valuable, that her choices carry responsibilities that are within her power, that her achievement is within her own control, can all help girls to respect the self-agency they possess. Through being encouraged to talk about her own personal values and beliefs, the spiritual core of her evolving self, the young female can recognize additional skills which will help her negotiate challenges and withstand pressures.

Teachers should plan proximal goals that allow students to reach success and then provide the vital feedback that secures self-agency and allows the learner to build greater efficacy. This two-fold process of proximal goals and feedback ultimately enhances productivity in all learners (Bandura, 1997). Teachers must be alert and knowledgeable in order to capitalize on ways to help students design and develop their own goals. Along with that, teachers can also have students design evaluation measures to see if the outcomes are what they expected and desired.

Training young males to respect the qualities of women through studying selected curriculum materials is also important. The goal is to help all students learn to delight in their strengths and trust in using their powers in ways that enhance personal achievement. Using case studies and guided brainstorming, teachers can help students see a range of alternatives to problems and help them capitalize on their own abilities.

Teachers can check their own words and body cues. Are there different messages sent to boys and girls through pitch of a voice, its tone or in open or closed body movements? Are different degrees of difficulty involved in the questions we pose to girls and boys in class? Teaming up with another teacher can help when one acts as an observer and gives feedback to the other colleague on classroom interactions, questioning techniques and gender-related expectations.

Female students prefer a conversational style of learning over confrontational debates. Through opportunities to interact with others, get their hands on experiments and other applied activities, or through selected, relevant stories, they come to dig deeper and apply new knowledge that connects them to the outside world. Teachers need to use strategies that help girls move through these pathways. Helping young female students evolve from external motivation to self-regulated learning based on recognized personal needs is an essential goal for all educators.

In adolescence, girls need to learn to trust their own voice and know that it is possible to be connected and independent at the same time. Teachers might encourage keeping an 'I am female' journal as a means of reflecting on personal voice. Involvement in young women's leadership or service organizations can help girls hone valuable skills in goal-setting, planning and organizing

Girls can also learn that networking is an important skill that will be used throughout their lifetime. Bibliotherapy – learning through reading about the life passages of others – can open new potential for sharing self and developing new special strengths. Seeing how others learn to accept mistakes and failure can lead females to positive ways of managing their own lives.

Lastly, teachers can remember the forgotten force in education of girls: grandmothers. As co-educators, these women can work with teachers to use their store of experience to show females different ways to control and shape a life. Grandmothers can emphasize respect for self, confidence in choices, learning how to question, consider career options and finding a balance in one's life. These wise women provide a key to eternity and are a resource that all educators should consider using.

Summary

Girls and adolescent females need to recognize that their lives are not pathways to one permanent, single ambition. Research shows that women experience a continuity of refocusing and redefining self through multiple, overlapping experiences. Their lives provide complex colour filters through which young girls can reflect their own achievements.

The Spiral Model of Female Achievement draws together the multiple attributes that evolved from research on high-ability women. Expanding on Bandura's self-efficacy research, and supported by literature on constructs of success, the model illustrates the complementary and recip-rocal factors which emanate from the lived lives of women who believe that what they do can make a difference in the world.

Educators can learn from the experiences described by women who have broken stereotypes, who have fought to balance families and careers and who have achieved an exemplary sense of self-agency. They believe that being female was the most important strength – an attribute that allowed them the delight of living a rich life combining the best of intellect and emotion, action and reflectiveness, social justice and personal respon-sibility. This is their legacy for those women who follow.

Acknowledgement

Grateful acknowledgement for support in this research is given to the Social Sciences and Humanities Research Council , Canada.

Epilogue

In 1990, Passow, in an overview of research, stated that we still did not know what provision to make to motivate the more able learner or how to educate those who were socially and culturally disadvantaged under-achievers. Now that we are in a new millennium I think we can claim that we do know how to address these problems. This knowledge must still, however, become a 'grand narrative' or 'zeitgeist' if it is to become accepted by mainstream educators. The cycle of development and imple-mentation in education according to Cooper (1999) seems to operate on a 50-year pattern. It would be disappointing, and for the learners devas-tating, if gifted education were to follow this pattern.

We do know what to do and how to do it. The next problem is to work on spheres of influence to ensure that these changes take place. In the methods proposed we can see that the education of the gifted and talented needs to take place at a foundation level alongside other children in school. Instead of differentiation of the curriculum, we need to make schools and the education they provide inclusive by differentiating the teaching methods and then build other strategies upon this.

All learners need to experience an education which is supportive and valuing, whatever their differences. To achieve this, general education needs to be made more flexible. Access to special provision where it is useful should be based on the principles of inclusion and self-referral and use authentic or performance-based assessment to provide feedback to both learners and teachers. Learners need opportunities to contribute their own views on the value and appropriateness of the education they are receiving.

Regrettably, the findings in this book are in direct contravention to state systems of education in many countries of the world. However, these systems result in widespread underfunctioning, both overt and covert, with creative, imaginative and autonomous learners particularly at risk. It is time for change. If we get it wrong and move further towards indoctrination as education, we develop a population which cannot question what 'authorities' say and do, and what role models portray. We become gullible and lose the capacity for independent thought, and refer back to custom and practice and old routines even when inappropriate.

Is it intentional that the stifling of the ability to think in 'real-world terms' seems to be in progress? If so, it can lead to an 'overdomesticated' population rather than a self-actualized one, according to Maslow (1949) such a long time ago. Surely we must learn from the 'education' systems that have underpinned the war-ridden history of the 20th century and look forward to what should be. Must education even now be a subversive activity?

References

Adams J, Eyre D, Howell J, Raffan J (1987) The Village of Eddington. Wisbech: Learning Development Aids.

Adey PS (1991) Pulling yourself up by your own thinking. European Journal for High Ability 2: 28–34.

Adey PS (1992) The CASE results: Implications for science teaching. International Journal for Science Education 14: 137–46.

Adey PS, Shayer M (1994) Really Raising Standards: Cognitive Interventions and Academic Achievement. London: Routledge.

Alberta Community Development (1995) Raise Young Voices High: A Resource for Gender Socialisation. Edmonton, AB: Government of Alberta.

Allcock, P (2000) Handwriting speed and learning difficulties. Unpublished MA dissertation. London Middlesex University.

Alpern S (1993) In the beginning: A history of women in management. In A Fagenson (ed.) Women in Management: Trends, Issues and Challenges in Managerial Diversity. Women and Work: A Research and Policy Series, Volume 4. Newbury Park, CA: Sage, pp. 19–51.

Alston J (1993) Assessing and Promoting Handwriting Skills. Stafford: National Association of Special Educational Needs.

Alston J, Taylor J (1987) Handwriting Theory and Practice. London: Croom Helm.

Ambrus Z (1935) Eloszo (Preface). In Anatole France. Budapest: Feher Kovon, Revai.

American Association of University Women (1995) How Schools Shortchange Girls: The AAUW Report. New York: Marlowe & Co.

Arnold R (1997) Raising Levels of Achievement in Boys. Windsor: Education Management Information Exchange/National Foundation for Educational Research.

Arnot M, Gray J, James M, Rudduck J, Duveen MG (1998) Recent Research on Gender and Educational Performance. OFSTED Reviews of Research. London: The Stationery Office.

Arter J, Spandel V (1992) Using portfolios of student work in instruction and assessment. Educational Measurement: Issues and Practice (spring).

Askew S, Ross C (1988) Boys Don't Cry: Boys and Sexism in Education. Milton Keynes: Open University Press.

Astin H (1990) Educating women: A promise and vision for the future. American Journal of Education (August): 479–93.

Augur J, Briggs S (eds) (1991) The Hickey Multisensory Language Course (2nd edition). London: Whurr.

Ausubel DP (1968) Educational Psychology: A Cognitive View. New York: Holt, Rinehart and Winston.

Avery LD (1998) The international professional perspective: Reflections on the Third International Mathematics and Science Study. Gifted and Talented International 13(1): 40–3.

Baddeley A (1990) Human Memory: Theory and Practice. Boston, MA: Allyn and Bacon.

Bandura A (1986) Social Foundations of Thought and Action: A Social Cognitive Theory. Englewood Cliffs, NJ: Prentice-Hall.

Bandura A (1995) Self Efficacy in Changing Societies. New York: Cambridge University Press.

Bandura A (1997) Self Efficacy: The Exercise of Control. New York: Freeman and Co.

Bannatyne A (1974) Diagnosis: A note on recategorisation of the WISC scaled scores. Journal of Learning Disabilities 2: 272–4.

Barnard HC (1961) A History of English Education (2nd edition). London: London University Press.

Barron F (1968) Creativity and Personal Freedom. New York: Van Nostrand.

Barton JM, Starnes WT (1989) Distinguishing characteristics of gifted and talented/learning disabled students. Roeper Review (Special Issue: Gifted Students with Disabilities) 12(1): 23–8.

Becker BJ (1990) Item characteristics and gender differences on the SAT-M for mathematically able youth. American Educational Research Journal 27(1): 65–87.

Belenky MF, Goldberger NR, Tarule JM, Clinchy BV (eds) (1986) Knowledge, Difference and Power: Essays Inspired by 'Women's Ways of Knowing'. New York: Basic Books.

Benbow CP, Stanley JR (1983) Sex differences in mathematical reasoning ability: More facts. Science 222: 1029–31.

Benn C (1982) The myth of giftedness. Part two. Forum 24: 78–84.

Bennett N (1986) Co-operative learning. Children do it in groups or do they? Paper presented at the Division of Educational and Child Psychology Conference, British Psychological Society, London, April.

Biddulph S (1998) Raising Boys: Why Boys are Different and How to Help Them Become Happy and Well-Balanced Men. London: Hawthorn.

Billings AG, Moos RH (1981) The role of coping responses and social resources in attenuating the stress of life events. Journal of Behavioural Medicine 4: 139–57.

Bireley M, Languis M, Williamson T (1992) Physiological uniqueness: A new perspective on the learning disabled/gifted child. Roeper Review 16(3): 101–7.

Black H, Black S (1990) Understanding Metaphors. New York: Critical Thinking Press.

Black P, Willam D (1998) Inside the Black Box: Raising Standards Through Classroom Assessment. London: School of Education, King's College.

Blagg N, Ballinger M, Gardner R (1993) Somerset Thinking Skills Course: Handbook (2nd edition). Taunton: N. Blagg.

Blatchford P (1991) Children's writing at 7 years: Associations with handwriting on school entry and pre-school factors. British Journal of Educational Psychology 61: 73–84.

Block AA (1997) I'm Only Bleeding: Education as the Practice of Violence Against Children. New York: Peter Lang.

Bloom BS (ed.) (1956) Taxonomy of Educational Objectives, Volume 1. London: Longman.

Bloom BS (1985) Developing Talent in Young People. New York: Ballantine.

Borland JH (1996) Gifted education and the threat of irrelevance. Journal for the Education of the Gifted 19: 129–47.

Bowers S, Wells L (1988) Ways and Means. Kingston: Kingston Friends Workshop Group Publication.

Bray R, Gardner C, Parsons N (1997) Can Boys Do Better? Leicester: Secondary Heads Association Publication.

Briggs J (1990) Fire in the Crucible. Los Angeles, CA: J.P. Tarcher.

Briskin L, Coulter R (1992) Feminist pedagogy: Challenging the normative. Canadian Journal of Education 17(3): 247–63.

Bronson C (1992) Arts Connection National Diffusion Network, Washington, DC.

Bryant PE (1992) Arithmetic in the cradle. Nature 338: 712–13.

Burbridge L (1992) New Economic Trends for Women's Employment: Implications for Girls' Vocational Education. Working Paper series No 247. Wellesley, MA: Center for Research on Women, Wellesley College.

Burnhill P, Hartley J, Fraser L, Young D (1975) Writing lines: An exploratory study. Programmed Learning and Educational Technology 12(2): 84–7.

Burton D, Anthony S (1997) The differentiation of curriculum and instruction in primary and secondary schools. Educating Able Children (spring) (issue 1): 26–34.

Butler-Por N (1987) Underachievers in School: Issues and Interventions. London: John Wiley.

Cahoone L (ed.) (1996) From Modernism to Postmodernism: An Anthology. Oxford: Blackwell.

Caplan P (1993) Lifting a Ton of Feathers: A Woman's Guide to Surviving in the Academic World. Toronto: University of Toronto Press.

Cassidy, S (1999) Girls now beat boys at A-level. Times Educational Supplement (6 August): 7.

Chalmers GS (1977) Reading Easy 1800–1850. A Study of Reading. London: Broadsheet King.

Chomsky N (1968) Language and Mind. New York: Harcourt, Brace and World.

Ciccocioppo L (1998) Cracking the 'glass ceiling'. Folio (20 March): 3.

Clark B (1986) Optimising Learning: The Integrative Education Model in the Classroom. Columbus, OH: Merrill.

Coil C (1992a) Motivating Underachievers. Beavercreek, OH: Pieces of Learning.

Coil C (1992b) Becoming an Achiever. Beavercreek, OH: Pieces of Learning.

Collins W, Gunnar MR (1990) Social and personality development. Annual Review of Psychology 41: 387–419.

Commission of European Communities (1988) Social Europe: Report on the Fight Against Literacy Supplement 2/88. Brussels: Commission of European Communities.

Connell RW (1989) Cool guys, swots and wimps: The interplay of masculinity and education. Oxford Review of Education 15: 291–302.

Cooper P (ed.) (1999) Understanding and Supporting Children with Emotional and Behavioural Difficulties. London: Jessica Kingsley.

Cowdery LL, Montgomery D, Morse P, Prince-Bruce M (1983–7) Teaching Reading Through Spelling (TRTS). Kingston: Learning Difficulties Research Project.

Cowdery LL, Montgomery D, Morse P, Prince-Bruce M (1984) TRTS: The Foundations of the Programme. Kingston: Learning Difficulties Research Project.

Cromer JP (1990) Someone to look up to. Parents Magazine (December).

Csikszentmihalyi M, Rathunde K, Whalen S (1993) Talented Teenagers: The Roots of Success and Failure. New York: Cambridge University Press.

Csikszentmihalyi M, Rathunde K, Whalen S (1997) Talented Teenagers – The Roots of Success and Failure. Cambridge: Cambridge University Press.

Cumbria Education Service (2000, in preparation) Now, Bernard! Gender Friendly Approaches to Raising Achievement in Key Stage 2 English. Carlisle: Cumbria Education Service Able Pupil Project.

Daniels JC, Diack H (1958) The Standard Reading Test. London: Chatto and Windus.

Davies J, Brember I (1998) Boys Outperforming Girls: An Eight Year Cross-sectional Study of Attainment and Self Esteem in Year 6. Manchester: Manchester University School of Education.

de Alencar EMLS (1990) Training teachers to teach for creativity. European Journal for High Ability 1(1/2): 222–8.

de Alencar EMLS (1999) Teaching for creativity. Keynote presentation, World Council for Gifted and Talented Children, Biennial International Conference, Istanbul, 2–6 August.

de Bono E (1983) CoRT Thinking. Oxford: Pergamon.

Deci E (1988) Intrinsic motivation and gifted learners. 10th International Bulgarian Symposium on Education, Plovdiv, October.

De Corte E (1995) Learning and high ability: A perspective from research in instructional psychology. In MW Katzko, FJ Monks (eds) Nurturing Talent. Assen, The Netherlands: Van Gorcum, pp. 148–61.

De Mink F (1995) High ability students in higher education. In MW Katzko, RF Mönks (eds) Nurturing Talent: Individual Needs and Social Ability, Volume 1. Assen, The Netherlands, Van Gorcum, pp. 168–76.

Denton C, Postlethwaite K (1985) Able Children: Identifying Them in the Classroom. Windsor: NFER/Nelson.

Department of Education and Science (1977) Gifted Children in Middle and Comprehensive Schools. London: HMSO.

Department of Education and Science (1981) The Education Act. London: HMSO.

Department for Education and Employment (1994) The Code of Practice. London: HMSO.

Department for Education and Employment (1995) The National Curriculum for England and Wales. London: HMSO.

Department for Education and Employment (1997) Excellence for All Children. London: The Stationery Office.

Department for Education and Employment (1999) Excellence in Cities. London: The Stationery Office.

Desforges C (1998) Learning and teaching: Current views and perspectives. In D Shorrocks-Taylor (ed.) Directions in Educational Psychology. London: Whurr, pp. 5–18.

Dick T, Rallis S (1991) Factors and influences on high school students' career choices. Journal of Research in Mathematics Education 22(4): 281–92.

Dickens MN, Cornell DG (1993) Parent influences on the mathematics self concept of high ability adolescent girls. Journal for the Education of the Gifted 17(1): 53–73.

Downes P (1994) The gender effect. Managing Schools Today 3(5): 7–8.

Dubbeldam LFB (1991) Literacy and socio-cultural development. Paper given at the international conference Attaining Functional Literacy: A Cross-cultural Perspective. Tilburg, The Netherlands.

Early GH (1976) Cursive handwriting, reading and spelling achievement. Academic Therapy 12(1): 67–74.

Economist (1999) Underperformance among working class boys, vagrancy and crime. Economist p. 36.

Education Reform Act (1988) London: Department of Education and Science.

Education Reform Act (1995) Revised by Sir Ron Dearing. London: Department for Education and Employment.

Eisner E (1994) The Educational Imagination (3rd edition). New York: Prentice-Hall.

Elwood J, Gipps C (1999) Boys, girls and literacy: Single sex pupils get the best results. National Literacy Trust Web pages (http://www.literacytrust.org.uk/)

English L (1992) Children's use of domain-specific knowledge and domain-general strategies in novel problem-solving. British Journal of Educational Psychology 42: 203–16.

Epstein D, Elwood J, Hey V, Maw J (1998) Failing Boys? Issues in Gender and Achievement. Buckingham: Open University Press.

Eyre D (1997) Able Children in Ordinary Schools. London: Fulton.

Farmer D (ed.) (1993) Gifted Children Need Help? A Guide for Parents and Teachers. Strathfield, NSW: Australian Association for Gifted and Talented Children.

Feuerstein R (1995) Mediated Learning Experience. Keynote presentation, Mediated Learning Experience Conference, February, London, Regents College.

Feuerstein R, Rand Y, Hoffman MB, Mitter R (1980) Instrumental Enrichment. Baltimore, MD: University Park Press.

Films for the Humanities and Sciences (1998) Sexual Stereotypes in Media: Superman and the Bride. Fort Erie, ON: Films for the Humanities and Sciences.

Flach F (1988) Resilience: Discovering a New Strength at Times of Stress. New York: Fawcett Columbine.

Flanders NA (1970) Analysing Classroom Behaviour. New York: Addison-Wesley.

Flavell JH (1979) Metacognition and cognitive monitoring. American Psychologist 34: 906–11.

Folkman S, Lazarus RS, Dunkel-Schetter C, DeLongis A, Gruen RJ (1986) The dynamics of stressful encounter: Cognitive appraisal, coping and encounter outcomes. Journal of Personality and Social Psychology 50: 992–1003.

Ford DY (1995) A Study of Achievement and Underachievement among Gifted, Potentially Gifted, and Average African-American Students. Research Monograph 95128. Storrs, CT: The National Research Center on the Gifted and Talented, University of Connecticut.

Fowler WF (1990) Talking from Infancy: How to Nurture and Cultivate Early Language Development. Cambridge, MA: Brookline Books.

Frater G (1997) Improving Boys' Literacy: A Survey of Effective Practice in Secondary School. London: The Basic Skills Agency.

Freeman J (1991) Gifted Children Growing Up. London: Cassell.

Freeman J (1992) Quality Education: The Development of Competence. Geneva and Paris: UNESCO.

Freeman J (1994) Gifted school performance and creativity. Roeper Review 17: 15–19.

Freeman J (1996) Highly Able Girls and Boys. London: Department for Education and Employment.

Freeman J (1998) Educating the Very Able: Current International Research. OFSTED Reviews of Research. London: The Stationery Office.

Fuchs D, Fuchs L (1995) Counterpoint: Special education – ineffective? immoral? Exceptional Children 61: 303–6.

Gagné RL (1973) The Essentials of Learning. London: Holt, Rinehart and Winston.

Gallagher JJ (1995) Teaching the Gifted Child (5th edition). Boston, MA: Allyn and Bacon.

Gallagher JJ (1997) Preparing the gifted student as independent learner. In JA Leroux (ed.) Connecting the Gifted Community Worldwide, Selected Proceedings from the 12th World Conference of the WCGTC, Seattle, 29 July–2 August. Seattle, WA: World Council for Gifted and Talented Children, pp. 37–50.

Galloway D, Godwin C (1987) The Education of Disturbing Children. London: Longman.

Gardner H (1983) Frames of Mind: The Theory of Multiple Intelligences. New York: Basic Books.

Gardner H (1991) The Unschooled Mind. New York: Basic Books.

Gardner H (1993) Multiple Intelligences: The Theory in Practice. New York: Basic Books.

Geschwind N (1984) The biology of cerebral dominance. Implications for cognition. Cognition 17: 193–208.

Gibbs G (1990) Summary poster. Oxford: Oxford Brookes University Staff Development Centre.

Gibbs G (ed.) (1994) Improving Student Learning: Theory and Practice. Oxford: Oxford Brookes University Staff Development Centre.

Gibbs G (ed.) (1995) Improving Student Learning: Through Assessment and Evaluation. Oxford: Oxford Brookes University Staff Development Centre.

Gilligan C (1982) In a Different Voice. Cambridge, MA: Harvard University Press.

Gilligan C (1991) Women's psychological development: Implications for psychotherapy. In C Gilligan, A Rogers, D Tolman (eds) Women, Girls and Psychotherapy: Reframing Resistance. New York: Harrington Park Press, pp. 5–32.

Gilligan C (1994) Women's place in man's life cycle. In L Stone (ed.) The Education Feminist Reader. New York: Routledge, pp. 26–41.

Gilligan C, Lyons N, Hanmer T (1990) Making Connections: The Relational Worlds of Adolescent Girls at Emma Willard School. Cambridge, MA: Harvard University Press.

Gillingham AM, Stillman BU, Orton ST (1940) Remedial Teaching for Children with Specific Disabilities in Reading, Spelling and Penmanship. New York: Sackett and Williams.

Gillingham AM, Stillman BU, Orton ST (1956) Remedial Teaching for Children with Specific Disabilities in Reading, Spelling and Penmanship (5th edition). New York: Sackett and Williams.

Goldberg ML (1965) Research on the Talented. New York: Teachers College, Columbia University.

Goldberger NR (1996) Looking backward, looking forward. In NR Goldberger, JM Tarule, BV Clinchy, MF Belenky (eds) Knowledge, Difference and Power: Essays Inspired by 'Women's Ways of Knowing'. New York: Basic Books.

Golombok S, Fivush R (1994) Gender Development. Cambridge: Cambridge University Press.

Gross MUM (1993) Exceptionally Gifted Children. London: Routledge.

Grossman H, Grossman S (1994) Gender Issues in Education. Needham Heights, MA: Allyn and Bacon.

Grubb J (1999) Boys in brief: Reduced research on gender and underachievement. Times Educational Supplement (4 June): 30.

Grumet M, Macedo E (1996) Power and education: Who decides the forms schools have taken, and who should decide? In J Kincheloe, S Steinberg (eds) Thirteen Questions: Reframing Education's Conversations. New York: Peter Lang.

Gubbay SS (1975) The Clumsy Child. London: WB Saunders.

Gyarmathy E (1995) Developmental learning disabilities and giftedness. In Book of Abstracts, VIIth European Conference on Developmental Psychology in Krakow, Poland, p. 178.

Hagen JW, Jongeward RH Jr, Kail RV Jr (1975) Cognitive perspectives on the development of memory, strategies in acquisition and retrieval. Organisation and retrieval processes. In HW Reese (ed.) Advances in Child Development, Volume 10. New York: Academic Press.

Halford GS (1993) Children's Understanding: The Development of Mental Models. Hillsdale, NJ: Erlbaum.

Hall C, Coles M (1999) Children's Reading Choices. London: Routledge.

Hanna PR, Hanna JS, Hodges RE, Rudork EH (1966) Phoneme-Grapheme Correspondence as Cues to Spelling Improvement. Washington, DC: US Office of Education.

Hany EA (1997) Modelling teachers' judgment of giftedness: A methodological inquiry of biased judgment. High Ability Studies 8(2): 159–78.

Hargreaves D (1984) Improving Secondary Schools. London: Inner London Education Authority.

Harris S, Nixon J, Ruddock J (1993) School work, homework and gender. Gender and Education 5: 5–9.

Heilbrun CG (1987) Writing a Woman's Life. New York: Ballantine.

Hendryx W (1993) Make your child a self starter. Reader's Digest (January): 21–4.

Hernstein R, Murray C (1994) The Bell Curve: Intelligence and Class Structure in American Life. New York: The Free Press.

Herskovits M, Gyarmathy E (1995) Types of high ability. Highly able children with unbalanced intelligence structure. European Journal for High Ability 6(1): 38–48.

Hibbett A, Fogelman K (1990) Future lives of truants, family formation and health related behaviour. British Journal of Educational Psychology 60: 171–9.

Hiller A (director) (1984) Teachers (Film).

Hirsch ED (1993) Esprit de core. Core Knowledge Foundation Newsletter No 1 October: 1.

Hirsch ED (1996) The Schools We Need. New York: Doubleday.

HMI (1986) Lower Attaining Pupils Project (LAPP). London: HMSO.

HMI (1992) Provision for Highly Able Pupils in Maintained Schools. London: HMSO.

HMI (1996) Annual Report of the Chief Inspector for Schools in England. London: HMSO.

HMI (1997) Annual Report of the Chief Inspector for Schools in England. London: The Stationery Office.

Holland V (1998) Underachieving boys: Problems and solutions. Support for Learning 13(4): 174–8.

hooks b (1994) Teaching to Transgress: Education as the Practice of Freedom. New York: Routledge.

Horgan D (1995) Achieving Gender Equity: Strategies for the Classroom. Toronto: Allyn and Bacon.

Hundeide K (1991) Helping Disadvantaged Children. London: Jessica Kingsley.

Hyde JS, Fennema E, Lamon S (1990) Gender differences in mathematics performance: A meta-analysis. Psychological Bulletin 107(2): 139–55.

Jarvis P (1992) Paradoxes of Learning: On Becoming an Individual in Society. San Francisco, CA: Jossey-Bass.

Javits JK (1988) Gifted and Talented Students: Education Act of the United States. Washington DC: Public Law 100–297.

Johnson LG, Evans RW (1992) Hemispheric asymmetry and recategorised WISC-R patterns in learning disabled and non disabled children. Perception and Motor Skills 74(1): 77–8.

Kaplan LD, Kaplan C (1997) Democracy, meritocracy, and the cognitive élite: The real thesis of the Bell Curve. Educational Theory 47: 425–31.

Karnes MB, Johnson IJ (1991) Gifted handicapped. In N Colenangelo, GA Davis (eds) Handbook of Gifted Education. Boston, MA: Allyn and Bacon.

Kaufman A (1979) Intelligent Testing with the WISC-R. New York: Wiley.

Kellmer-Pringle M (1970) Able Misfits. London: Longman.

Kelly GA (1955) The Psychology of Personal Constructs, Volume 1. New York: Norton.

Kemnitz TM, Martin EG, Hegeman KT, Hickey JC (1982) Management Systems for Gifted and Special Educational Programs. New York: Trillium Press.

Kessler RC, Price RH, Wortman CB (1985) Social factors in psychopathology: Stress, social support and coping processes. Annual Review of Psychology 36: 531–72.

Kimball M (1994) The worlds we live in: Gender similarities and differences. Canadian Psychology 35: 388–404.

Kleinfeld J, Yerian S (eds) (1995) Gender Tales: Tensions in the Schools. New York: St Martin's Press.

Knight P (1992) How I use portfolios in mathematics. Educational Leadership 99(8): 71–4.

Krishnamurti J (1974) Krishnamurti on Education. Chennai, India: Krishnamurti Foundation India.

Landrum GN (1994) Profiles of Female Genius. Amherst, NY: Prometheus Books.

Lasch C (1995) The Revolt of the Élites and the Betrayal of Democracy. New York: W.W. Norton.

Lasonen J, Burge P (1991) Women in the workplace: Vocational education and segregated division of labour. Paper presented at the American Vocational Convention, December, Los Angeles, CA.

Laszlo M (1987) Children with perceptuomotor difficulties in schools. Times Educational Supplement (3 September): 22.

Learning Difficulties Research Project (1999) Occasional Reports. Maldon: Learning Difficulties Research Project.

Lee-Corbin H , Denicolo P (2000) (in press) Factors associated with achievement and underachievement in able children. Educating Able Children.

Lerner J (1971) Children with Learning Disabilities. Boston, MA: Houghton-Mifflin.

Leroux JA, Butler-Por N (1996) Keeping faith in ourselves: A comparative study of Canadian and Israeli women's perceptions of their achievement Gifted and Talented International 9: 167–71.

Leroux J, McMillan E (1993) Smart Teaching: Nurturing Talent in the Classroom and Beyond. Markham, ON: Pembroke Publishers.

Lewis M, Macedo D (1996) Power and education: Who decides the forms schools have taken, and who should decide? In JL Kincheloe, SR Steinberg (eds) Thirteen Questions: Reframing Education's Conversations. New York: Peter Lang, pp. 31–58.

Leyden S (1985) Helping the Child of Exceptional Ability. London: Routledge.

Licht BG, Dweck C (1987) Sex differences in achievement orientations. In G Arnot and G Weiner (eds) Gender and Politics of Schooling. London: Hutchinson.

Lincoln YS, Guba EG (1985) Naturalistic Inquiry. Beverly Hills, CA: Sage.

Lipman M (1991) Thinking in Education. Cambridge: Cambridge University Press.

Loewen JW (1995) Lies My Teacher Told Me: Everything Your American History Textbook Got Wrong. New York: New Press.

Luke A (1995–96) Text discourse in education: An introduction to critical discourse analysis. In M Apple (ed.) Review of Research in Education, Volume 21. Washington, DC: American Educational Research Association, pp. 3–48.

MacDonald A, Saunders L, Benfield P (1999) Boys' Achievement, Progress, Motivation and Participation. Slough: NFER.

Maker CJ (1982a) Curriculum Development for the Gifted. Rockville, MD: Aspen.

Maker CJ (1982b) Teaching Models for the Education of the Gifted. Rockville, MD: Aspen.

Maker CJ (1992) Intelligence and creativity in multiple intelligences. Identification and development. Educating Able Learners pp. 12–19.

Maker CJ, Neilson AB (1996a) Curriculum Development and Teaching Strategies for Gifted Learners (2nd edition). Austin, TX: PRO-ED.

Maker CJ, Neilson AB (1996b) Teaching Models in the Education of the Gifted (2nd edition). Austin, TX: PRO-ED.

Maker CJ, Neilson AB, Rogers JA (1994) Giftedness, diversity and problem-solving. Teaching Exceptional Children (fall): 4–19.

Margolin LM (1994) Goodness Personified: The Emergence of Gifted Children. Hawthorne, NY: Aldine and Gruyter.

Marland S (1971) Education of the Gifted and Talented: Report to the Congress of the United States by the US Commissioner of Education. Washington, DC: US Government Printing Office.

Marton F, Saljo R (1984) Approaches to learning. In F Marton, J Hownesell, NJ Entwistle (eds) The Experience of Learning. Edinburgh: Scottish Academic Press.

Mascie-Taylor CGN (1989) Biological and social aspects of development. In N Entwistle (ed.) Handbook of Educational Ideas and Practices. London: Routledge, pp. 992–1004.

Masson A, Hornby E (1986) Counselling women: Different ways now. Guidance and Counselling 1: 54–8.

Mayer RE (1992) Thinking, Problem Solving, Cognition. Oxford: Freeman.

McCalope M (1991) Fear of acting white. Jet (September): 2.

McCrae RR (1984) Situational determinants of coping responses: Loss, threat and challenge. Journal of Personal and Social Psychology 46: 919–28.

McGuinness C (1999) From Thinking Skills to Thinking Classrooms: A Review and Evaluation of Approaches for Developing Pupils' Thinking. Research Report RR115. Crown Copyright. Norwich: Department for Education and Science.

McLeod J, Cropley A (1989) Fostering Academic Success. Oxford: Pergamon.

Measor L, Sikes P (1992) Gender and Schools. New York: Cassell.

Mehler J, Pupoux E (1994) What Infants Know: The New Cognitive Science of Early Development. Oxford: Blackwell.

Meno Research Project (1998) Problem Solving: Preparing for the Assessment. Cambridge: Cambridge University Local Examinations Syndicate, Thinking Skills Service.

Messer DJ (1994) The Development of Communication: From Social Interaction to Language. Chichester: Wiley.

Miles MD, Huberman AM (1984) Qualitative Data Analysis: A Sourcebook of New Methods. Newbury Park, CA: Sage.

Millard E (1997) Differently Literate: Boys, Girls and the Schooling of Literacy. London: Falmer.

Miller JB (1986) What do we mean by relationships? Work in Progress No 22. Wellesley, MA: Stone Center Working Paper Series.

Miller JB (1994) Women's psychological development: Connections, disconnections and violations. In MM Berger (ed.) Women Beyond Freud. New York: Brunner/Mazel, pp. 79–97.

Mills CJ, Ablard KE, Stumpf H (1993) Gender differences in academically talented young students' mathematical reasoning: Patterns across age and subskills. Journal of Educational Psychology 85(2): 340–6.

Mirkin M (ed.) (1994) Women in Context: Towards a Feminist Reconstruction of Psychotherapy. New York: Guilford Press.

Mishra SP, Lord J, Sabers DL (1989) Cognitive processes underlying WISC-R performance of gifted and learning disabled Navajos. Psychology in the Schools 26(1): 15–23.

Mittler P (1990) Editorial Foreword. In D Montgomery (ed.) Children with Learning Difficulties. London: Cassell.

Moi T (1985) Sexual/Textual Politics: Feminist Literacy Theory. London: Routledge.

Molnar A, Lindquist B (1989) Changing Problem Behaviour in Schools. San Francisco, CA: Jossey-Bass.

Montgomery D (1977) Teaching pre-reading through training in pattern recognition. The Reading Teacher 30(6): 216–25.

Montgomery D (1981) Education comes of age. School Psychology International 1: 1–3.

Montgomery D (1983) (2nd edition 1999) Learning and Teaching Strategies: Study Skills. Maldon: Learning Difficulties Research Project.

Montgomery D (1984) Evaluation and Enhancement of Teaching Performance. Maldon: Learning Difficulties Research Project.

Montgomery D (1985) The Special Needs of Able Children in Ordinary Classrooms. Maldon: Learning Difficulties Research Project.

Montgomery D (1989) Managing Behaviour Problems. Sevenoaks: Hodder and Stoughton.

Montgomery D (1990) Children with Learning Difficulties. London: Cassell.

Montgomery D (1991) Special Needs of Able Children in Ordinary Classrooms (2nd edition). Maldon: Learning Difficulties Research Project.

Montgomery D (1993) Learner managed learning in teacher education. In N Graves (ed.) Learner Managed Learning: Policy, Theory and Practice. Leeds: Higher Education for Capability/World Education Fellowship, pp. 59–70.

Montgomery D (1994) The role of metacognition and metalearning. In G Gibbs (ed.) Improving Student Learning: Through Assessment and Evaluation. Oxford: Oxford Brookes University Staff Development Centre, pp. 227–53.

Montgomery D (1995a) Critical theory and practice in evaluation and assessment. In G. Gibbs (ed.) Improving Student Learning: Through Assessment and Evaluation. Oxford: Oxford Brookes University Staff Development Centre, pp. 88–105.

Montgomery D (1995b) Social abilities in highly able disabled learners and the consequences for remediation. In MW Katzko, FJ Monks (eds) Nurturing Talent: Individual Needs and Social Abilities. Assen, The Netherlands: Van Gorcum, pp. 226–38.

Montgomery D (1996) Educating the Able. London: Cassell.

Montgomery D (1997a) Spelling: Remedial Strategies. London: Cassell.

Montgomery D (1997b) Developmental Spelling: A Handbook for Teachers. Maldon: Learning Difficulties Research Project.

Montgomery D (1998) Reversing Lower Attainment. London: David Fulton.

Montgomery D (1999) Positive Appraisal Through Classroom Observation. London: David Fulton.

Munro J (1996a) Gifted Students Learning: Basing the Teaching of Gifted Students on a Model of Learning. Melbourne: Educational Assistance.

Munro J (1996b) Social, Constructivist and Information Processing. A Teacher Friendly Model of Learning. Melbourne, Ed. Assist.

Munro J (1996c) A Learning Base for Education of the Gifted and Talented Students. Seminar Series Paper Number 56. Melbourne: IARTV.

National Excellence (1993) National Excellence: A Case for Developing America's Talent. Washington, DC: US Government Printing Office.

National Literacy Trust (1999) Boys and Writing. National Literacy Trust on the web (http://www.literacytrust.org.uk/)

Neisser U (1967) Cognitive Psychology. New York: Appleton Century Crofts.

Newell A, Shaw JC, Simon HA (1961) Computer simulations of human learning. Science 174: 2011–17.

Nisbet J (1993) The thinking curriculum. Educational Psychology 13(3/4): 281–90.

Norman DA (1977) Notes towards a complex theory of learning. In AM Lesgold, JW Pellegrino, SD Fokkema, R Glaser (eds) Cognitive Psychology and Instruction. New York: Plenum.

Northern Ireland Council for the Curriculum Examinations and Assessment (1999) Focus on Boys: Guidance on Improving Attainment, Particularly in Literacy. Belfast: Council for the Curriculum Examinations and Assessment.

Nunes T, Schliemann AD, Carraher DW (1993) Street Mathematics and School Mathematics. Cambridge: Cambridge University Press.

Office for Standards in Education (OFSTED) (1993) Boys and English 1988–1991. Report No 2/93. London: HMSO.

OFSTED (1995) Guidance on the Inspection of Secondary Schools. London: HMSO.

OFSTED/Equal Opportunities Commission (1996) The Gender Divide. London: HMSO.

Ognibene E (1983) Moving beyond 'True Woman' myths: Women and work. Humboldt Journal of Social Relations 10(2): 2–25.

Ohio Council of Coordinators for the Gifted (1989) Ohio Gifted Students Course of Study. Ohio: Council of Coordinators for the Gifted in Ohio.

Ontario Women's Directorate and Education Ministry (1995) The Joke's Over. Toronto, ON: Government of Ontario.

Pagano J, Miller J (1996) Women and education: In what ways does gender affect the educational process? In JL Kincheloe, SR Steinberg (eds) Thirteen Questions: Reframing Education's Conversations. New York: Peter Lang, pp. 139–56.

Papert S (1980) Mindstorms. Brighton: Harvester.

Parent A (1995) David. A case study. Flying High (issue 2): 26–32.

Passow AH (1990) Needed research and development in teaching high ability children. European Journal of High Ability 1: 15–24.

Patchett RF, Stansfield M (1991) Subtest scatter on the WISC-R with children of superior intelligence. Psychology in the Schools 29(1): 5–11.

Paul RW (1990) Critical thinking in North America. In AJA Binker (ed.) Critical Thinking: What Every Person Needs to Know to Survive in a Rapidly Changing World. Sonoma: Sonoma State University, Centre for Critical Thinking and Moral Critique, pp. 18–42.

Pearlin LL, Schooler C (1978) The structure of coping. Journal of Health and Social Behaviour 22: 2–21.

Peters ML (1967) Spelling Taught or Caught? London: Routledge and Kegan Paul.

Peters ML (1985) Spelling Taught or Caught? (2nd edition). London: Routledge and Kegan Paul.

Peters ML, Smith B (1993) Spelling in Context. Windsor: NFER/Nelson.

Piaget J (1952) Origins of Intelligence in Children (2nd edition). New York: International Universities Press.

Pickering J (1997) Raising Boys' Achievement. Stafford: Network Educational Press.

Piirto J (1994) Talented Children and Adults: Their Development and Education. New York: Macmillan.

Piirto J (1997a) Precepts for the curriculum for the talented. The Journal Portfolio 13: 10–17.

Piirto J (1997b) Twelve issues: Postmodern curriculum thought and the education of the gifted. Paper presented at the National Association for Gifted Children Conference, Little Rock, AR, November.

Piirto J (1998a) Understanding Those Who Create (2nd edition). Tempe, AZ: Gifted Psychology Press.

Piirto J (1998b) Review of the Book – Curriculum Development in the Postmodern Era. Gifted Child Quarterly 42: 130–3.

Piirto J (1999) Talented Children and Adults: Their Development and Education (2nd edition). Columbus, OH: Prentice-Hall/Merrill.

Piirto J, Fraas J (1995) Androgyny in the personalities of talented teenagers. Journal of Secondary Gifted Education 6(2): 93–102.

Pinar W, Reynolds W, Slattery P, Taubman P (1995) Understanding Curriculum: An

Introduction to the Study of Historical and Contemporary Curriculum Discourses. New York: Peter Lang.

Pipher M (1994) Reviving Ophelia: Saving the Selves of Adolescent Girls. New York: Ballantine.

Poorthuis GMT, Kok WAM, van Dijk L (1990) An instrument to analyse curriculum materials for the gifted. Paper presented at the 2nd European Conference of ECHA, Budapest, 25–8 October.

Prentice S (1996) Addressing and redressing chilly climates in higher education. College and University Teachers' Bulletin: Status of Women Supplement 43(4): 7–9.

Pyke S (1997) Education and the 'Woman Question'. Canadian Psychology 38: 154–63.

Qualifications and Curriculum Authority (1998) Can Do Better: Raising Boys' Achievement in English. London: Qualifications and Curriculum Authority.

Qualifications and Curriculum Authority (1999) Improving Writing at Key Stage 3 and 4. Sudbury: Qualifications and Curriculum Authority.

Radford J (1990) Child Prodigies and Exceptional Early Achievers. London: Harvester Wheatsheaf.

Ralph JB, Goldberg MI, Passow AH (1966) Bright Underachievers. New York: Teachers College Press.

Raven JC (1988) The Raven's Progressive Matrices. Oxford: Oxford Psychologists Press.

Rawlings A (1996) Ways and Means Today. Kingston: Kingston Friends Workshop Group. (Available from Kingston Friends Workshop Group, 78 Eden Street, Kingston upon Thames, Surrey, UK.)

Reinen I, Plomp T (1993) Some gender issues in educational computer use: Results of an international comparative survey. Computers in Education 20(4): 353–65.

Reis S (1991) The need for clarification in research designed to examine gender differences in achievement and accomplishment. Roeper Review 13(4): 193–206.

Renzulli JS (1977) The Enrichment Triad. A Model for Developing Defensible Programs for the Gifted and Talented. Mansfield Center, CN: Creative Learning Press.

Renzulli JS (1995) New directions for the schoolwide enrichment model. In MW Katzko, FJ Monks (eds) Nurturing Talent. Individual Needs and Social Ability. Assen, The Netherlands: Van Gorcum, pp. 162–7.

Renzulli JS, Reis SJ (1989) The Schoolwide Enrichment Model. Mansfield Center, CT: Creative Learning Press.

Ridehalgh N (1999) A comparative study of the effectiveness of three dyslexia programmes. Unpublished MA dissertation. London: Middlesex University.

Riding RJ, Rayner S (1998) Cognitive Styles and Learning Strategies. London: Fulton.

Roaf C (1998) Slow hand. A secondary school survey of handwriting speed and legibility. Support for Learning 13(1): 39–42.

Roeders P (1995) Student-assisted education – the active way of differentiation in the classroom: Basic concepts and effects. Paper presented at the European Seminar of ECHA, Antwerp, April.

Rogers C (1985) Freedom to Learn in the 80s. New York: Macmillan.

Rogers KB, Span P (1993) Ability grouping with gifted students: Research and guidelines. In KA Heller, FJ Monks, AH Passow (eds) International Handbook of Research and Development in Gifted Education. Oxford: Pergamon, pp. 585–92.

Ross P (1993) National Excellence: A Case for Developing America's Talent. Washington, DC: Office of Educational Research and Improvement.

Rowe A (1993) Introduction. In J Austen, Northanger Abbey. Ware: Wordsworth Editorial, pp. v–xii.

Rowe KJ (1991) The influence of reading activity at home on students' attitudes towards reading, classroom attentiveness and reading achievement: an application of structural equation modelling. British Journal of Educational Psychology 61: 19–35.

Royce-Adams R (1975) Columbus to Aquarius. Dryden Press, p. 145.

Royce-Adams R (1977) Developing Reading Versatility. New York: Rinehart and Winston.

Sadker M, Sadker D (1995) Failing at Fairness: How America's Schools Shortchange Girls. New York: Charles Scribner's Sons.

Sadler K (2000) Attributions and solutions for the underachievement of able pupils. Educating Able Children 4(1).

Sapon-Shevin M (1994) Playing Favourites: Gifted Education and the Disruption of Community. Albany, NY: State University of New York Press.

Sassoon R (1987) Handwriting. A New Perspective. Cheltenham: Stanley Thornes.

Schmidt P (1993) Seeking to identify the gifted among LEP students. Education Week 12(35): 12–13.

Schneider FW, Coutts LM (1985) Person orientation of male and female high school students to the educational disadvantage of males? Sex Roles 13(1–2): 47–63.

Schlosser C (1999) Facilitation of career success: Canadian and Finnish women. Unpublished doctoral dissertation, University of Alberta, Edmonton, Canada.

Schoemaker MM, Calverboer AS (1994) Social and affective problems of children who are clumsy. How do they begin? In SE Henderson (ed.) Developmental Co-ordination Difficulties. Special Issue of Adaptive Physical Activity Quarterly 11: 130–44.

Schonell FJ, Schonell EE (1946) Diagnostic and Attainment Testing (4th edition). Edinburgh: Oliver and Boyd.

Scollay S (1994) The forgotten half: Are US schools shortchanging girls? The American School Board Journal (April): 47–8.

Scottish Education Department (SED) (1978) The Education of Pupils with Learning Difficulties in Primary and Secondary Schools: A Progress Report by HMI. Edinburgh: HMSO.

Shannon C (1993) Parents and teachers in partnership. Gifted Child Today (Nov/Dec): 16–19.

Shaw GA, Brown G (1991) Laterality, implicit memory and attention disorder. Education Studies 17(1): 15–23.

Shore BM, Tsiamis A (1986) Identification by provision. In KA Heller, JF Feldhusen (eds) Identification and Nurturing the Gifted. Berne: Huber.

Siegler RS (1991) Children's Thinking. Englewood Cliffs, NJ: Prentice-Hall.

Silverman LK (1989) Invisible gifts, invisible handicaps. Roeper Review (Special issue: Gifted students with disabilities) 12(1): 37–42.

Silverman LK (1991) Helping gifted girls reach their potential. Roeper Review 14(2): 122–3.

Simon BL (1987) Never Married Women. Philadelphia, PA: Tempole University Press.

Simonton DK (1988) Scientific Genius. A Psychology of Science. Cambridge: Cambridge University Press.

Sisk D (1991) Minority strength checklist. Leadership training for gifted students.

Paper presented at the World Council for Gifted and Talented Children Conference, The Hague, The Netherlands.

Sisk D (1999a) Socio-economic development of gifted students. Gifted Education International 14 (in press).

Sisk D (1999b) Step-Up/Even Start II: Final Even Start Report. Austin, TX.

Skelton C (1998) Feminism and research into the masculinities and schooling. Gender and Education 10(2): 217–27.

Skilbeck M (1989) School Development and New Approaches to Learning: Trends and Issues in Curriculum Reform. Paris: Organisation for Economic Co-operation and Development.

Skinner BF (1967) Science and Human Behavior. New York: Macmillan.

Skoe E, Marcia J (1993) A measure of care-based morality and its relation to ego-identity. Merrill-Palmer Quarterly 37(2): 298–384.

Slattery P (1995a) A postmodern vision of time and learning: A response to the National Education Commission Report – Prisoners of Time. Harvard Educational Review 65: 612–33.

Slattery P (1995b) Curriculum Development in the Postmodern Era. New York: Garland.

Smith JN (director) (1995) Dangerous Minds (Film).

Spalding RB, Spalding WT (1969) The Writing Road to Reading. New York: Whiteside and Morrow.

Span P (1995) Self regulated learning. In J Freeman, P Span, H Wagner (eds) Actualising Talent: A Lifelong Challenge. London: Cassell.

Spearman C (1927) The Abilities of Man. New York: Macmillan.

Stanovich K (1993) The consequences of literacy. Invited Lecture, British Psychological Society Annual Conference, April.

Steele C (1992) Race and the schooling of black Americans. The Atlantic Monthly 269: 68.

Steinke J, Long M (1995) A lab of her own? Portrayals of female characters in children's educational science. Paper presented at the annual general meeting of the International Communication Association, Albuquerque, NM.

Stephenson J, Weil S (1988) Launch of 'Higher Education for Capability'. London: Royal Society for Arts.

Sternberg RJ (1986) Beyond IQ. A Triarchic Theory of Intelligence. New York: Cambridge University Press.

Stewart WJ (1977) Sex Differences and the School. ERIC database, Document (RIE). New York: Delmar.

STRANDS (1991) Spelling Teaching for Reading and Needs of Dyslexic Students. Winchester: Hampshire Local Education Authority.

Strauss A, Corbin J (1990) Basics of Qualitative Research. London: Sage.

Street BV (1990) Cultural Meanings of Literacy. Paris: UNESCO, IBE.

Supplee PL (1990) Reaching the Gifted Underachiever: Program Strategy and Design. New York: Teachers College Press.

Suter D, Wolf J (1987) Issues in the identification and programming of the gifted/learning disabled child. Journal for Education of the Gifted 10(3): 227–37.

Sutherland M (1990) Education and gender differences. In N Entwistle (ed.) Handbook of Educational Ideas and Practices. London: Routledge.

Swartz RJ, Parks S (1994) Infusing the Teaching of Critical and Creative Thinking into Elementary Instruction. Pacific Grove, CA: Critical Thinking Press and Software.

Tannenbaum AJ (1983) Gifted Children: Psychological and Educational Perspectives. London: Macmillan.

Tannenbaum A (1986) The enrichment matrix model. In JS Renzulli (ed.) Systems and Models for Developing Programs for the Gifted and Talented. Mansfield Center, CT: Creative Learning Press, pp. 391–429.

Tannenbaum AJ (1997) Programs for the gifted: To be or not to be. In JA Leroux (ed.) Connecting the Gifted Community Worldwide. Selected Proceedings from the 12th World Conference of the WCGTC, Seattle, 29 July–2 August, pp. 5–36.

Terman LM (1925) Genetic Studies of Genius, Volume 1. Stanford, CA: Stanford University Press.

Terman L (1954) The discovery and encouragement of exceptional talent. American Psychologist 9: 221–30.

Third International Mathematics and Science Survey (TIMSS) (1997) Third International Maths and Science Study, 1995. Cheshunt Hill, MA: TIMSS Study Centre, Boston College.

Thomas F (1998) Une question de writing. Support for Learning 13: 43–5.

Thomas L, Augstein S (1975) Reading to Learn Project Report. Uxbridge: Brunel University, Centre for Human Learning.

Thomson ME (1990) Evaluating teaching programmes for children with specific learning difficulties. In PD Pumfrey, CD Elliott (eds) Children's Difficulties in Reading, Spelling and Writing. London: Falmer, pp. 155–71.

Tizard B, Hughes M (1984) Young Children Learning: Talking and Thinking at Home and School. London: Fontana.

Tomini B, Page S (1992) Vocational bias and gender: Evaluations of high school counsellors by Canadian university undergraduates. Canadian Journal of Counselling 26: 100–6.

Turnbull S (1993) The media: Moral lessons and moral careers. Australian Journal of Education 37: 153–68.

Tyler R (1949) Basic Principles of Curriculum and Instruction. Chicago, IL: Chicago University Press.

UNESCO (1988) Compendium of Statistics on Literacy. Paris: UNESCO Office of Statistics

UNESCO (1994) The Salamanca Statement and Framework for Action on Special Educational Needs. Paris: UNESCO.

Van Tassel-Baska J (ed.) (1988) Comprehensive Curriculum for Gifted Learners. Needham Heights, MA: Allyn and Bacon.

Van Tassel-Baska J (ed.) (1994a) Comprehensive Curriculum for Gifted Learners (2nd edition). Needham Heights, MA: Allyn and Bacon.

Van Tassel-Baska J (1994b) Planning and Implementing Curriculum for Gifted Learners. Denver, CO: Love.

Van Tassel-Baska J (1998) Girls of promise. In J Van Tassel-Baska (ed.) Excellence in Educating Gifted and Talented Learners (3rd edition). Denver: Love, pp. 129–43.

Vellutino FR (1979) Dyslexia. Research and Theory. London: MIT Press.

Vellutino FR (1987) Dyslexia. Scientific American 256(3): 20–7.

Visser J, Rayner S (1999) Emotional and Behavioural Difficulties: A Reader. Birmingham: Q.Ed.

Voigt J (1994) Negotiation of mathematical meaning and learning mathematics. Educational Studies in Mathematics 26: 275–98.

Vygotsky LS (1978) Mind in Society: The Development of Higher Psychological Processes. Cambridge, MA: MIT Press.

Vygotsky LS (1984) Mind in Society: The Development of Higher Psychological Processes (Reprint). Cambridge, MA: MIT Press.

Waller E (1973) The Problem of Handwriting. Boston, MA: Allyn and Bacon.

Warrington M, Younger P (1996) Gender and achievement: The debate at GCSE. Education Review 10(1): 22–7.

Waters E, Wippman J, Stroufe LA (1979) Attachment, positive effect and competence in the peer group: Two studies in construct validation. Child Development 50: 821–9.

Watson J (1996) Reflection Through Interaction. London: Falmer.

Wayman J (1991) If You Promise Not to Tell. Beavercreek, OH: Pieces of Learning.

Wedell K (1973) Learning and Perceptuomotor Disabilities in Children. Chichester: Wiley.

Weil P (director) (1989) Dead Poets Society (Film). Touchstone Video.

Welch L (1990) Women in Higher Education: Changes and Challenges. New York: Praeger.

Wetherington E, Kessler RC (1991) Situations and processes of coping. In J Eckenrode (ed.) The Social Context of Coping. New York: Plenum Press, pp. 13–29.

Whitmore JR (1982) Giftedness, Conflict and Underachievement. Boston: Allyn and Bacon.

Wilgosh L (1993) The underachievement of girls: A societal rather than a gender issue. Education Canada (spring): 18–23.

Wilgosh L (1996) Underachievement of women and girls: Some societal and feminist views. Education Canada (fall): 25–31.

Wilgosh L (1999) Maximising achievement of adolescent girls. Paper presented at the 13th World Conference of the World Council for Gifted and Talented Children, Istanbul, August.

Yewchuk CR (1986a) Gifted/learning disabled children: Problem of assessment. In A Cropley, K Urban, H Wagner, W Wierczerkowsky (eds) Giftedness: A Continuing Worldwide Challenge. New York: Trillium Press, pp. 40–9.

Yewchuk CR (1986b) Identification of gifted/learning disabled children. School Psychology International 7(1): 61–8.

Yuill N, Easton K (1993) Joke comprehension. The Lancet 342: 858.

Zarit SH, Todd PA, Zarit JM (1986) Subjective burden of husbands and wives as caregivers: A longitudinal study. The Gerontologist 26: 260–6.

Zeidner M, Scheleyer E (1999) The big fish-in-little-pond-effect for academic self concept, test anxiety and school grades in gifted children. Contemporary Educational Psychology Vol 24, pp. 305–29.

Index